ARCTIC HOMESTEAD

ARCTIC HOMESTEAD

THE TRUE STORY OF ONE FAMILY'S
SURVIVAL AND COURAGE IN THE
ALASKAN WILDS

Norma Cobb
AND Charles W. Sasser

St. Martin's Press
New York

www.stmartins.com

Book design by Michelle McMillian

Library of Congress Cataloging-in-Publication Data

Cobb, Norma.
    Arctic homestead : the true story of one family's survival and courage in the Alaskan wilds / Norma Cobb and Charles W. Sasser. —1st ed.
        p. cm.
    ISBN 0-312-26198-5
    1. Frontier and pioneer life—Alaska—Minook Creek Valley. 2. Minook Creek Valley (Alaska)—Biography. 3. Minook Creek Valley (Alaska)—Social life and customs. 4. Cobb family. I. Sasser, Charles W. II. Title.

F912.M55 C64 2000
979.8'7—dc21   00-031733

First Edition: October 2000

10 9 8 7 6 5 4 3 2 1

To my family: Les, Sid, Sean, Tom, Cara, and Cora; who shared all our dreams and adventures . . .

To my grandchildren: Cassandra and Caje Cobb; Ira and Norma Gene Cobb; Jared Dulinsky; Joey Williams; Aaron, Grady, and Chantell Dollison; and Haley Johnson; that they may understand . . .

And most of all to God, who stood by us during the trying years of discovery in a wild and untamed place . . .

NORMA COBB

And to my wife, Donna Sue . . .

CHARLES W. SASSER

AUTHOR'S NOTE

In this book I have endeavored to render the truth as accurately and vividly as possible. This is my story, but it is also the story of my family and others who played major or minor roles in the events narrated.

Dialogue and events are reported to the best of my recollection. While the content is accurate, naturally I cannot be certain every quote is entirely accurate word for word or that my interpretation of events will be exactly the same as someone else's. Much time has passed since many of these events occurred.

In some instances, events have been condensed, compressed, or rearranged as necessary for brevity and clarity. Life is so full that to give a complete accounting of it in sequence would require a book much longer than this one and would render it unreadable.

Many of the names in this book have been changed.

—NORMA COBB

INTRODUCTION

Colorado rancher and friend Scotty Anderson introduced me to Norma and Lester Cobb at the Lost Creek Ranch in Minook Valley in the spring of 1998 during one of my frequent forays to Alaska to hunt, fish, climb mountains, and hike the wonderful bush country. Alaska remains one of the few places left on earth where there are almost no fences and wildlife outnumbers humans. Les is today a big-game hunting guide, a tall, brash, leather-tough man of whom it is said that if you have a choice between fighting an enraged grizzly or taking him on, you might be safer choosing the bear. Norma is a sensitive, spiritual woman whose observations about the raw Alaskan wilderness express her love for and appreciation of it. She handles the business end of the operation while also serving as hostess, camp cook, and wrangler.

Even today, their nearest neighbor, a "fair weather" neighbor at that, is eleven miles away down a muddy road Les maintains himself. From the nearest settlement at Eureka, an old gold mining camp that is now all but a ghost town, the road punches through willows and alder brush, cuts across high tundra, curves around spectacular mountain peaks, tops Dead Horse Pass, then drops abruptly into a lost valley so stunning it takes away your breath. Minook Valley is one hundred and fifty miles northwest of Fairbanks, south of the Arctic Circle, and four directions from literally nowhere.

The valley is wide and green with fir, spruce, birch, cottonwood, larch, and willow. Snowcapped peaks surround and protect it from the fierce winds of winter. It is dissected by a pair of fast, clear-running streams. Lost Creek rushes into Minook Creek, from which the valley acquired its name, and Minook tumbles merrily toward the Yukon River nineteen miles away.

"If we hadn't found this valley, *nothing* could have induced me to stay in Alaska," Norma contends today. "But it stole my heart the moment we came to the top of the pass and I saw it for the first time."

In spite of its isolation, indeed because of it, Minook Valley carries a rich history. Early Athabascan tribes used it as a route to reach the Yukon and its salmon harvests. In the late 1800s, gold rush pioneers walked the Minook Trail between diggings at Rampart on the Yukon and Eureka farther south. Jack London penned some of his famous Alaskan short stories while weak from scurvy only a short distance from the Cobb homestead. Wyatt Earp and his wife, Josie, were stranded at Rampart over a winter when their steamboat froze up on the river. Tex Rickard ran a saloon along the Minook Trail before becoming America's leading boxing promoter and building Madison Square Garden. Iditarod winners Susan Butcher and Rick Swenson live and train in the area around Eureka.

Lost Creek Ranch is the only occupied homestead remaining in the valley. The log cabin is squat, solid, and massive, built to endure far into a new millennium. It melds naturally into the terrain, at peace with the timber and mountains and tundra, a symbol of the indomitable human spirit and the pioneer creed. Although still rough and primitive, it now includes comforts only recently acquired and which are taken for granted by most Americans.

Electricity, for example, is supplied by an oil-fueled generator. The indoor plumbing uses water pumped directly from Lost Creek—another true luxury. Les climbed a seven-thousand-foot peak, Norky's Mountain, to erect an antenna for relaying telephone signals, providing telephone access to the outside world for the first time.

Norma, now in her fifties, is a dark-haired, attractive woman only slightly over five feet in height. Spiritwise, characterwise, she is every inch the stature of her burly six-two husband. She was the last woman in America to sign up under the U.S. Homestead Act of 1862 to become a homesteader. Mrs. Cobb is a true pioneer.

Les Cobb is a rough-talking, easy-laughing man more at home on a game trail than on a city street. Together, twenty-six years ago, dragging along with them their five small children, they set out from the lower United States in quest of an American dream that had all but died after the opening of the American West—the opportunity to have free land if they would but settle on it and build a home.

I have sat many evenings with the Cobbs around the warm cradle of the woodstove in their cabin and listened to tales of when this valley was *really* virgin and they first hiked into it from trail's end. That was when it was occupied solely by moose, black bear, grizzly, wolverines, and, along the Yukon, a few Indians and Eskimos who spoke in hushed tones of a "Bushman," a huge, hairy manlike creature who stole children.

Their odyssey began in the autumn of 1972. Newly married with five small children between them from previous relationships, they were barely eking out an existence in the Lower Forty-eight. They realized the only way they could ever afford to own a farm of their own was to take the trail of pilgrims and pioneers before them and set out to find America's last frontier.

Most of the only remaining land available for homesteading lay north of Fairbanks in Alaska near the Arctic Circle. It was a raw and lawless country, a transplanted piece of the Old West where grizzlies outnumbered settlers twenty to one, where outlaws and thieves robbed new settlers, attempted to burn them out or jump their claims, and where the only law was the one a man wore on his hip or pegged above his cabin door.

The Cobbs were *chechakos,* tenderfeet, in a land that consumed even toughened settlers. Outlaws stole their supplies. Seven-year-old Sean was accidentally gun shot. Winter's snow collapsed the roof of their first cabin. They built too near the creek and spring thaw threatened to flood them out. Bears prowled the woods and stalked the children, clacking their teeth as agitated and aggressive bears will. Packs of hungry timber wolves lurked outside the firelight. The legendary Bushman of native lore waited in the forest shadows, watching. Starvation and loneliness were constant companions. Everything about the new land seemed to be in conspiracy to defeat them.

Subjected to severe deprivations and dangers, young and pretty Norma Cobb, small-town girl from Wichita, Kansas, learned to build cabins, skin beavers, tan bear pelts, make a campfire, mush sled dogs, shoot a rifle, fight both men and wild animals, suture wounds, treat illnesses, cook a moose or a bear or a grouse, home-school her brood, fight forest fires, and cope with the isolation of the long, dark Arctic winters.

Through the Cobbs' tales and Norma's journal, which she so graciously provided, emerged what I recognized as one of the truly great adventure odysseys of modern times—the story of Norma Cobb, the last woman to homestead the Alaskan wilderness. I am privileged to help bring Norma's wonderful story to life.

—CHARLES W. SASSER

What went ye out into the wilderness to see?

—St. Matthew

ARCTIC HOMESTEAD

PART I

The hope I dreamed of was a dream . . .

—Christina Rossetti

1

Being isolated and lonely is different from being in town and lonely. Few people can take it. They fall apart each in his own way just as I began to fall apart the moment Les pushed back his plate and looked at me across what remained of supper's black bear roast.

"Norma . . . ?"

I slowly laid down my fork and, before he could continue, warded him off with both palms. I didn't want to hear it.

Even the children stopped eating. Early October's first snowfall murmured in the darkness against the spruce log cabin. Silence fell around the table, so that the fire in the wood-burning oil drum roared like a grizzly coming down the stovepipe and the whisper of snow on the black windows became as ominous as gossip at a funeral wake.

The way Les looked at me, half apologetically, half triumphantly . . . Panic leered from shadows resurrected to life by the uncertain flicker of the oil lamp. Tears blurred my vision. It wasn't as though I hadn't known tonight or a night like tonight eventually had to come. Sometimes I blocked from my mind things I didn't want to happen. I didn't trust myself to speak. I knew I might say things I surely would come to regret in hindsight. The hush built.

Lester Cobb was one stubborn man. I knew it when I married him, but I married him anyhow. He had dark hair and a magnificent beard. At six feet two, he towered over me by nearly a foot. He made me feel protected and diminished at the same time. It was his attitude as much as his size. He thought he could conquer the world, and if he couldn't conquer it he would bluster his way through. I could never win an argument with him. He would have his way tonight, as he had his way in most things.

Anger, resentment, loneliness, flared deep inside my soul, fueled by emotion with which I was well acquainted after nearly three years homesteading the Alaskan wilderness—*raw fear*. My husband was going to abandon me and our five small ones in the middle of the northern wilds with wolves literally at the cabin door and snow bringing the long darkness of the Arctic winter. Suddenly, I let it all out from a bitter deep spring inside.

"You can't go and leave me out here all by myself with five kids. Lester, *anything* could happen!"

"Honey . . ." Les began.

"It won't do, Les."

Last August while prospecting for gold, Les met a man named Gary Streicher. Streicher was putting together an oil field service company to construct iron islands—oil derricks—in Prudhoe Bay. They could only be erected when the bay was frozen over, from October to April. They were built right out on the ice, then drilled and anchored to the bottom of the bay. Come spring thaw, people who didn't know wondered how they got out there like that in the middle of the water. Streicher had hired my do-it-all husband to ramrod the operation over the winter.

Rough as a Cobb. That was what people said about Les. The expression somehow expanded to include the children and me after we migrated to Alaska. It became "Lester and Norma, the Cobbs, and their five little Kernels." Rough or not, we were still *chechakos*, tenderfeet. Other bush people were predicting we would never make it as pioneers. We were lucky, they said, if this land didn't kill us all. Which it might do yet—starting this winter after Les abandoned the children and me.

"Honey, either I take the job to earn enough money to see us over," Les argued, "or we give up right now and move back to Colorado . . ."

Sid, the eldest of the brood at nearly thirteen, sat very straight and stiff. He folded his hands in his lap, squared his shoulders, and looked across the table at Les. His face turned pale; Sid loved it in wild and isolated Minook Valley.

Sean, ten, exchanged uncertain glances with seven-year-old Tommy. Things had started out rough for Sean, but the valley had been the first real home he had known in his short life. Tommy got up and as self-appointed protector to the twins, Cara and Cora, moved around closer to them. They temporarily suppressed their endless tittering and picking at each other. At four years old, nearly five, they were already a riotous and rebellious pair. Their bottom lips swelled in mirror images of defiance and resistance to whatever decision we reached. To please was never an objective in their lives. They were just like their father.

The Kernels seemed to realize that we Cobbs were confronting another landmark obstacle in pioneering.

"Honey . . ."

"Les, it's our first wintering over. And to do it out here by ourselves, without you . . . We're not ready."

"Honey, the cabin is finished—"

"The roof fell in on the last one when it snowed."

"All the food supplies are in—"

"Remember how bears broke into the other cabin and ransacked it?"

"The bears are hibernating. Firewood is all bucked up for the winter—"

"What if we run out of food? Can't you wait until spring and get another job?"

"Norma, we *have* to have the money—"

"What about the Bushman? He chased Sid. He's stolen some of the Indian kids."

Les threw up his hands in exasperation. "The *Bushman*! God help the Bushman if he should run into you!"

Grinning like that, Les had the look of a rough-and-ready TV villain, even down to the mischievous devil-may-care twinkle in his blue-gray eyes. The way that man could grin!

"Grinning won't work this time, Lester," I warned him. I turned to the children. "Kids, finish eating and go to your loft. Fur is going to fly. Your father is deserting us."

"I am not *deserting*—"

"I'm scared," Tommy whispered, wide-eyed and looking around at the window for prowling bears and Bushmen.

If I were to be honest with myself, I had to admit Les had a point. We *were* all but broke, again. If he turned down this job, with its really good pay, he would undoubtedly have to hike out of the valley and look for employment come spring, when he was *really* needed to work the homestead. There were cabins to build, the airstrip to finish, some gold prospecting to do. We had only three more years, a little over, to "prove out" our homestead claim before it actually became ours. Les insisted that about all he had to do in the winter was lie around, eat, and, weather permitting, run a trapline with Sid and Bony Newman the Eskimo.

But the important thing to me was that he would be *here,* with us, when it really mattered. I actually pretended all summer, even knowing differently, that I was going to spend the long, snug, romantic winter cocooned up with my husband and children. I thought we would have plenty to keep us busy—books, home-schooling the children, trapping furs for making mukluks and caps and robes, training the sled dogs so we would have transportation.

I had tried to ignore the growing restlessness I saw forming in Les as winter approached. Winter and cabin walls were hard on men, especially high-energy men like Les. They started getting restless in September and early October. I suspected the threat of cabin fever, of being confined with women and children, was the reason men took to traveling and trapping as soon as the streams froze and there was enough snow on the ground for dogsleds.

Summers were visiting time for people in the bush. It was as if everyone tried to cram in enough living between June and September, like bears gorging themselves fat for hibernation, to last them from October to May. All the socializing pretty much ended in September as people left the bush country for the safety and comfort of towns. The Westbrooks, our only neighbors in the valley, had left weeks ago; it was uncertain if they would ever be back. The last visitors we'd had were John Shilling, who worked a gold mine claim downvalley toward the Yukon River, and was on his way out to Fairbanks, and Ted and Steve, the district's roaming schoolteachers who delivered materials for home-schooling the children. There wouldn't likely be anyone else out this way until thaw breakup in the spring.

Autumn was a lovely time of year, what with the brilliant new golden drapery donned by the aspen and birch and larch on the hillsides and the broad-leafed cottonwoods along Minook Creek, and the crisp fall mornings during which the air itself seemed to crackle. Behind the beauty, however—especially this year—it seemed to me there lay a mounting anxiety. Pine squirrels went into a final frenzy of food gathering; bears headed higher up, walking fast, to search for dens; ducks and geese chattered excitedly as they fled south; ermine, snowshoe hares, and grouse hurriedly changed into their winter colors. They knew winter was coming. So did I. They were preparing for it. I tried to ignore it, knowing Les would leave for the winter but hoping up to the last minute he would reconsider.

By the end of September, the sun hung so low in the sky that its rays could not reach over the mountaintops. It circled around and around the unseen horizon outside Minook Valley, sinking lower and lower, pursued by the darkness. We would not see it—or Les—again until spring.

It was a tense evening after the children went to their loft. The argument between Les and me went on until the fire died down and the grizzly stopped coming down the stovepipe. I kept on at him even though I knew he was going to do what he said he *had* to do, no matter how much I protested. Leave me out here with five little kids. With an old battery-powered car radio our single link to the outside world—and a *one-way* link at that. My heart beat wildly to the rhythm of *What if? What if . . . ? What if . . . ? What if . . . ?* So many things could happen to us!

"Our survival at homesteading depends on me getting a winter job," Les insisted.

The man was immovable, like the mountain peaks. I may as well have been outside shouting at the snowstorm or at the thick imperturbable spruce with their deep shadows.

The evening ended on a sour note. I finally surrendered out of sheer exhaustion as I knew I would. As Les knew I would. What hurt as much as his determination to leave was the look of excitement, of *happiness,* on his face. I was afraid with a woman's keen intuition, deep in my soul, that if he left us like this, things would never again be the same between us, that it would be a winter to haunt us for the rest of our lives.

"When are you leaving?" I asked with a final, tearful sigh.

"Tomorrow. I'll never get out once snow closes Dead Horse Pass."

IT WAS STILL SNOWING the next morning when he departed to walk the eleven miles over the pass. I was reserved, resigned to our fate. The kids stood very quiet at the door, the twins and Tommy clinging to me. Les hoisted his pack without looking directly at any of us. He *ought* to feel guilty.

"Are you coming back?" Tommy asked, pleading.

"Hey! Don't I always come back?"

"What if something gets us?" whispered Sean, always the worrier. He still had nightmares about the bear that almost got him at the creek.

Les shot me a sharp look, blaming me for transferring my own fears to the children.

"Nothing will get us," I scolded with more confidence than I felt.

Les tightened his pack straps and turned to Sid. A rough hand fell on the boy's shoulder.

"Keep your rifle handy, son," he said.

Sid squared himself with pride and newfound responsibility. Sometimes I thought quiet Sid was the most responsible member of the entire Cobb clan, Lester included. Watching the exchange between father and son, the passing of the sword, as it were, made me realize how fast the boy was growing up out here. Much of the child had already left his face. It now cut a profile as thin and sharp as a skinning blade. In his eyes already appeared the faraway Alaska look. Wolves and grizzlies had that look. Les said it came from gazing into free and wild places where a man could be a man.

Finally, there was nothing left but goodbyes. Kisses and hugs stiffly delivered and received.

"We're Cobbs," Les said in parting. "We're homesteaders—and we're here to stay."

Then he turned and began walking rapidly with his pack away from Minook Creek. Snow swirled around his tall figure, its vortex sucked him into it, and he was gone. The mountains blurred by the snowfall seemed to rise higher and higher until they blocked out the sky and I thought they might suffocate me. Tears like icicles touched my cheeks. Twin terrors of loneliness and fear started growing in my belly like the unwanted fetus of a monster, whose very presence I heard in the whisper-walking of snow on the cabin roof, whom I sensed lurking in the deep shadows of spruce across the creek where they were a part of the changing light and the texture of the air itself.

"Maybe it'll keep the wolves back if I put some traps around the cabin," Sid proposed, covering his uncertainty with the thin flash of a grin. "I reckon they're going to get mighty hungry before the winter's over. Snow is coming early. Two or three more days like this and we won't be able to get in or out of the valley until spring thaw."

Jack London wrote that there were a thousand ways this country could kill you—and each way was more horrible than the last.

2

Odd that it was *I,* not Les, who came up with the idea of homesteading. I was not the pioneering type; at least I didn't think I was. I was a small-town girl from Wichita, as in *The Wizard of Oz*. Like most young females of my generation, I grew up aspiring to the title *Mrs.* as the pinnacle of female success—a little house in the suburbs, a hardworking and faithful hubby, two-point-two children . . .

Right out of high school, I ended up with a tract house, a husband who was neither particularly industrious nor faithful, and, soon, three kids. I divorced my husband in the spring of 1971. Good riddance. He was just as happy to be rid of me and his three rough-and-tumble sons as I was to be rid of him. We were holding him back, he said. Turned out the only thing we were holding him back *from* was commitment to various institutions for treatment of his mental condition and insanity. The boys and I never saw him again.

Reflecting back, I decided it was probably the breakup of my marriage that made it easier, perhaps even inevitable, for me to entertain the idea of new frontiers. After my divorce, I was more than ready to begin life again—somewhere far away from the bad memories. I felt *compelled* to go out and start fresh.

I bundled Sid, eight, Sean, five, and Tommy, three, into what amounted to my share of the wrecked marriage's assets—a metallic-blue

1966 Ford Mustang Fastback—and headed . . . west. Where else? Had Americans not always turned west in search of new lives?

We first settled in Denver. That proved to be transitory. I was a small-town girl with small-town ways and habits. I was out of my pond in Denver. I picked us up and moved to Longmont, a much smaller town, where I soon hooked a job working a cash register at a truck stop. I barely earned sufficient wages to satisfy four hungry mouths and make ragged ends meet.

I was twenty-seven years old, divorced, uneducated, the single mother of three—and I was going nowhere fast. I was a dead-end woman at a dead-end job in a dead-end corner of nowhere—a brutal but honest assessment of my life. Exhausted, discouraged, and frustrated, I prayed every night for God to let me see a better way. A single thought nagged at me: *There has to be more to life than this.*

Sometimes Destiny has to kick you in the seat of the pants to get your attention. Not that I recognized the grease monkey from the truck garage next door as Destiny. He looked more like Trouble. As it turned out, he was a cowboy-type recently off a Colorado cattle ranch, so tall he bumped his head on the doorway when he came in, broad shouldered, with a dark magnificent beard and a direct blue-gray gaze that proved hard to ignore. He walked with a brash, swaggering gait that turned out to conceal an inherent shyness.

He kept coming into the truck stop to drink coffee and, I correctly suspected, to attract my eye. He started off exchanging a few comments with me at the register, then gradually got around to introducing himself and asking my name. It took him almost a month and forty gallons of coffee to get that far. His name was Lester Cobb.

"My pop named me Lester after my granpaw. Granpaw was an early settler in Colorado."

"I see."

"Norma is a real pretty name. I notice you a lot. You're always friendly and smiling at people."

I smiled. "You do drink a lot of coffee."

"I come in for lunch and on my coffee break. That's when I notice you."

"I notice you noticing me."

The big guy actually blushed. I was going to burst out laughing if he kicked the toe of his shoe on the floor and said, "Gee whiz!"

"Uh . . . Norma. Maybe . . . You know . . . ?"

I said it for him, laughing merrily, *"Gee whiz!"*

He grinned sheepishly. That man could really light up a grin.

"Norma, if you ever get a break . . . I mean, uh . . ." He finally blurted it out. "Maybe you could have coffee with me?"

I did. About forty more gallons of it. In the process I learned that the beard covered up a baby face; he was only twenty-one, six years younger than I. His live-in girlfriend had packed up and split just before last Christmas and left him in sole custody of six-month-old twin daughters, Cara and Cora. A single parent like me, he struggled to make ragged ends come together. His dream was to own a little farm or ranch of his own, if he could ever afford it.

"That's something that doesn't seem to be in the foreseeable future," he admitted ruefully.

I thought this was going nowhere. The age difference between us seemed too great. Gradually, however, age vanished as a point of contention between us. I was small and dark haired and looked even younger than he. I was the one carded at the door, not Les, whenever we went dancing at a club. We became close. One night, Les said, "Norma, I love you. We oughta be practical too. Between us, we got five kids. If we was to put 'em all in one pot . . . ?"

The seven of us, a large ready-made family, moved into a rented hundred-year-old farmhouse that was rumored to be haunted by the ghost of the rancher who died there. It was shortly thereafter that the dreams began. The same one almost every night. Les and I and the five kids were in the wilderness somewhere building a log cabin and growing vegetables. I assumed it was in Canada. The sun shone and we were happy as we worked clearing our land.

I always awoke feeling contented and fulfilled, but also confused. Where were those dreams coming from? If anyone should be having them, it was Les. He was the wanderer, the adventurer. I attempted to dismiss them as an aberration disrupting the building of my "normal" life.

Yet they persisted, and in their persistence stirred something sleeping in my soul and awoke it into a slightly scary stranger. I searched for answers. Was this God's way of booting me in the seat of the pants, I asked myself? His way of answering my prayers and showing me a better way? Was God revealing my Destiny?

What else *could* it be?

I sat suddenly upright in bed in the middle of one night and shook Les awake. I was so excited. The answer had come to me as clearly as a verse from Exodus.

"The ghost again, honey?" Les mumbled drowsily.

We sometimes heard unexplained sounds in the night, footfalls and banging, although the rancher's ghost had never actually appeared.

"Lester, listen to me—"

"Go back to sleep, Norma. He's a Casper."

"It's not that, Les! I *know* what we're meant to do. I think God is showing me our destiny."

"Tell me about it in the morning, honey."

"Lester!"

He started off half listening with his eyes closed and his head on the pillow. His eyes slowly opened. By the time I finished explaining, he was sitting upright in bed. We were both chattering at once.

"Homesteading?" Les said. "Canada?"

I could almost feel him rolling the words around in his head, tasting them, savoring their flavor of adventure and challenge. Clearly, the idea titillated his imagination.

"We oughta do it!" he declared, embracing it. "It'll be good for the kids."

"It'll be good for the family."

A thought stopped him. "You can still homestead in Canada?"

"I'm sure you can. It's a big country with lots of open land."

I turned on the bedside lamp and ran to get the atlas with a map of Canada. Les's eyes blazed with energy. We devoured the map, marking likely spots of sparse population. There *was* lots of open country.

"With five kids to feed," Les said, mulling it over, "all we're ever going to do down here is work for wages and exist hand to mouth, paycheck to paycheck. We'll never be able to afford a farm of our own. We'll never have anything."

With that, we took my dream, shared it, and it became *our* dream. From the moment it became *ours,* Destiny was set as surely as if God Himself directed it. How naïve and young we were.

We simply assumed there was Canadian land for the taking. That was what "everybody" said, and "everybody" couldn't be wrong. Canada was still the Old West; it needed settlers to make it grow. We heard all you had to do was find a good site with plenty of grass and water on it and pitch camp. Why, it would take us no time until we had our own cabin and no mortgage to tie it up for thirty years. It would be our own piece of earth upon which to raise kids and crops and a future. We could work hard and have something. No one could ever come around and kick us off. All we had to do was get there.

"A new land!" Les shouted. "We're pioneers!"

It *felt* right. We began immediately making plans, sitting at the kitchen table and compiling a rough list of reasons why we should go ahead with it. I taped the list to the door of the fridge where it became our constant motivator:

1. Society making it hard to raise a large family
2. Schools getting bad educationally and morally
3. Want to get closer to nature and God
4. Want our faith to come alive
5. Want to raise our kids the old way, not influenced by the new ways taking shape
6. Want to teach our kids responsibility and common sense
7. Don't like what's happening in the cities
8. Don't like the pollution of environment and health
9. Would be a great challenge to us all
10. Want to be free to do as we please
11. Want a strong family relationship
12. Want to give kids land in the country where they have a choice on how to live
13. Les wants to work for himself, not others

My parents and Les's were vocally and ardently opposed to the entire plan.

"Why do you want to go out to that godforsaken country?" my father demanded. "You can't grow anything out there. You'll get everybody killed."

Our folks obviously thought Les and me reckless and uncaring parents, taking the children into some wild land to live in isolation. No doctors, no schools, and only wild animals for neighbors. Why, we didn't even know where we were going, other than *somewhere* in Canada.

Only Les's little grandmother sympathized. Les had grown up with her tales of how she and his grandfather had gone against *their* parents' wishes and moved west to Colorado where, through strength and perseverance, they eventually built a vast farm of over two thousand acres. Little Grandma took my hand and Les's.

"Do it," she said to us. "Don't let the against-ers ruin your chances. You're the only one in the family, Lester, who is going to make it. And you're both going to have a good time."

As for the children, Sid, now nine, was the most enthusiastic; he consumed books and magazine articles on dog mushing and big-game hunting. Cara and Cora, still in diapers and not yet talking, sensed adventure looming but had little idea of what it was. Tommy the toddler was only slightly more aware. Six-year-old Sean chased after Sid to bombard him with endless questions. *Mightn't we freeze to death in the winter? Won't the bears and wolves get us? What will we eat?*

Sean was the family worrier. Les said the reason he remained so thin was because he worried himself skinny.

LES AND I WERE MARRIED on October 20, 1972, at a local justice of the peace. Two weeks later, to the day, everything we no longer needed or couldn't take with us had been sold off and the money socked for our impending journey to Canada. Our entire stash came to less than one thousand dollars.

We set out for Canada on a November morning so frosty even words crackled in the air, and so clear you could almost see an echo bounce off the snowcapped Rockies. Our caravan sat parked in front of the old farmhouse while we scurried around making last-minute checks. Everything we thought we might need in clearing land and building a new home in the wilderness filled the box bed of the old green Ford two-ton truck Les had bought and repaired. Les would drive it and lead the way, towing behind it his Willys Jeep that, in a more cavalier spirit and time of the sixties, he had hand-painted a background red sprinkled with giant white daisies. I would bring up the rear at the wheel of my Mustang. It seemed an extravagant vehicle for pioneers, but I couldn't stand to part with it. We could always sell it if we got into trouble and needed cash.

The route we mapped out led west to California, then north through Oregon and Washington to British Columbia. We would pick out land once we got there. Grinning, Les commented on how much we resembled a caravan of Okies fleeing the dust bowl. Right out of *The Grapes of Wrath*.

The enormity of our undertaking, maybe even the foolhardiness of it, had crept cold and slithering into bed with me the night before we departed. Trembling, I curled up as close to Les as I could get.

"Are you afraid?" he asked, whispering.

"Oh, Les! Are we doing the right thing? It's . . . Everything is so unknown . . . so *uncertain!*"

After a long pause during which I feared he was also having second thoughts, he asked, "Would you rather not go?"

A question so bluntly worded was enough to bring me back on track. Of course we were going. We were committed.

"That's my girl," he said, kissing me.

Les was not a man to entertain doubts. He knew only one way to look—straight ahead. This was going to be the grandest adventure of his life.

"We've burned all our bridges behind us," he said. "We have only one way to go now. North."

3

The way North, the generic term we adopted for our destination, turned into an unexpectedly hard journey, and a long one. Early pioneers who headed west with their cornmeal, barrels of pickled pork, and everything else crammed into their prairie schooners suffered from mountains, dust storms, illness, blizzards, accidents, and hostile Indians. The Cobbs with our cornmeal, canned goods, and everything else packed into the box of the two-tonner Ford suffered from mountains, storms, illness, freezing weather, mechanical breakdowns, and thieves.

Les gave the vehicles a last-minute tinkering underneath their hoods before the seven of us split up between the truck and my Mustang and piled in to begin the trip. Eager Sid wore his cap with the earflaps and hurried everyone along. The other two boys were a bit quieter than normal, little Sean wearing a worrier's crease in his brow. Cara and Cora seemed in such awe of the undertaking that they forgot to be unpleasant. Les slammed the truck's hood, stretched his back, and cast me a long, searching look. I batted my eyes nervously to clear them. Les's gaze shifted in the direction of Wolf Creek Pass, our first rally point at the top of the Rocky Mountains.

"Let us all join hands," I suggested, "and ask God to keep us safe on our journey and to guide us in the right direction."

The two-ton truck, loaded down as it was and towing Les's psychedelic Willys, sucked gas as through a water hose. Food, flats, engine trouble, and other minor crises accumulated to suck cash from our trip sock the same way. Morale plummeted after one particularly trying day when a car burglar broke into the Jeep while we slept at a roadside park and stole most of our tools and some of Les's hunting guns. It was apparent by the time we reached California four days into the journey that we had naïvely underestimated expenses. Although God may have showed me the way in my dreams, it seemed He was now going to test us to make sure we were worthy.

We needed more money to continue the trip. Les hunched down into his broad shoulders and seemed disappointed but not defeated. He looked around in Chino, California, and landed a job as a garage mechanic while I rented a small house in a working section of town.

"Three or four weeks," Les calculated, "and we'll have enough dough to move on."

Weeks passed—and turned into the spring of 1973.

"We're never going to reach Canada at this rate," Les fretted. "Rent and hungry mouths eat up everything we make."

We had to focus. Les took on extra work. The kids and I contributed to the trip sock by going around to Dumpsters and pilfering discarded items, which we then cleaned and repaired for resale at garage sales and flea markets. California was so rich and wasteful that its residents seemed to think nothing of throwing away useful stuff, some of which were genuine treasures.

One Saturday afternoon a woman stopped by the resale table Les and I had set up at a flea market. We fell into eager conversation with her after we discovered she was a Canadian schoolteacher traveling in the United States on sabbatical. She looked skeptical when we revealed we were homesteaders on our way to Canada. Les whipped out the magazine clipping on homesteading he carried around in his shirt pocket for inspiration.

"How long ago was this piece published?" she asked.

Les admitted he had torn it from a magazine that may have been four or five years old.

"Well . . ." She appeared uncomfortable, like someone delivering sad news about a next of kin.

"Well . . . *what?*" I asked, more sharply than I intended.

"Don't you know?" It was obvious we didn't. "Homesteading in Canada is closed to noncitizens. It's been closed for quite a while."

Even the twins playing and bickering underneath the table fell silent. Seven pairs of eyes regarded her with disbelief.

"It's not true," Sid breathed, his eyes filling.

"Well . . ." She looked ready to bolt. "You might try up around the Peace River area. There are some squatters there. Homesteading is officially closed, but if you get far enough into the outback you can settle and the government probably won't run you off."

I was almost in shock. Could I be mistaken about where God was directing us? Had I misinterpreted my dreams? Should we give it up? Should we turn back?

Les and I avoided each other's eyes for the next several days while questions and doubts prompted some soul-searching. At least I searched my soul, tormented and uncertain about the decision we had made. But if my husband and I shared one trait, it was that from our common German ancestry we were both hardheaded, stubborn as only Bavarian peasant stock could be. Resolve slowly returned and our spirits lifted.

If homesteading required *squatting* on government land, then that was what we would do. Les was right: We had burned all our bridges behind us. North was the only direction we had left. Homesteading had become more than a dream; it became our quest for the Holy Grail. Don't confuse us with the facts, our minds were made up.

In spite of its hardships, our venture had inspired my sister Susie and her husband John to pull up stakes in Arizona and launch an adventure of their own. They had no children to hold them back. They stopped to visit us in Chino on their way to Anchorage, Alaska.

"Maybe you-all should come with us to Alaska," Susie suggested. "You could meet us up there next spring."

Les and I talked it over. The threat of long, cold, dark winters put us off. Besides, neither of us was willing to concede failure so readily.

"We feel we should give Canada a chance first," I said. "If they refuse us settlement, we can head on up to Alaska and see how you're faring. That way we'll hit all the bases on the way."

Les sold both his psychedelic Willys and my baby-blue Mustang. Was this not an emergency? We replaced the two vehicles with a cheap 1949

Ford pickup and had some money left over to contribute to the trip sock. Gradually, through the efforts of the entire family, the sock filled up again, coin by coin, a dollar bill at a time. Even Sean regained hope that we were not to be stuck in Chino forever.

In June, supplies partly replenished, the Cobbs set out North again driving the two-tonner and the '49 pickup. We had been on the road for nearly eight months.

"Are we going to make it this time?" Sean worried.

AS IT TURNED OUT, Sean's skepticism was more than warranted. In Washington State, the three youngest—Tommy, Cara, and Cora—contracted whooping cough and became too ill to travel. Les pitched our tent in a vacant field south of Seattle where we intended to camp out until the children got better. Instead of recovering, however, the poor things suffered repeated relapses. So young they were, and so sick. Vomiting in their sleeping bags, unable to hold down food and drink. They wasted away in that tent in the field in the rain.

Once again I had second thoughts. Specters of accusation and guilt arose to haunt my sleep. I said nothing to Les about my misgivings; I knew he was wrestling with his own. Besides, *my* dreams were what had landed us here.

This time Les sold the '49 pickup and most of our remaining furniture in order to pay doctor bills and buy supplies while we were stalled. That left us with the two-tonner, our clothing, a few personal possessions, and a trip sock so flat it could have been ironed.

"The only thing I can see to do," Les said, fighting to conceal his disappointment, "is to settle here over the winter, get a job, regroup, and head out again next spring."

We were bogged down for the second time since leaving Colorado. Les landed another mechanic's job and we rented a small house; it was all we could afford. Life for the rest of the summer turned almost normal. Come September I even enrolled the kids in public school.

There were days when I even wished we might put down roots right where we were and give up my foolish dreams; we should never have started out like this in the first place. I had accepted that we would face hardships. I simply failed to realize they would start so soon, even before we reached North. What prevented my suggesting quitting was that my dreams had kindled even bigger dreams in my husband. I sometimes caught him standing outside when he came home from work, gazing north with that restless pioneer look of longing in his eyes. *Give up* was not part of this man's vocabulary. I felt guilty for even considering it.

One evening in late October while I was washing dinner dishes, Les called out excitedly from the living room. "Norma! Honey, come here right now!"

There was a program on our black-and-white garage-sale TV about Alaska and homesteading. Until that moment, we had thought little about the origin of *homesteading* or what it meant, other than free land. We were to receive a quick eye-opening history lesson that changed our lives, as it were.

According to what we learned, Congress had passed the U.S. Homestead Act in 1862, which provided that any person over age twenty-one who was head of a family and either a citizen or an alien who intended to become a citizen could obtain free title to 160 acres of government land if he or she lived on the land for five years and improved it. Sponsors of the law hoped it would help landless workers obtain *homesteads*—small farms—of their own while serving the purpose of settling and taming the West.

Between 1862 and 1900, nearly a half million Americans obtained free land. Although the U.S. Government would not end homesteading in the Lower Forty-eight until 1976, still nearly three years away, virtually all suitable land had long ago been gobbled up. That left only Alaska. Most homesteading in the U.S. and its territories had occurred there since 1900. But that was also about to end. Because of land claims by native Eskimos, Indians, and Aleuts, homesteading would be suspended in Alaska at the end of the year.

By January 1, 1974, less than three months away, there would be no more free government land, ever, in the United States of America.

"Homesteading in *Alaska*" Les whispered, looking at me, as though this were the first time we had even thought about it.

Both of us had kept up the pretense that everything would go well for us in Canada, that like the boll weevil "looking for a home" in the old folk song, we would also find a home. Doubts had secretly tormented Les as much as they had me.

"We still have time," Les said. "We can still do it—in *Alaska*. John and your sister are already in Anchorage."

Simply hearing that there actually *was* free land, if only for a short time longer, rekindled all the old dreams. Canada was not a sure thing; Alaska was. I thought seeing the TV program at this particular time was an omen. God had been right in directing us toward homesteading; we had merely been mistaken about *where* He meant.

We had to get started right away, no matter that winter was coming on. Our journey North turned into a race against time. Posting Alaska or Bust! signs on either side of the two-tonner Ford strengthened our resolve and seemed to offer good insurance against further catastrophe. On November 2, 1973, almost exactly one year from the day we first set out from Colorado, the seven Cobbs and Kernels piled into the cab of the big truck. Les cranked over the engine.

"I think we're gonna make it this time," young Sid commented. "We've already been busted enough."

THE ALCAN HIGHWAY stretched unpaved for most of its nearly two thousand miles. November was not the ideal time of year to be traveling north. Autumn rains and snow threatened to take the bottom out of the mud road, and there was always the hazard of getting snowed in out in the middle of the wilderness where traffic might not pass for days. However, we had no choice except to press on. We had less than two months to get there, find a homestead, and file on it with the government.

Although accustomed to winter weather in Colorado, we found ourselves quite unprepared for the meteorological vagaries of the North Country. The temperature in Canada our first full day driving north of the border was a pleasant forty-five degrees. The mercury started dropping that night after we pulled to the side of the road and prepared beds and pallets in the truck's uninsulated box bed shelter. Freezing snow began falling. We huddled together like puppies for warmth. The temperature plunged to *twenty below*.

"I'm *freezing*!" Sean cried. "Are we already in Alaska?"

The seven of us crowded into the truck cab in order to utilize our combined body heat in the more confined space. That was how we slept for the next five nights, piled up together on the seat and on the floorboard.

It was wonderful country though, rugged and breathtaking. It challenged the eye with magnificent vistas of conifer-furred valleys dusted with snow. Waterfalls cascaded off mountainsides in frozen crystal tiers. Les sucked his lungs full of the crisp, scented air.

"Taste it!" he exhorted. "It's the taste of *freedom!*"

We were going to be heartbroken, devastated, if we got there and couldn't find land.

Another thing besides the meteorology for which I found myself unprepared was the effect the land began exerting on my husband. Les always spoke of himself as a "one-way cut of cloth." He was very physical, very strong, and very macho, an outdoors type who never particularly learned to tolerate crowds and who wanted things to go his way even if he had to beat them into submission. Not an educated man at all, but practical and a survivor. I accepted that about him when I married him.

What I could not accept was the way this rough side began subtly overpowering the laughing, sensitive side that I also knew and loved. Maybe it was something in the northern air. Perhaps it had to do with the stress of traveling in cramped quarters with a wife and five exuberant kids. Whatever it was, it was as if he took off one coat and put on the coat of a rough, tough, macho bushman. His voice turned brusque, booming, and demanding. By the time we crossed the border into Alaska, I saw more of noisy Mr. Hyde than I saw of gentle Dr. Jekyll.

"Stop ordering us around, Lester!" I protested. "Whatever happened to kindness and consideration?"

"I'm getting us there, aren't I?" he responded peevishly.

I hoped his condition proved temporary.

Thirty-five dollars remained in the trip sock when we rolled into Anchorage on November 8 and linked up with my sister and her husband. The city was a bit disappointing, especially for Les and Sid. We expected Dawson City during the Yukon gold rush. Wooden sidewalks and mud and dogsleds hitched outside saloons. Instead, Anchorage was a modern city in spite of the fact that moose sometimes wandered into town and caused traffic jams and you could get eaten by a bear ten minutes outside city limits. There were movies, department stores, and traffic lights.

"You won't find any homesteading around Anchorage," we were informed. "You have to go farther north than this. North of Fairbanks, up near the Arctic Circle. But you can't get there from here this time of year. There aren't many roads—and what there are of them are starting to get snowed in and closed for the winter. You'll have to wait until spring thaw."

Spring! We *couldn't* wait until then. Time was running out on us. We had to locate a homestead before January 1. The thought that we had come all this way, only to be defeated at the end, was so unbearable we refused to entertain it. There must be a way to get there. Skis? Snowshoes? Dogsled? A wing and a prayer?

We would not be defeated.

4

Anchorage sprawled at the interior end of Cook Inlet, protected from the severe blasts of the Arctic winter by giant mountain ranges—the Wrangells, the Alaska Range, and the Talkeetna Mountains. The climate there was much milder than in other areas outside the valley. Winter had already arrived ahead of us in Anchorage, with first snowfalls. We were advised that the farther north you went, the more savage winter became. Fairbanks lay north another 325 miles, while virtually all the remaining available government land lay beyond Fairbanks even closer to the Arctic Circle.

Les talked to the Federal Bureau of Land Management and learned that it was possible to beat the January 1 homesteading deadline through a process called a "dry claim." The BLM maintained maps showing lands still available for settling. A prospective pioneer could pick out his 160 acres on the map, sight unseen, and lay claim to it on the promise that he would start "proving" it as soon as weather permitted. To make our dry claim, however, we would have to appear in person at the Fairbanks BLM office.

"I have a map showing where all the land is," Les declared. "Honey, the roads are hazardous. If you and the kids will stay with your sister, I'll see if I can get to Fairbanks and file. If it's humanly possible, I'll take a look at the land first."

Off he went in the two-ton Ford, using the last of our trip sock money for gasoline, while the children and I camped out in the tiny Airstream camper trailer John and Susie dragged up from Arizona. I would be a nervous wreck until he returned.

The road to Fairbanks was still passable. Negotiating the Elliott Highway farther north remained questionable. I was so relieved when Les returned three days later jubilant and full of grins. He had successfully filed on 160 acres located in the Manley Hot Springs region 150 miles west-northwest of Fairbanks and less than 75 miles south of the Arctic Circle. The "Far North Country." Our prospective new homesite was about a mile past Unanimous Creek. It was bush country and largely unsettled, for good reason as we were to discover.

"Did you see it?" I asked him.

"Honey, it's wonderful country."

"You *saw* it then?"

"You and the kids are gonna love it."

We now had land, a start on a new life. We were soon-to-be *homesteaders* who wouldn't be able to set foot on the new farm until after spring thaw. In the meantime, we had to survive through the winter in Anchorage with no money left, no place to stay, and no jobs.

Sean the family worrier summed it up. "*Almost* busted."

5

Les clung to the attitude that you could envision *anything* in Alaska and make it happen, that it was a wide-open frontier waiting to be conquered. Maybe you could, but it took time. We tightened our belts and our resolve and prepared to hang on. We had made it this far.

Our first priority was shelter. We latched onto a rundown four-room house by promising to pay rent as soon as Les found winter employment. Food was an equal priority—although, as Les pointed out, we weren't going to starve. Alaska was a well-stocked larder filled with meals on hoof and paw. He took his .22-caliber rifle, the only firearm to have survived the roadside theft en route to California, and supplemented our meager tablefare by hunting snowshoe rabbits. We had rabbit fried, rabbit broiled, rabbit baked, and rabbit dumplings and stew. We used everything about the rabbit except his snowshoe—and Sid carried one of those in his pocket for good luck.

"We're going to need all the good luck we can get," Sean fretted.

"I keep seeing this ol' moose hanging around out there where I'm rabbit hunting," Les said. "There's enough beef there on the hoof to last us until spring."

We couldn't afford a hunting license. Besides that, moose season was closed. It was risky enough for Les to hunt rabbits without a license.

"Poaching?" I cried in alarm.

"The *first* pioneers never even heard of a license," Les complained.

"It's against the law to shoot the moose, Lester. You could go to jail."

Les had this way of rolling his shoulders forward and thrusting out his chin whenever he was spoiling for a fight. "It's against the law to let my family starve too," he said.

He shot the moose. I knew he would. He pumped the giant animal full of lead from the small-caliber .22. He skinned it, field-dressed it, and drove back to town in John's pickup to get our Ford truck with the enclosed bed. The boys were excited over the kill. They had never seen a moose close up. Sid, Sean, and little Tommy clambered into the truck with Les and went back to help load the huge carcass. Les said they were going to have to learn how to take care of game for when we started homesteading in the spring.

They were on their way home, rejoicing over the triumph and anticipating moose steaks, when a state trooper eased in behind the truck. Les's heart dropped when the policeman lit up his emergency pull-over lights. There was no way we could afford a traffic fine.

Apparently, a traffic violation wasn't the purpose for the stop.

"What do you have inside the truck?" the trooper demanded.

Les shot a guilty look at the box bed's closed doors and froze. He had no way of knowing whether someone had spotted him loading the moose or whether the patrolman was simply nosy and checking for contraband, hoping to get lucky. Whichever, the outcome likely meant Les's spending the winter in jail. Poaching big game was serious business. The kids and I would have to return to Colorado or to my dad's place in Wichita, if we could get there. It meant starting the trek all over again come spring—if we still had the energy for it.

The three silent little boys huddled around Les. They looked even more guilty than he, if that were possible. Reluctantly, Les opened the double doors of the box bed and stepped back to let the officer see inside. What could he say? There lay the moose carcass, all the evidence the trooper needed for an arrest.

"Will you let me take my boys home first?" Les asked, assuming the worst.

The trooper was a seasoned Alaska hand who had undoubtedly handled situations like this before. He looked at Les. He looked at the dead moose. His eyes drifted carefully across the three small boys standing in a stairstep row. Skinny kids with thin hatchet faces, needing haircuts, hands hanging straight by their sides out of the frayed sleeves of soiled and worn coats. They weren't starving, of course, but they were so thin they looked like they were starving.

"We were going to eat it," five-year-old Tommy muttered in a small voice.

The remark could not have been better timed or delivered. The trooper sighed deeply, his eyes remaining on the children. Then he seemed to make up his mind. He reached and slowly closed the truck doors.

"Get out of here," he said to Les.

A moose is an incredibly big animal. We put it in the bathtub while we cut it up and packaged it for freezing. It was an old brute, and awfully tough, but still a welcome respite from snowshoe hare.

"We'll eat good like this all the time," Sid murmured around a full mouth, "when we finally move onto our own homestead."

6

We made it through the winter. Les landed another mechanic's job and we began to restock for when spring came. The first thing we bought was another pickup truck, a used white Ford Ranger. Gradually, by shopping wisely and doing without, we accumulated many of the supplies, material, and livestock necessary for when we moved onto our land: building materials, tools; hunting guns; canned and packaged foodstuffs; old schoolbooks so the brood could continue studying in the bush; eight rabbits to begin our farm; six potential sled dogs, which included a black yearling malamute named Black, a bitch husky named Lady and her four puppies; and one cat, Callie, which Cara and Cora took turns dragging around by her neck. As "homesteading" day approached, conflicting emotions of excitement, confusion, and expectations mounted in the family. It looked as if we were finally going to make it, with God's help.

Not that the winter had not extracted casualties. Long, dark, cold winters, we discovered, frequently unraveled relationships not strong enough to weather them. My sister Susie and John had intended going north with us to help. Instead, they announced they were returning to Arizona where they would divorce within a short time. I thanked God that the Cobbs, who had endured so much during the journey, seemed to have been strengthened and tempered by hardship.

Taking the places of John and Susie were Arnold Cranick and his wife, Betty. Arnold worked with Les as a mechanic at the Anchorage Yellow Cab Company. I met the Cranicks a short time before we planned to take off.

I liked little of what I saw. Les was too quick to accept people for what they appeared to be on the surface. My husband had this bold, confident manner that attracted other men to want to grow big beards like his and join him in adventuring. Not all such men were honorable, and Les asked few questions. I always looked deeper, was more cautious. Something about Arnold Cranick spelled trouble with a capital *T*.

He was about thirty, a big man, bigger than Les, with a dark mustache that refused to soften the thin cruel line that was his mouth. I thought he looked brutish. He had hard, mean-looking eyes and a bottle of booze always lurking within reach, the odor of which seemed to mist from his pores. Men like that, it seemed, always married short, dumpy women with hair bleached so often it looked like straw. That was Betty. She uttered conversation at the rate of about two words an hour as long as her husband was around, and only then after looking to him for permission.

"It's too late for them to file for land," I hedged.

"They'll check around and see if they can take over somebody else's homestead," Les said. "Besides, we can help each other."

You rarely said no to Les. You just didn't. The man was a force of nature.

On March 31, as Alaska started shaking itself free of snow and thawing out its bones to the first thin rays of sun coming back north, we packed our few worldly possessions into the pickup and the box bed of the old two-ton Ford and set out for Fairbanks and points north. The Cranicks showed up for the trek driving a small, tan Chevy pickup. Arnold had cut the bed off it and used it as the chassis for constructing a rickety-looking camper trailer, which he towed behind what was left of the truck.

"Looks like a junk pile pulling a junk pile," Sid aptly described it.

I gave a sigh of relief as we struck the blacktop road that led to Fairbanks. Les handled the big truck with part of the kids; I followed in the pickup with the remainder, along with six dogs, eight rabbits in cages, and Callie the cat in the cab; and the Cranicks brought up the caravan's tail. We had either been on the road or stalled somewhere along it for nearly a year and a half. Pioneers, but still not pioneers. You had to *get* there first.

Fairbanks was a flourishing little town what with the oil boom and construction of the Alyeska oil pipeline. Beyond it, however, civilization pretty much stopped. The pavement on the inappropriately named Elliott *Highway* soon petered out and became mud ruts so narrow one car had to pull over and stop when meeting another vehicle. The road was sloppy and slick with sides piled car-rooftop high with dirty snow that sucked you in like a magnet if you got too close. It curved and roller-coastered through a land whose vastness gave the impression of driving directly into the sky. Evergreen spruce as thick as dog fur covered rolling and craggy hills; creeks and muskeg swamps were splotched with willow, cottonwood, and alder thickets. The terrain seemed to stretch on like that forever without changing, except for some rudimentary sign here and there—a trail, a rough-hewn sign posting someone's homestead, an abandoned vehicle—to mark the outer limits of civilization. I felt . . . lost in space. There was no other way to describe it. Yet, lost in a calm and peaceful way.

The terrain as we traveled north became less commanding, less imposing than the giant snowcapped mountain ranges south of Denali and on toward Cook's Inlet. Shorter growing seasons and the ring of permafrost circling the Arctic cap stunted vegetation. Trees were shorter and tougher looking. Only in the protected valleys did spruce grow to cabin-building size or stands of birch tower in white and ghostly battalions along clear-rushing streams of melted snow. We had been told that the land beyond the Arctic Circle became flatter than in Kansas and so barren the clouded breath of a far-distant caribou or wolf stood out like a frozen question mark.

"Will there be enough big trees on our place to build a cabin?" I asked Les during a rest break.

"I'm sure there will be," he evaded.

We camped alongside the road and slept in the big truck's covered bed. The aurora borealis flooded the sky with colors unimaginable to a Kansan or Texan. We stood together in awe, faces lifted in tribute. The twins hid behind Les and me, hugging our legs and peeking out with their little eyes wide and their mouths open but speechless for a change. With the northern lights God gives an artist's touch to His creation. He steals your breath and runs it shimmering across the sky. Eskimos say that the "People Up There" are holding a festival and chasing bears. The lights are the lights of the hunters.

Arnold, who had lagged behind all day, complained of how he couldn't safely get any speed pulling his homemade camper because his pickup was too lightweight and unbalanced. The camper weaved and jerked him dangerously from side to side. He narrowly avoided several disasters.

"Norma's truck is much heavier," Les offered. "We'll let her pull the camper tomorrow."

"That's right!" I scolded Les when we were alone. "The wife always gets the worst. Everybody else gets better."

Les attempted to mollify me. "You're a much better driver," he said.

"Humph!"

I TOOK THE LEAD the next morning pulling the Cranicks' trailer. Les brought up the rear in the two-tonner in the event either of the pickups experienced mechanical trouble. The road, if it could still be dignified with the title, grew progressively worse. I drove white-knuckled. We were finding out that when weather conditions were nice in Anchorage and to the south of Fairbanks, the spring breakup of ice and snow in the far north interior was only beginning. I was a raw bundle of nerves, what with the hazardous road, pulling the trailer, and the kids pestering me and wanting to know when we were going to get there. Poor things had been hearing about this mysterious "homestead" for going on two years while we slowly worked our way north toward it. By now, it probably seemed as elusive and mythical to them as the tower from which Rapunzel let down her hair or the castle at the top of Jack's beanstalk.

A diesel tractor-trailer sloshing south from the oil pipeline forced me to crash off the road into a snow berm. At least he was decent enough to stop and pull me out. Les called a break until I controlled my trembling.

"How much farther?" I asked him.

"It's past the Top of the World," he said.

"The Top of the World?"

"It's called the Top of the World because from up there you can see out all over the world."

"Okay. *Then* how much farther?"

"We go through Minto, then Eureka. We're real near then."

"Is Eureka a town?"

"Well . . ."

I was beginning to get suspicious. "Does the road go to our land?"

Les remembered something urgent to be done underneath the hood of his truck. I followed him. All four kids followed me.

"Does the road . . . ?" I said, starting over, distinctly enunciating each syllable as though trying to pin down an evasive child.

"I'm sure there's a trail," he said.

"You're *sure* there's a trail," I repeated numbly. "Lester! Don't you know?"

He slammed the truck's hood. "Well, we'd better be going."

The Top of the World *did* provide a breathtaking view of the Saw-tooth Mountains in one panorama and the Minto Flats in another. It was a country so big it stole words and swallowed them when you tried to describe it. It was wide and dark green with spruce laid out against the dazzling white of unmelted snow. Scores of frozen lakes glittered like a handful of diamonds cast from the heavens.

During our lunch stop, Les continued to evade and avoid questions about our new land. He hurried to finish eating, then got up, brushed crumbs out of his beard and wiped his hands on his jeans.

"I'd better take the lead vehicle from here on," he said. "The road gets worse."

Little worrier Sean expressed it for all of us. "How can it get any worse?"

"Lester?" I said. The tone of my voice warned him I would tolerate no more of his dodging.

He looked up over me and past my left shoulder. "I haven't actually been beyond this point," he finally admitted.

It took me a moment to collect my thoughts. I murmured in disbelief, "Today is April Fool's Day. Tell me this is an April Fool's joke?"

"This was as far as I could make it the last time," he explained sheepishly. "The roads and trails were all closed. I had to go back and file a dry claim. Honey . . . ?"

"Don't give me that grin, Lester. How could you let me think you'd actually *seen* our land?"

"I never really lied to you, honey. I—"

"You just let me think what I wanted to think."

He threw up his hands. "C'mon, everybody. Let's go to our new home. Norma, everything's gonna be all right."

I felt . . . lost in space. *Really* lost this time.

7

Alaska is a quiet land whose very immenseness seems to absorb all sound. Years later I was reminded of this when I saw a science fiction movie that asked the question, Does anyone hear you if you scream in space? The answer as it pertained to Alaska was: No! No one would hear. The roaring and grinding of our engines as we negotiated roads now more appropriately termed *trails* slapped back at us from silence as thick as the fog clutched deep in the forest. I felt like jumping out of the pickup and screaming to relieve tension.

So, go ahead. Scream. No one would hear.

Les's big truck in front of me picked up speed as gravity pulled it down a long steep decline. Mud and melting snow spumed from its tires, splashing against a steep rise of forest on the right while raining out onto the tops of spruce in a canyon on the other side. The heavy vehicle caromed down the slope, going faster and faster, fishtailing and sliding and slinging so much mud it almost disappeared into it.

I screamed. He wasn't going to make the corner at the bottom.

"He's a goner!" Sean morosely predicted.

Then, I was busy with my own problems and unable to dwell on Les's. Like some gluttonous monster, the decline sucked my pickup down the slippery slope after the truck. I fought the wheel to avoid disaster. The Cranicks' old trailer kept trying to overtake me and pass. I glanced in my rearview mirror in time to see it whip almost sideways alongside.

I twisted the wheel. The pickup's rear end with trailer attached endeavored to swap ends with the front. Pickup and trailer slid and roared and bulldozed down the hill amid flying mud and children's cries of panic.

"*We're* goners!" Sean screeched.

Luck more than skill negotiated us to the bottom where Les had managed to make the curve after all and stop on a level stretch. He and Sid jumped out of their truck as I ploughed up behind them. Cora and Tommy had been thrown to the floorboard where they were actively and noisily attempting to extricate themselves from each other. Sean braced himself wide-eyed against the dash, frozen to it. Callie the cat had all claws sunk into the seat, while the dogs in their cages in back were barking with excitement. They probably thought it was great fun.

"Whew!" Sean exhaled when we came to a stop.

"Lester!" I scolded. "We could have all been killed."

He checked us over, then said matter-of-factly, "We weren't. I was going one hundred miles an hour down that hill. My brakes wouldn't hold. We're going to have to take it easier."

There were times when I could have choked him.

The Cranicks in their pickup with Cara made the downhill trip with no problems. After all, I was pulling their trailer. Sean transferred to their cab to ride with Cara; it seemed safer. That left Sid with Les, Cora and Tommy with me.

We proceeded in that harrowing fashion deeper into Alaska's thawing and muddy heart. The day compressed itself into growling engines as we crept and fought our way up and down and around. White knuckles gripping steering wheels. Berms of dirty snow. Forested valleys in spectacular panorama of Wild America. And above all, that oppressive silence that threatened to absorb us molecule by molecule.

I wondered if we were lost. I could have strangled Lester for having pretended all winter that he had actually gone out to our land, set foot on it and knew where it was.

"The road's much better than this in the summer," Les consoled us.

I couldn't resist digging at him. "How do you know since you've never been out here to see it?"

The road, if it could be called that, twisted and climbed around the crest of a mountain. Deep snow still covered the ground and road at this altitude. The world dropped off on one side and plummeted sheer into a deep valley that broadened out into a green and white picture postcard.

I shifted into low gear on the downhill grade and crawled the pickup along the side of the mountain as tentatively as a caterpillar moving upside down on a piece of glass. Lady and Black and the pups howled into the abyss. Who would have thought less than two years ago that this little Kansas girl was capable of testing her nerve and prowess under pressure like this?

The pickup began to accelerate. When I tapped the brakes to slow it down, the homemade trailer under its own momentum pushed the rear of the pickup sliding toward the edge of the precipice, threatening to commit suicide and take us with it. I had no choice but to let up on the brakes and pray we rode it out.

We built up speed quickly, making it even more hazardous to attempt to use brakes. Breath froze in my throat like a handful of snow when I saw the curve coming up. It twisted sharply to the right, around the cone of the mountain, while directly ahead in our pathway lay open valley and cloudy sky.

"Mommy!" Cora shrieked.

Our parents were right. I panicked. We *were* all going to be killed.

I tapped the brakes, attempting to slow us down. That was a mistake. The trailer attempted to pass the pickup and take wing out over the canyon. Pickup and trailer were joined at the hip like Siamese twins. Where one went, both went.

The curve and the emptiness beyond it seemed to telephoto in toward me until it filled the windshield. Somehow I was aware of the cat hunched up on the seat with all her hair sticking out like quills on a frightened porcupine. Tommy and Cora grabbed each other. Their conjoint screaming merged into a high thin note of despair and stark terror.

We were going off the edge! There was no way to stop us!

Bursting snow canceled all vision as the Chevy exploded through the snow berm wind-piled along the cliff's edge. I experienced the sensation of falling. *God, forgive me for bringing my children . . .* There was sky on all sides and the timbered valley far below, as though we had taken off in an airplane.

Then . . . *we stopped falling!*

It took a moment for time to catch up and for me to realize what had happened. The trailer that seemed so bent on destroying us had now saved our lives. The Ranger had gone halfway out over the edge of the cliff and was teetering in space, balanced there and held by the counter-balance of the trailer which remained on the road.

I took a moment to gather my senses. I saw my white-knuckled hands still gripping the steering wheel. Slowly, as though in a dream, I turned my head to look at Cora and Tommy. They still hugged each other and seemed afraid to move, terrified that anything they did might upset the balance we had achieved through some miracle. Their faces were pale and their eyes wide enough to fall into.

"Don't move, kids," I whispered hoarsely and unnecessarily.

When I shifted my weight, the pickup seesawed ever so slightly. The children whimpered and trembled. In back of us, the dogs started carrying on again.

We couldn't get out of the Ford because both doors opened into nothing but air. Unnecessary movement might upset the equilibrium and send us plunging on to our early deaths.

"Please don't move," I pleaded with the kids. "Everything's going to be all right. Daddy will get us out."

For the first time, I think, I appreciated something in Les that must have been there all along but which was only recently being brought to the surface by adversity. I sensed in Les a newfound competence and confidence that came along with the annoying "bushman attitude" he had acquired since we crossed over into the North Country. It was a com-forting feeling at a time like this to know that my brawny bearded hus-band would indeed rescue us if it were at all humanly possible. Les was pioneer stuff.

He appeared with Arnold Cranick at the edge of the cliff. Hiding his apprehension, he assured us we would be back on firm earth within a few minutes. Working quickly, he and Arnold rigged chains to the Ranger's rear bumper and attached them to the two-ton truck. It wasn't long until he had us pulled safely back onto the road. I collapsed in Les's arms, forgiving him his attitude and his misleading me about seeing our land and anything else he might have done for as long as I had known him. I was so thankful that the two kids and I were still alive. All five children crowded around in a family hug fest.

"I've had it. I can't go any farther today," I cried. "We're going to have to spend the night here."

We built a campfire, ate what we could in weary silence, then crammed into the back of the two-tonner to sleep. Temperatures plummeted to zero degrees Fahrenheit beneath a clear sky where the aurora borealis chased the stars, but no one noticed. Shivering from cold, clutching the five children around Les and me to share our warmth, I whispered a prayer as the others slept.

"Lord," I murmured earnestly from the doubts growing deep in my soul, "haven't You tested us enough—or are You trying to drive us back?"

8

I wrestled with God and my own misgivings for most of that cold, sleepless night in the back of the truck. "Lord, did You *really* mean for us to come into this hard and forsaken land?" I beseeched Him. My faith in God was like that. I talked to Him, argued with Him, chatted, cried, scolded . . . Like Noah and Moses in the Old Testament. They, too, had had their doubts, had questioned God, and themselves. "Are we walking in the wilderness, Lord? Is this part of Your purpose?"

The list of homesteading incentives we taped to the fridge back in Colorado, and which I tucked into a copy of *Swiss Family Robinson* to bring with us, seemed incredibly fanciful in the hard light of reality. Our families were right when they objected to our migrating. It *was* dangerous. We *were* naïve. We could have been killed today. Had I misinterpreted my dreams after all?

Come morning, there was a bright April sun made even brighter by its reflection off the snow. I accepted it as a good sign. Even the three-year-old twins were more loving and less contentious than normal. They both hugged me good morning.

"We wuv you," Cara said.

"I love you. All of you."

"Will we get there today?" Sean wondered.

Of all the children, only Sid seemed to enjoy the adventure. He was enough like Les to be his own blood son. He took the .22 rifle and went off grouse hunting while Les and Arnold worked underneath the hood of the Cranicks' pickup. It kept stalling out.

"Why don't you and Betty take the three younger ones and drive on ahead to Eureka?" Les suggested, obviously sensing that I needed a break after the tribulations of the past few days. "We need some supplies. Leave the trailer. Arnold can pull it. If there's nothing in Eureka, go on to Manley Hot Springs where there's at least a trading post."

He straightened from underneath the hood of Arnold's truck. Grease smudged his forehead. Excitement sparked in his eyes as he looked toward the northwest.

"We should get there by this afternoon," he said. "Our own home."

Our own home. It sounded good. A bath, if only in a creek, or, better, in water heated over a campfire, also sounded good. So did a real meal cooked over the same open fire. Les figured we should have a log cabin erected within a couple of months or so after we reached our land. That meant real beds, a stove to keep us warm nights, a kitchen and table. Amenities that were necessities in normal life but which you didn't miss until you no longer had them.

Les's enthusiasm was contagious on such a bright spring morning. I felt much better when Betty and I along with Tommy and the twins piled into our white pickup and set off to find civilization, unencumbered by the camper trailer. A place where there were other people! Maybe we could sample a hamburger again, or a candy bar and Coke. How you missed the little things you once took for granted.

It was such a wonderful day I thought nothing could dampen my enthusiasm.

Eureka offered little in the way of civilization. It wasn't a town, merely a few abandoned and decaying miners' cabins, a few others occupied but looking as if they should be abandoned. Betty and I were both disappointed. Eureka was the nearest settlement to our homestead, which, according to Les's map, lay about ten miles north of it.

"It's like everybody got up and left after the gold claims played out," Betty offered. "I read that there used to be a lot of gold in this area. I bet there still is."

"That's why the place looks so prosperous," I scoffed. "It's fools' gold."

"*Real* gold, Norma. Nome up north had the biggest gold strike of all.

Bigger than the Klondike was. They found gold lying around on the beach!"

Betty could talk when she was away from Arnold.

"Wouldn't it be something if we struck gold?" she said with a get-rich-quick expression.

"I wouldn't count on finding it lying around on the beach. You'd have a better chance in Las Vegas."

"A girl can dream."

Yes. A girl could dream.

I turned the pickup south and drove over a slightly better road for another twenty miles until we reached Manley Hot Springs. Manley was booming with all of a dozen or so residences, a trading post next to a grass airstrip, and the Roadhouse, where you could pick up your mail at the post office window, order a genuine steak, or look over mammoth tusks and wolf furs on display in the window.

Manley, I was to learn, was first known as Tunalelten, "where the water is hot," by indigenous Athabaskans who had lived here for as long as fourteen thousand years. The Koyukuk and Tanana groups still lived in the area. The first non-Indian to settle here was old "Dad" Karshner who established an agricultural homestead at the sacred hot springs in 1902. The resulting small settlement was known simply as Hot Springs until 1957 when the postmaster, Gus Benson, got tired of local mail being sent half a continent away to Hot Springs, Arkansas, and decided to add *Manley* to *Hot Springs* for clarification.

Frank Manley—some said it was an alias to protect him from the law in Texas—was a local entrepreneur who developed the town and gold fields during the brief gold boom of 1907. Like so many Alaskan outposts, the town prospered, then gradually died. Its only attraction now, aside from the trading post and the Roadhouse, were the commercial hot springs. Settlers came from all around to bathe in them.

Electricity and the only telephone in town turned the trading post into a veritable light in the wilderness, the social center not only of Manley villagers but also of the few pioneers scattered within a hundred-square-mile radius. It consisted of several shelves stacked with nonperishable basic commodities, plus candy bars up front, a fridge stocked with beer and soft drinks, and a round table and chairs for customers to socialize. Two men sitting over beers at the table attracted our attention. The twins, never timid, stalked up to the first locals we had so far encountered and boldly looked them over.

"These your kids?" the shorter of the two men growled, looking at both Betty and me.

He appeared perhaps thirty-five years old and was maybe an inch or two taller than me. He wore a battered felt Stetson, jeans tucked into the tops of cowboy boots, a flaring red mustache, and a revolver in a holster belted around his hips. The other man was about the same age, but tall and skinny. He also wore a gun. I felt as though I had been unexpectedly transported back in time to a Dodge City saloon into which Wyatt Earp would walk at any moment.

I acknowledged Cara and Cora were mine.

"Don't you teach 'em it ain't polite to stare at people?" Shorty asked.

Frontiersmen, I soon came to realize, were a contentious, gravelly lot.

I grabbed the girls' hands and dragged them away to buy us all Cokes and candy bars. The clerk seemed cold and withdrawn, apparently as suspicious of strangers as any Ozark hillbilly. While he was taking our money, the telephone rang and he answered it.

When he hung up, he walked out to the gunslingers. "There's been an accident up on the side of the road, according to CB radio. They're on their way to Manley now. Jeff, see if you can round up B. J. It looks like they're gonna need his bush plane to get to a doctor."

I experienced a slight twinge of alarm, but immediately dismissed it as tension left over from the past few days. News certainly traveled fast for an area that had only two or three telephones. The clerk and the locals, unreceptive to begin with, now turned downright unfriendly. Like they hadn't time to waste on a passel of kids and two nosy women. We took our drinks and candy and drove to the bridge over the Manley Slough to wait for Les and Arnold and the two older boys.

We were parked there only a few minutes when a red pickup came barreling down the road, spraying mud like a Kansas tornado. It took the one-lane bridge in a single leap, all four tires taking to the air. It hit hard on the road, engine still gunned out.

"That's Les in the pickup!" Betty cried.

I went cold. *The accident!*

Somehow, in spite of the dread that clamped my heart in a fist of ice, I got the pickup started and turned around to chase after Les.

The red truck slid to a stop in front of the trading post. Les jumped out of the passenger's side with a blanketed bundle in his arms. The driver, a stranger, ran around to help him.

I braked hard, throwing mud, and let momentum propel me out the door, my eyes riveted on the blanket in Les's arms. I ran toward it, then began screaming Sean's name.

His little face looked so pale against the dark blanket. His eyes were hooded to near-lifeless slits. Blood soaked the blanket, stained Les's hands, and even smudged his beard. The man's eyes looked more haunted and anguished than I had ever seen them.

I became completely hysterical, rushing at my husband and attempting to wrench Sean from his arms.

"What has happened to my son?" I bellowed from reserves of pain and fear.

9

Jeff Stoddard, the shorter of the two gunslingers, rounded up the pilot B. J. Baker from his isolated cabin on the outskirts of Manley and rushed him to the trading post.

"It's another sign," B. J. said. At the time I was too distraught to question what he meant. Later I learned how B. J. looked upon virtually every uncommon occurrence as another sign that the End of the World was near. The Alaskan bush seemed to breed and attract eccentrics.

B. J.'s plane, which some men dragged out onto the grass strip to be ready for him, was an ancient tail-dragging Piper Cub equipped with only two seats. The nearest medical help, a village clinic, was in Tanana, some fifty miles away by air. B. J. had never flown there before and wasn't sure how to get there. Bush pilots flew by the seat of their pants, not by charts. A local named Martin Ott volunteered to show him the way and hold Sean during the flight. Sean was in shock and still losing blood.

"I'm going with my son!" I insisted.

B. J. stuck out his hairy jaw. "Lady, do *you* know the way to Tanana?"

"No, but—"

"Lady, the kid's been gunshot. You know what that means? I seen people shot before. If you want him to die, you'll stand here and fuss with us. Otherwise, we gotta get going."

I blubbered helplessly as Les thrust Sean into Martin Ott's arms. The two strangers quickly climbed into the airplane with my baby. Sean's face resembled a bar of carved soap, his sharp little features having relaxed and melded together from shock. I feared I would never see my son again as the plane lifted off the grass strip and became a speck in the sky heading south. I continued to stare long after it vanished, frozen in place by dread and fear. Les put his arms around me.

"Honey, Carl has taken Betty and Tommy and the girls back to his place. Do you want to go there to wait?"

"Carl?" I murmured, still numb. I had no idea how long I had been standing there.

"Carl Nicholas. I stopped at his place in Eureka looking for help. He drove us to Manley."

"I'm staying right here." The airstrip and the phone at the trading post were my last and only links to my son. I had no intention of giving them up.

My thoughts were jumbled and confused and twisted; I was prepared to lash out. What kind of place had we come to—where men wore guns and the nearest medical facility was fifty miles away? Where the roads were bogs and the people seemed rough and uncaring? Somehow, I had conjured up an idyllic image of homesteading as being a little like farming in the Midwest, minus the conveniences. It had been that way in my dreams. The reality was proving to be quite different. What a fool I was. Already I was losing one of my children—and we hadn't yet reached our homestead.

"What happened?" I finally managed to ask Les. "How was my son shot?"

As though hearing it might take away some of the horror of the unknown, maybe even undo what had happened.

Les explained how Sean had been sitting in Arnold's pickup while the men worked underneath the hood and Sid, back from hunting, watched. Arnold's .357 Magnum revolver lay on the floorboard. Sean scooted across the seat to get out of the truck. In doing so, he inadvertently knocked the pistol out onto the ground. It discharged, a freakish once-in-a-million accident, and the bullet ripped into my seven-year-old's frail little chest.

"Norma, I had rather it was me that was shot," Les agonized.

The minutes, the hours, dragged as we waited through the afternoon, waiting for news, good or bad. We sat side by side on the wooden porch at the trading post, too deadened to speak. Rugged-looking men and women with harsh, severe faces nodded to us in guarded sympathy as they came and went and discussed the tragedy among themselves in hushed tones. I glanced up frequently to search the skies for the returning airplane.

The first news we received came from the clinic in Nenana. Sean was still alive! All the clinic could offer was emergency first aid, as there was no doctor in residence. B. J. and Mr. Ott took off again in the Piper Cub to deliver Sean to the nearest hospital in Fairbanks, one hundred and fifty miles away.

That meant another seemingly endless wait before we learned to our relief that Sean was still hanging on when the plane landed in Fairbanks. He was taken immediately to surgery.

"If he makes it out of surgery and survives the night, he has a chance," we were informed via the single telephone line between Fairbanks and Manley.

I CANNOT RECALL a longer night, or a darker one, even though daylight persisted until near midnight and returned gray again a few hours later. Locals who had seemed so cold and aloof at first now rallied to help any way they could. Jeff Stoddard and his taller gunslinger partner, Joe Pumper, both of whom were gold miners, drove out to the roadside where Sid and Arnold Cranick had been left and brought them back to Carl Nicholas's house in Eureka. Carl had already been of such assistance in alerting Manley to have a plane ready and then speeding Les and Sean to it. He now offered to let us stay in a tiny camper trailer in the trees behind his cabin until things settled down. I finally relented to Les's coaxing and spent the rest of a sleepless night in the camper.

The next morning as Les and I were driving into Manley, we encountered the local state trooper on his way to Eureka to inform us of Sean's condition.

"It's a miracle," he said. "Your boy's still alive."

I broke down with relief. "I have to be with him, Les. Somehow I have to get there."

A bush pilot in Manley who had a son Sean's age offered to fly me to Fairbanks while Les stayed in Eureka and took care of the other kids.

Although it was only the second time I had ever flown, the first time in a small airplane across vast wilderness, I jumped at the chance.

As soon as we landed in Fairbanks, I hurried directly to the hospital. I had to see for myself that my little boy remained alive. He was pale and unconscious. He looked so tiny and vulnerable lying in that sterile bed with tubes and lines running from every orifice. Tears blurred my vision. I placed my ear close to his lips to satisfy myself that he was still breathing.

"It *is* a miracle," the doctor confirmed. "The bullet punctured his lungs, diaphragm, and the edge of his heart. With injuries like that, he should never have made it alive to the hospital. Strictly speaking, even if he did make it he should have been a vegetable for the rest of his life but . . ."

I held my breath. He smiled reassuringly, looking a bit befuddled. "But . . . it looks like everything is functioning properly. He's going to make it. I don't understand how."

"Prayer," I explained, crying softly. "Prayer."

10

Sean underwent two surgeries and remained in intensive care for five days. He stayed in Fairbanks Memorial for another five days after that, an unsmiling and withdrawn little boy intimidated by all the attention and from being hooked up by line and catheter to machines obviously frightening to a seven-year-old. Scars left by the bullet and subsequent surgeries horrified him the first time he saw them. They ran in a large half-moon from underneath his arm to the middle of his belly. I prayed for both his physical and emotional recovery.

While people on America's "Last Frontier" may appear rough and uncaring on the surface, I discovered they had a way of rallying when someone needed help. Even back in Kansas and Colorado, folks would never have extended themselves like these did. I was a stranger in a strange town with only fifty dollars to my name and the clothing I wore. Patricia Weld of the medical records department, who lived three blocks from the hospital, took me in, knowing only that I had an injured son and nowhere to stay. Doctors said they would arrange payment of Sean's medical bills since Les and I were without jobs and low on money.

"It's the bush way," Jeff Stoddard later explained in all candidness. "Alaska is a place where you're expected to be independent and care for yourself when you can. But if you got real trouble and need help, then you got friends and neighbors. Even if they do live thirty or forty miles away."

While I remained at Sean's bedside in Fairbanks, Les in Eureka accepted Carl Nicholas's hospitality and moved the rest of our Kernels, along with rabbits, dogs, and cat Callie, into a spare camper trailer parked in the aspen about a hundred yards behind Carl's two-room log cabin. It was an old dilapidated miner's camper that Carl had salvaged from somewhere. It had one small room equipped with a bed, a sagging sofa, a wood-burning stove, and a kerosene cooking range of sorts. Arnold and Betty Cranick set up camp in their own homemade camper directly behind Carl's place. The Cobb homesteaders were stalled while we waited for Sean's recovery.

Sean and I rejoined the family on April 12 after another bush flight from Fairbanks. All our new friends—Jeff Stoddard and Joe Pumper, the gunslingers; B. J. Baker; Martin Ott; Carl Nicholas; as well as Les, Sid, Tommy, and the twins—greeted us at the Manley grass strip. Only the Cranicks were conspicuous by their absence.

"Arnold thinks we blame him for the accident, since it was his gun," Les explained. "I've tried to tell him it couldn't be helped. We don't see much of him. Him and Carl spend most of their time up in the main cabin, drinking."

"Are you all going to keep staying at Carl's?" Joe Pumper casually inquired.

It wasn't like we had other choices at the moment. Living in the back of the two-tonner without beds, heat, and a means to cook our food was out of the question during Sean's recuperation. It would be at least two or three weeks before he could travel.

"Are you all sure you want to stay there?" Joe proceeded in a tone that carried a subtle warning.

"What do you mean?" I cried, alarm sensors sounding.

Joe declined to go on. I couldn't blame Arnold for what had happened, as much as I would have liked to, but the incident certainly did little toward improving my evaluation of the man. It was common knowledge in the area that Carl Nicholas was an alcoholic; in Arnold Cranick he apparently found a soul mate. Les said the two of them had been drunk together most of the time I was gone. When Arnold was drinking, he grew surly, talked mean.

Helpless to do otherwise, I swallowed my sense of foreboding and disregarded intuition, which was telling me something was wrong. We would have to keep to ourselves away from Carl and Arnold, and make the best of things until Sean could travel again. Couldn't *anything* go right for us?

I was ready to give up and go home. If pioneering was like this, threatening the lives of my children in so many ways, then I was ready to head back to indoor plumbing, electric lights, television, and paved streets. If God *was* testing us, I'm sure He found me lacking. On the other hand, if He was telling us to go back, *that* I understood. Les sensed I was wavering.

"Honey, we can still do this," he lectured. "You'll see. Things are going to get better now."

"They couldn't get any worse."

"This is where we belong. You said so yourself."

That was before all this happened, when I was still naïve and ignorant about the dangers.

"A man can do great things in a country like this," Les said, pounding his chest. "I feel it in here, honey."

"And what can a woman do?" I countered.

"We're in this as a family, Norma," he argued. "You and me and the kids. We can build together . . ."

I left it at that.

Uneasy about the future and my lack of resolve, Les campaigned to restore my enthusiasm. He took me out to cabins Jeff Stoddard and Joe Pumper had built on their gold claims, to show me what could be done. Both men had built fine one-room log cabins of golden-colored spruce. They were snug and warm and set in idyllic surroundings with running water nearby and towering evergreens growing about. Joe was married to a quiet woman, Gloria, nearly as tall and lanky as he, while Jeff lived with his girlfriend. The girlfriend was thinking about moving back to the Lower Forty-eight, but Gloria insisted she would live nowhere but in Alaska.

"We can have a cabin just like these," Les proclaimed. "Only bigger, with a big loft for the kids."

I was unmoved.

"Norma, we're so near. This was your dream."

My dream was in danger of becoming a nightmare.

We had yet to even see our land. On a sunny morning so bright it was hard for our spirits to stay low, Les announced it was time we hiked in to take a look. It was easier to acquiesce than to resist.

After seeing to Sean's comfort in the camper and leaving Sid to watch after him and the three younger ones, Les and I eased the Ranger pickup through the ruts past Boston Creek, which was still frozen firmly enough to support vehicle traffic, and got out to hike the rest of the way. According to the map, our land lay a couple of miles off the trail, on the other side of a low mountain crest. Les was anxious to reach it.

He strapped on his .44 pistol as insurance against a bear attack, saying, "Boston Creek is starting to thaw and break up. We're going to have to start moving our stuff over here real quick."

I said nothing.

It was incredibly difficult walking. First of all, there was no trail. The extremes of Alaskan temperatures this far north—as hot as a hundred degrees in July and August, as low as sixty or seventy *below* in winter—alternately thawed and froze the soil and left it lumped and piled and in hummocks. On top of this lay a ground cover of moss, lichen, and partially decomposed plant material in a soft carpet nearly a foot thick in places. Long summer days during which the sun shone for nearly twenty-four hours intensified growth in plants adapted to thrive in soil both acidic and perpetually cold with scattered permafrost beneath the surface. Alders grew so thick in draws and drainages that you had to fight and climb your way through. Short, stunted spruce and firs covered the hillsides as thick as fur on a dog's back.

Following the map, we crested the mountain ridge and descended on its north face, the cold side of the mountain where the timber was even more stunted. Les stopped. He looked at the map, he looked around. There wasn't a tree within miles big enough to make a log for a cabin. There were no running streams, none of the idyllic scenery that surrounded Jeff's and Joe's cabins. Nothing, I thought, but the monotony of failed dreams.

"Is this it?" I asked, not wanting to believe it.

"It looked good on the map when I filed," Les murmured. He looked as though the entire mountain had fallen on top of him. I had never seen him like that before—grim and speechless, defeated, all the new bluster and confidence knocked right out of him by disappointment. No longer macho bushman. Only Lester Cobb, displaced mechanic and handyman.

I turned around and in silence started walking back to the pickup. The whole thing had been wrong. We were mistaken in thinking we could choose homesteading as an option. How could Les oppose returning home after a setback like this? We would have to return to Colorado. I would go back to being a cashier at a truck stop and my big brawny husband would reappear as defeated prince of the grease rack. Dead-end jobs in a dead-end corner of nowhere.

That evening among the Cobb clan crammed into the camper, I finally blurted out what Les and I were both avoiding: "We've made a terrible mistake. Let's get out of Alaska as fast as we can."

Sid looked alarmed. Les stared silently at his big hands.

"What else can we do, Lester?" I argued. "Are we going to sit here like the Cranicks and wait and hope for something to happen? You might as well go over to Carl's now and start sucking on the bottle. I'm a Kansas girl. I don't want to be around Arnold's sort of people or the sort of things that are going on around here. We're going home. Lester, are you listening to me?"

Les took a deep breath. He rose to his feet from the ratty sofa while the five kids and I watched him with bated breath. His head almost touched the ceiling and his broad shoulders appeared to fill the entire end of the room. He said not a word. He merely looked around at our faces, at the wood-burning stove chugging out heat and smoke, at the discolored and worn strip of carpet on the floor, the yellow flame guttering in the kerosene lamp, the broken window whose panes were held together by tape. Clearly, this wasn't what he had expected of homesteading either. We were all but out of money, Sean lay recovering from a gunshot that by rights should have killed him, and the dream of a homestead where we could eke out a living had exploded in our faces.

My heart went out to him. It was hard for a man like Les to admit defeat. But what more did it take to convince him that it was over?

He walked slowly outside and closed the door. When I peeped out the window a little later, after putting the children to bed, I saw him standing alone among the ghostly white-barked aspen with his face lifted toward the northern lights. The flickering colors of the sky played across the broad face and sparkled in his great beard.

11

The dream I had planted in Les, I planted deep. He brooded for the next few days, rarely saying a word, frequently going off by himself on walks and long hikes. Then one afternoon after being gone most of the day he burst into the camper with an exuberance and excitement absent in him since Sean's accident. The grin was back.

"Norma!" he shouted. "I've found the place!"

"I don't want to hear it."

"I've seen it, honey. It's a protected valley with two clear-water creeks flowing through it and full of spruce as tall as skyscrapers. Oh, honey, you'll love it! The Westbrooks and the Yagers are going to homestead there—and there's room for us."

I wasn't about to be set up for another fall. "It's too late to file a claim," I hedged.

"I've talked to Jeff and Joe Pumper. They say we can backdate. What we do is tell the government that we've been camping there since last year trying to decide if we really want to settle it. I've already used up my claim—but *you* haven't. *You* can file."

We had met the Westbrook and Yager families the same afternoon Les and I returned from our disappointing trek to see our land on the other side of the mountain. Having just arrived in Eureka, they were moving an old blue school bus and tents across Boston Creek glacier to the end of the road and setting up camp in preparation for clearing a trail and moving onto their homesites. At the time, I thought them as foolish as we had been.

They seemed like good, perfectly normal people, poor people like us who were attempting to make a new life for themselves. Roger Yager was nondescript in appearance, average height and weight, average brown hair thinning on top, average looking. He seemed jolly and talkative, rivaled only in his flow of words and laughter by his outgoing wife, Loni. Loni would have been rather plain except for her personality. They had four kids—Chloe, Ray, Morris, and Donnie, ranging in ages from Chloe's thirteen to Donnie's five.

Gary and Hazel Westbrook were bold and outspoken, both dark-haired and in their early thirties. They, too, looked as average as any couple I might have met on a street in Wichita. They had three offspring. Francis, eight, was the eldest; Robert, two, the youngest; and Kenneth somewhere in between.

The two families had become acquainted in Florida and decided to move to America's last frontier together. Unlike us, however, they had actually *seen* the land they were claiming beforehand. The men had come out last summer to inspect it and file before the January deadline.

"Norma," Les argued, "what harm can it do for you to go and at least have a look?"

I gave in to mollify him. He was hard to say no to. I remained skeptical, but it promised to be a welcome outing away from the camper trailer and the kids.

We set out early in the morning because it was a long hike in and out—eleven miles along a game trail from the end of the road past Boston Creek, up and over the mountains through Dead Horse Pass, then down into Minook Valley. There was no one living out there except for a seasonal miner or two at the far end of the valley and an Indian village, Rampart, farther north on the banks of the Yukon River.

Gary Westbrook produced a little medicine bottle and poured a small quantity of dust into his cupped palm. The sun caught the dust in a dull yellow sheen.

"It's *gold*!" Westbrook explained. "I panned it from the creek that runs through our property."

Les's eyes lit up. He looked at me: *See? We could be rich.*

I refused to be impressed. I had read that there was a *little* gold in many Alaskan tributaries. Sourdoughs grew old and bent and crippled from digging in the cold earth for the mother lode. In my opinion, only fools bet their lives on finding it.

Gary and Roger led the expedition; their wives stayed behind to pool all our children at their blue bus campsite. Westbrook pulled a sled loaded with supplies as he wanted to get into the valley and begin building a cabin as soon as possible. Roger was a bit more relaxed about it.

It was a wonderful morning, but I was none too hopeful about the journey. Les's excitement did little toward eliminating my doubts.

A lot of snow persisted at the higher elevations of Dead Horse Pass. We climbed up through the stunted spruce and birch, panting and laboring and kicking snow. Suddenly, we were at the top of the pass and I caught my first glimpse of the other side—into a world unexpectedly brightened and metamorphosed into something so awesomely beautiful that it actually took away my breath. I paused, stunned. Les stood and grinned that grin of his.

"Oh, Les . . . !"

"What did I tell you, huh? What did I tell you?"

The valley fell away at our feet, wide and almost a mile deep. It was covered with timber. *Big* timber. Giant spruce and fir with red trunks or gray trunks. Les said the valley's lower altitude, plus its being surrounded and protected from the north winds by soaring mountains whose crowns reached the sky, permitted growth of extraordinary abundance. I was anxious now to see it all. My mind lightened.

The trail led down from the pass and edged along the mountainsides as it descended. Each twist in the trail produced more wonderful panoramas. The jeweled glint of the sun through green boughs and white snow marked the route of Minook Creek as it tumbled its merry way toward the Yukon some twenty miles away downvalley toward the northwest.

The Westbrook and Yager claims lay along Minook Creek near the head of the valley. Les and I continued along the creek, deeper into the valley sheltered by magnificent Elephant Mountain looming above the timberline. We came upon another stream, which we called Lost Creek. It was clear, tumbling over rocks, and merged unceremoniously with Minook. At the junction of the two streams was a small meadow bordered by tremendous yellow- and red-barked spruce. Wild flowers—fireweed and tundra rose, asters and huge daisies—filled the meadow with glorious color. Walking among the spruce was like walking into a cathedral. It was warmer here, less wind, and the snow was melting fast. Dolly Varden and Arctic grayling darted in Minook Creek. Far down the valley we spotted a moose knee-deep in a marsh.

I fell in love with the valley. It was that simple. *This* was how I had seen it in my dreams. God, I thought, had been directing us here all along, testing us en route to make sure we possessed the pioneer mettle to withstand hardship before He put us in charge of one of His most delightful creations on the crust of the earth.

"Here we will build our cabin," Les shouted, throwing his arms wide in the little meadow.

"Yes," I agreed. "Home."

12

Excitement returned to the Cobb household in its temporary camper trailer headquarters. We were going homesteading after all. Since Les had already used up his filing option with his dry claim, it was up to me to file on the land in Minook Valley. We drove the Ranger to Fairbanks the next day and backdated my claim the way Joe Pumper recommended and received papers on eighty acres at the junction of Lost Creek and Minook Creek. We decided eighty acres as a T&M site—trade and manufacturing—would be easier to "prove out" during the required five-year period than a 160-acre agricultural site. Later, we were informed that I was the last woman to file a claim for land under the U.S. Homestead Act. That made me the last official woman pioneer in America. It made me feel I should be wearing a blue gingham bonnet and churning butter with a paddle dasher.

I felt good about life again after so many days of anxiety and uncertainty. I smiled at Les across the skillet of frying meat as I made supper for us in the cramped confines of Carl's camper trailer. He grinned back. The man was a good father to his daughters, full of patience and forbearance, and was proving equally good with my three sons. I couldn't have chosen a better husband than Lester Cobb with whom to migrate to the frontier with a passel of kids. Sometimes, I thought with a rush of affection, the man wasn't much more than a kid himself. There were ways in which I hoped he would never grow up.

The Cobbs were a rowdy, noisy lot when confined in so small a space. Les and the children were piled on top of each other on the sofa while I cooked. There wasn't room in the camper for all of us to be on our feet at the same time. The twins were quarreling over something or other and trying to attract Les's attention to settle their dispute. Sean, still weak and recovering from his wound, snuggled under Les's arm for protection while Sid plied us with questions about Minook Valley. When would they get to see it? Where would we build our cabin? When? Were there fish and gold in the creeks? Would we see Indians and Eskimos?

"Did you see any bears?" Tommy demanded in his shrill four-year-old voice. "Was there any bears? Is anybody listening to me? I wanna know was there any bears?"

We had a lot of planning to do. As it turned out, the decision on when and under what circumstances we left for our homestead was about to be made for us. There was a knock on the door. I opened it and there stood Arnold Cranick. The odor of alcohol preceded him.

The man had been acting strangely ever since Sean's accident on the road. I had never liked Arnold, even from the beginning, but it had nothing to do with Sean. The man was a bully. I liked him even less now that he had turned sullen and withdrawn and teamed up with Carl Nicholas every night to drink himself silly. The look on his face tonight was meaner than usual, almost hostile, as though something ate at him.

Not wanting to seem inhospitable, I invited him inside. "Arnold, how are you? Where's Betty? Would you like some supper? We don't have much, but you're welcome."

He grunted an unintelligible reply and turned to Les, who rose from the sofa to talk to him. As I resumed cooking, I overheard him murmur something about needing Les to help him with repairs to his truck. Les agreed to help, but said it would have to wait for a few days. We needed to move out of Eureka to the other side of Boston Creek before the spring breakup thawed out the stream and made it impassable. Arnold was drunk and not making much sense, so I paid little further attention until I heard his angry bark.

"I want to get this settled right now!"

From the corner of my eye, I glimpsed Arnold jerk out a pistol and point it at Les. Sean screamed; it was the same .357 Magnum that had discharged into his little chest. Sobbing hysterically, he threw himself facedown on the sofa to hide from it. I wheeled around from the stove.

"What's going on here?"

"It'll be all right, honey," Les cautioned, warning me by his tone not to make any sudden movements. He stood directly in front of Arnold, his palms upraised placatingly. "Come on, Arnold," he soothed. "What do you think you're doing? What's the gun for anyhow? Let's go outside. You can see what this is doing to the kids. Whatever it is, we can work it out."

Arnold looked livid, uncontrollable with drunken rage. "I want to get this settled. I want it settled," he raved insanely.

"What's the issue?" I demanded. "What're we settling?"

Neither Les nor I understood what he was talking about, other than it probably had something to do with guilt over Sean's accident blown out of proportion by alcohol. He simply was no longer rational. The man was obviously unpredictable, dangerous. The kids, except for Sean who was still screaming, huddled together in a frozen tableau of terror. Les played for time, trying to penetrate through the craziness in Arnold's eyes.

"Arnold, this doesn't make sense—"

Arnold's eyes narrowed. He raised the gun, pointed it at Les's face, and cocked the hammer. My husband was a crazy man's trigger squeeze away from dying.

I had grown up protected and naïve in Kansas. Never had I encountered violent people like this, never had I been forced to defend myself from anything. But now that my family was under threat, maternal instinct kicked in. I couldn't let my husband die while I cowered behind him like a frightened schoolgirl.

My eyes darted frantically about the kitchen. I had to have a weapon. I dismissed the axe leaning against the wall behind the woodstove. Too unwieldy, too far away. By the time I reached it and swung, Les could be shot.

The short-handled hatchet. Sid had left it on the counter. In one single desperate movement, I grabbed its handle and lunged at Arnold, swinging.

The sharp blade bit into his gun hand. Blood splattered. The blow deflected the pistol. It discharged with a deafening bark inside the confines of the camper. Les dropped to his knees as the bullet seared through his right shoe and into the floor.

Now the twins screamed. Sean plunged into fresh hysterics. Lady and Black and the pups chained outside started barking. Sid jumped up and ran to get the axe. Still brandishing the hatchet, I charged Arnold, threatening to cleave his skull with it. He was blubbering in pain and surprise and holding his hand, the gun still in it. Blood gushed down the length of the barrel as I pushed and shoved him out the door, mindless of my own safety, thinking only of my family.

"You lied to me!" he bellowed through his pain, shock, and anger. "Carl saw one of your letters. You accused me of shooting your son on purpose."

"That's crazy! If that was what we thought, you'd already be in jail. Get out! *Get out!*"

He stumbled backward into the darkness. I had found courage and strength I never knew I possessed.

"You shot at my family. You're not going to get away with this!" I shouted at him. "I'm driving to Manley and calling the trooper as soon as I take care of my family."

I slammed the door in his face.

Several gunshots cracked from outside. Dogs bayed frantically. We ducked instinctively. The kids howled and threw themselves on the floor. Les, now recovered, his wound only a grazed foot, grabbed his .44 Ruger and started outside. I blocked the door.

"It won't do any good to kill him or get yourself killed," I protested.

Les hesitated. He looked at me in an obviously different light, as though awed by the efficiency with which I had handled the affair. From outside, Arnold snarled threats of revenge, his voice receding as he hurried back toward Carl's cabin.

"This ain't over! You hear me, Cobb? This ain't over by a damned sight. You'll all pay for this."

I was trembling now in the aftermath. I could go for the police, but it probably wouldn't do any good. There was only one law enforcement officer, the Alaska state trooper, in the entire wide area between Fairbanks and the Arctic Circle. Trooper Ross couldn't handle everything himself. He probably couldn't get here before morning anyhow. By then we could all be dead. Besides, as we were learning, police pretty much let home-steaders take care of their own problems, anything short of first-degree murder. Fact was, the Alaskan bush remained virtually without law. A lawless land, a true frontier.

"We're not staying here another night," I decided. "Both of them, Carl and Arnold, are crazy drunk up in that cabin. We're not staying another minute."

Les misunderstood. He thought I meant I wanted to leave Alaska. I saw the look on his face and gave a rather bitter laugh.

"We've been through too much to give up," I said firmly. "We've had to fight every inch of the way. Nobody is going to run us away. We're staying and we're going home—to Minook Valley."

"Atta girl."

He stepped outside to check around. He returned shortly. I was calming the kids and trying to get them to eat something.

"Arnold shot out the tires on the pickup," he reported. "I'll fix the flats. You start packing. We're crossing Boston Creek tonight."

That was how we left Eureka. In the middle of the night with all our belongings and livestock tossed helter-skelter onto the pickup and into the two-tonner bed. Kids huddled nervously on the front seats, eyes wide.

We left with Arnold Cranick's threats hanging over us.

13

Springtime in Alaska was more commonly referred to as *breakup*. Ice that had kept the creeks and rivers captive the long, dark winter began to break up; snow melted; streams overflowed; birches, willows, alders, and larch tried on gowns of new leaves; clearings and little meadows filled with wild flowers. Daisies of enormous size, red flamers, lupines in many colors, lady's slippers, thistles, purple iris, and even gray-green orchids. Winds nearly as strong as any on the Kansas plains howled in the spruce, whipped through the alders, ate away at the ice and snow, and kept the mosquitoes temporarily at bay.

The camp at Boston Creek became a colony, what with the addition of the seven Cobbs to the Westbrooks' five and the Yagers' six. There were entire *towns* in the Alaskan bush with a population of less than eighteen. Roger Yager lent us his large military-style army tent; he and Loni and their brood moved into the blue school bus, which they had managed to get across Boston Creek before its breakup. The tent was like a palace compared to our own smaller tent. It had more room than Carl's camper trailer in Eureka, although it wasn't quite as comfortable.

We had encountered our tribulations, but God was seeing us through and making us stronger as a result of them. He had led us to Minook Valley, a spot of supreme natural beauty. All we had to do now was get moved into it. I knew I had the strength now to go on.

"We're the kind of people Alaska was created for," Les proclaimed. "People who were down on their luck, but are now struggling back."

Even the children seemed happier and more settled, what with having seven other kids their own ages with whom to play and share the adventure. The twins weren't nearly as moody and apt to leave stormlike havoc in their wake. Sid worked with the men, Tommy helped take care of the rabbits and dogs, and Sean was soon up and about, gaining strength daily. He was still our worrier though, having now added firearms to his list of anxieties.

I felt like a real pioneer as we launched the campaign to transport three large families and their homestead goods eleven miles through thick forest, across innumerable streams and freshets, over Dead Horse Pass, which was still clotted with sixteen feet of snow, and down the steep slope of the mountain into Minook Valley. It was truly a campaign in every sense too, with Les the general in charge. He was much more the outdoorsman than either Roger Yager or Gary Westbrook. He had worked farms and ranches most of his young life, and was a master mechanic who could fix anything from a broken axe to an airplane engine. A big, strapping man who would look at a mountain and decide he *could* move it.

His abrasive macho bushman manner sometimes wore a bit thin, but I felt confident of his leadership and proud of him for taking charge. Although the realization of the magnitude of the venture we had undertaken sobered me considerably, I was now as determined as Les that we would succeed.

Our first task was to break a trail and widen it in order to move vehicles and supplies to our homesites. Armed with axes and chainsaws, the modern pioneer's boon, the men and Sid hacked and beat at the brush in a road-building frenzy. They cut timbers and constructed rough bridges across streams rapidly filling with snow melt-off.

Boston Creek was the widest and most treacherous along the route. The State Road Department had left several large timbers there to be used in emergencies. Considering this an emergency, as we needed a road link to the outside, Les hooked the two-ton Ford to two of the timbers and dragged them across Boston to be used as tire runners for the bridge.

"We need horses!" Les boomed. "The first pioneers would never have made it to the West if they hadn't had horses."

We broke camp successively and moved it with the progress of the trail, advancing step by step toward our destination. In spite of the men's efforts, however, the "road" remained treacherous. Most of the time we transferred camp on our backs, making multiple slogging trips back and forth.

I remembered how my mother used to say, with a sigh, that a man worked from sunup to sundown but a woman's work was never done. Cooking, doing dishes, washing clothes, cleaning the kids, feeding the dogs, rabbits, and the cat. Chores that seemed simple with the conveniences of the Lower Forty-eight now took on complications. Water for cooking and bathing and drinking had to be hauled from the creeks. Cooking was accomplished over an open fire or on a two-burner Coleman camp stove. Bathwater, dish-washing water, and water for laundry was heated in a kettle over the campfire. Baking a cake for Tommy when we celebrated his fifth birthday on May 26 was out of the question. Instead, I fried him a huge flapjack pancake and found an old candle in the pickup glove compartment to stick in its center and light.

We were chronically low on both stores and cash. Les and Sid hunted for our meals, providing a fresh supply of snowshoe hare, spruce hen, which is a type of grouse, and an occasional porcupine for variety. Sean remained in camp when they hunted, still trembling at the sight of a gun. A homesteader we had met in Eureka brought out a fresh haunch of bear one night. He said he killed it after it broke into his cabin and was ransacking it. The meat was rich, red, and stringy. Neither Loni, Hazel, nor I had ever cooked bear before. In fact, I had yet to see one in the wild. Lacking other directions, we fried it like we did everything else. It wasn't moose, but it was a welcome respite from rabbit.

Each day brought more hard, backbreaking work—frontiersmanship on a grand scale. We zipped ourselves exhausted into our sleeping bags each night. Life nonetheless might have been pleasant, filled as it was with the anticipation and challenge of working toward our own land, had it not been for one war we seemed in danger of losing. That was the ongoing skirmish with mosquitoes.

They came in three versions, we understood, each more savage than the last, each strain thriving about three or four weeks in late spring and early summer. They were a simple fact of existence, like rain. Whenever the wind lay still, they attacked in sun-darkening hordes, at times settling like a flock of seagulls descending upon dead fish.

There were millions of them per square mile, a whining, living veil intent on mugging every living creature. They could suck as much as a pint of blood out of a moose *each day,* or stampede herds of caribou into panicky, aimless galloping. Bulls fled until they were exhausted. Prospectors caught in a mosquito storm were said to have been driven insane. Local legend had it that an animal or a human caught in the open could be sucked dry. Luckily for us, we were told, the worst infestations lasted no more than a month or so.

By the time we reached Dead Horse Pass and started clearing it of snow, it became plain that we were going to be unable to build a road into Minook Valley anytime in the near future. We would still be working on the road come winter, only to have the snows and breakup next spring obliterate all our efforts. We held a council during which it was decided we would abandon road-building for this year and concentrate instead on constructing our cabins before winter came. We would pool our labor to build one cabin at a time. Typically, Les acceded to erecting ours last.

The Yagers and Cobbs decided to camp at the higher altitudes of Dead Horse Pass, away from the hordes of mosquitoes, and walk in the six miles each day to work on the cabins. The Westbrooks wanted to live on their site. They loaded what provisions they could on a sled, rounded up eight-year-old Francis and their two younger sons, and disappeared over the pass with Gary and Hazel pulling while the children pushed. The next time we saw them, they complained of a bear having ripped into their tent and ransacked it for food.

"Always carry a gun," Gary warned from the experience. "The bears are out of hibernation. Their tracks are everywhere. They seem to be very aggressive."

What kept me going through the hardships was the realization that after all these months on the road since leaving Colorado, we *were* making progress toward homesteading. Plus, even through the muck and the labor and the mosquitoes, there was the incredible beauty of it all. I never failed to be filled with awe and appreciation by standing at the top of the pass and looking down into *our* valley. Our little clan of colonists had it all to ourselves.

It stretched thirty-three miles long, from its one end all the way north to the Yukon River. Squadrons of mountains on either side of the valley marched backward in file to the end of the horizon. They were green, topped with white, turning to blue, turning to misty gray in the far distance. Mountains of infinite variety, of changing color according to the time of day or the silvery-gray misting of the short nights. They were like silent, powerful sentinels, protecting us from the worst storms and from the outside world. This valley was a precious, special place that possessed a unique and tranquil magic in the presence of towering conifers and ferns and the ever-present rippling of our own two little creeks.

Only during some nights around a campfire was I struck by the enormity of this country and our undertaking. I would either shiver and hug myself or move nearer the rock that was my husband. In many ways, Alaska was still an unknown and terrifying land. After all, it had only achieved statehood slightly over a dozen years ago. A comparatively mere handful of people populated its vast territory. It was said only daring men and women came to challenge it, and that those who refused to obey its harsh rules fled if they could retreat before it killed them.

"The Yagers and Westbrooks are talking about going home to Florida at the end of the summer and coming back next spring," Les confided to me one night. "They won't be wintering over."

He sounded pleased. I felt my heart start to race.

"We'll be all alone?" I whispered after a long while.

"I really don't expect them to last out here anyhow. Sooner or later, we'll have the valley all to ourselves."

Total isolation?

"Les . . . ?"

His answer was a long snore. I lay looking up into the darkness of the tent.

14

I was beginning to understand that frontiers by their very nature attracted adventurers and other people seeking to start their lives fresh away from crowds and the constraints of civilization. Included were the more unsavory elements from society's fringes, who frequently turned isolated communities into lawless, savage places where "an eye for an eye" literally prevailed. Men wanted for crimes in the Lower Forty-eight could sometimes hide out in Alaska for years. Often in the bush, there was no law except frontier law. You took care of disputes yourself. Even killing was not always out of the question. A corpse dumped in the wilderness seldom lasted more than a few days before bears, wolves, and wolverines obliterated all sign that the victim had ever existed. Even the bones would be crunched and digested. When we got to know the gunslingers Joe Pumper and Jeff Stoddard better, they talked of having "taken care" of several problems with meddlesome government busybodies and undesirables who were never heard from again.

All this took some getting used to.

Although Les and I desired nothing more than to be left alone to pursue our own goals, our introduction to the bush and our far-flung neighbors, first through Sean's accidental gunshot, then through the hatchet encounter with Arnold Cranick, made us look rather like shady and undesirable characters. Especially since we Cobbs were in the bush and unable to defend ourselves while Arnold Cranick continued to hang around Eureka and Manley spreading his hate of us like poison ivy. Carl Nicholas apparently supported him. To my horror, I learned that I was becoming known as "Hatchet Lady" because of what Arnold claimed was my unprovoked attack of him.

"He'll get tired soon enough and move on," Les predicted.

Arnold was a dangerous drunk and probably a real criminal, for all we knew. He had built imagined slights into a festering grudge against us, then turned that grudge into a campaign of vengeance. Arnold was not going to go away without first causing Les and me trouble.

Les kept our old rattletrap Ford Ranger pickup parked on the Eureka side of Boston Creek at trailhead so that we could hike down to it, then use it to drive to the trading post at Manley or to occasionally enjoy the hot springs there. On one of our trips in to "civilization," we learned that Arnold and Carl Nicholas had gone to Trooper Ross to complain that we had stolen Road Department timbers in order to build a personal bridge across Boston Creek.

Trooper Ross confronted Les with a long-suffering sigh. "The state said if those timbers are not placed back where you found them, you'll have to pay five hundred dollars for each timber."

Five hundred dollars! We hadn't seen that kind of money since before we left Colorado.

"They'll be put back," Les assured him.

Before he could make good on his promise, however, both timbers disappeared. Footprints, tire marks, and dragging sign at Boston Creek gave evidence of how someone had chained onto the heavy logs at the bridge and pulled them away. Joe Pumper found one of them seven miles away on the trail that led to his and Jeff Stoddard's gold mines. He was miffed.

"Why did you pull them out my way to connect me with your problems?" he demanded of Les.

"*I* didn't," Les replied, thrusting out his chin and rolling his shoulders forward in that way of his that said he had about had enough.

"Arnold and Carl are telling around that you stole the timbers and hid them."

All this did little to improve the Cobbs' reputation. Still trying to avoid a confrontation with the man who had, inexplicably, declared himself our nemesis, Les recovered both timbers and dragged them back to their original location near Boston Creek. He left alone in the Ranger pickup to report to Trooper Ross at his home and station that lay on the Elliott Highway south of Manley.

The Elliott Highway, which was not really a highway, ended in Manley; there was no other major road going farther into the interior or toward the Arctic Circle. Manley in many respects was literally the end of the line. As Les passed through Manley and picked up the highway south, a glance in his rearview mirror showed him Arnold's old brown pickup falling in behind. That this was no mere coincidence quickly became obvious when Arnold's pickup narrowed the gap between them and roared up onto Les's bumper.

Les sped up. Arnold kept pace, gesticulating and gesturing threats through his windshield. The road was narrow and slippery with snowmelt and runoff. Within seconds the two pickups were screaming down the road at nearly a hundred miles per hour, blasting up tornadoes of Alaskan mud. It was as if Arnold were bent on self-destruction and intended taking Les with him. He was crazy.

Arnold weaved back and forth on Les's bumper, then gunned up alongside at a widening in the road. Les saw him brandishing a pistol, pointing it through his mud-splattered side window. He thought he was about to be shot.

Reflexively, in self-defense, he whipped the Ranger's wheel to drive his pickup into Arnold's Chevy and perhaps cause him to lose control. Arnold avoided the trap and pulled ahead, kicking up an avalanche of slime that caked Les's windshield and all but blinded him. Determined to run no further, to make his stand, Les let off the gas and pulled to a stop. He reached for the .44 Ruger Blackhawk he always carried in its holster.

Fortunately for one or both, Trooper Ross happened to be driving up the road toward Manley. Arnold saw him and accelerated away.

"I'm the only law up here," Trooper Ross explained to Les, confirming what we had already heard about frontier law. "It's impossible for me to handle all the disputes among the homesteaders. You have to take care of yourself. Anything short of murder."

Arnold was a bully who took advantage of the lack of law to throw his weight around. Sooner or later, Manley Hot Springs would get fed up with him and band together to ride him out of town on a rail. But until then, it was obvious he intended making life miserable for the Cobbs. He boasted around at the Roadhouse that Alaska wasn't big enough for both Les and him; he wasn't going to stop until Les was gone.

Although I made Les promise to avoid confrontation, it was clear he would be pushed no further. Les being Les, macho frontier bushman and all that, was heading inexorably toward High Noon. Pride. That's something about a man. Pride and testosterone.

I was scared to death for him and what might happen. But there was nothing I could do to stave off an eventual showdown. Except pray. Pray that it wouldn't happen, but if it did happen that my husband would be spared. I shuddered and went pale every time Les drove into Manley to pick up our mail or purchase staples at the trading post. I even made excuses for him not to have to go. But you couldn't shelter a man like Les that way. He always tossed his holstered forty-four onto the seat of the pickup.

"I won't let another man dictate to me what I can or cannot do, where I can or cannot go," he stubbornly declared.

15

According to BLM regulations, a homesteader filing on an eighty-acre T&M (trade and manufacturing) site was allotted a period of five years to develop it, after which he received clear deed only to that portion of the property he had actually improved. You couldn't simply build a cabin in the middle of the eighty acres and call it "developed." Les and I decided to build a series of cabins, starting with the family cabin, and eventually launch our own business in the outdoors tourist and hunting-guide industry.

The land had to be posted in order to constitute a legal claim. Les chopped stakes and in true pioneer fashion we walked off as accurately as we could eighty acres lying between the toes of Elephant Mountain on the east and across Minook Creek to the rise of Norky's Mountain on the west. We filled out claim papers, placed a copy in a sealed Kerr canning jar, and attached the jar to our southeast post, as required.

"This piece of the world is officially *ours!*" Les boomed. He grabbed me around the waist and in his exuberance swung me off my feet and in circles until we both collapsed from laughter.

Sid, Sean, and Tommy grinned foolishly. Cara and Cora, independent, willful, and precocious as always, rolled their eyes at the folly of adults. Even though they weren't yet three, most people took them for at least four or five. Big girls, they took after their father. Almost three going on teenagers, I always said.

"Silly," Cora said to Cara. "Silly people."

Although we had agreed with the Westbrooks and Yagers to pool labor and raise one family's cabin at a time, it wasn't turning out that way. Human nature was geared toward self-interest, not toward socialism and communism. You put more effort toward your own welfare and concerns than you ever would toward the common interests. I remembered a story about other pioneers that applied as much to Minook Valley as it did to Plymouth Rock.

When pilgrims on the *Mayflower* arrived in the New World in 1620, they came under a contract that stated that everything produced would go into a common store; each member was entitled to one common share. All the land they cleared and the houses they built likewise belonged to the community. What happened? Many of them starved to death. Their leader, William Bradford, found that under this form of pure socialism, even the most creative and industrious people had no incentive to work any harder than anyone else.

"For this community was found to breed much confusion and discontent," Bradford wrote, "and retard much employment that would have been to their benefit and comfort. For young men that were most able and fit for labor and service did repine that they should spend their time and strength to work for other men's wives and children without recompense . . ."

So, Bradford tried something different. He assigned each family its own plot of land to work and permitted the family to market its own crops and products. The result was that the Pilgrims grew more food than they could eat.

"They had very good success," wrote Bradford, "for it made all hands industrious, so as much more corn was planted than otherwise would have been."

The discontent in Minook Valley began immediately when the Yagers and Westbrooks quarreled over which of their cabins we should construct first. While Les may never have heard of William Bradford and the experiment in socialism at Plymouth Colony, he was an intuitive man who saw the shortcomings in the commune system. It simply wasn't going to work. At this rate, the summer would pass and *none* of the cabins would be up. In exasperation, he gave up attempting to work with our neighbors.

"Fine, *fine*," he exclaimed, throwing up his hands. "The Cobbs will start on our own cabin until you two decide what you want to do."

In hindsight, the decision turned out to be the best for us. Les was a dynamo, a hard worker, who could accomplish more in one day than an ordinary man could in two or three days. The walls of our cabin began growing while the Westbrooks and Yagers were still quibbling over how it should be done.

We designed a cabin twenty feet wide by thirty feet long, with a small loft sleeping area for the kids. The logs would be arranged vertically instead of horizontally, as there was no way Les with only the help of a small woman and a ten-year-old boy could raise a cabin of logs twenty and thirty feet long. It would have a slanted shedlike roof running from ten feet in height facing the little meadow away from the creek down to a five-foot backside wall overlooking Minook and its tumbling water where Les and the boys regularly hooked Dolly Varden trout and grayling for supper. The roof of slanted logs would be packed with sod and tundra to repel rain and snow and serve as insulation against the winter cold. It was the old pioneer way of doing things. It was also the economical way. We had little money to buy city-style roofing, nor had we the means of hauling such supplies to the building site even were we to dig up the money.

Before anything else, I insisted on one convenience—a privy, an outhouse toilet. Grinning and teasing, Les started to work. Soon, we had a tiny beautiful house in the woods. It had four slab-log walls to break the wind and a sod roof to keep out the weather. Les bragged that it was one of only a few genuine two-holers north of Fairbanks. It made me feel Uptown Charlie.

All this time the Westbrooks were living in their tent in the valley, braving the bears and laboring on their cabin. The Yagers and we Cobbs maintained camp at the blue bus at the top of Dead Horse Pass. As long as we continued to camp there and hike into the valley each day to work, we maintained a road-and-trail line back to civilization. Reaching Manley and supplies would be much harder once we made the final move; in fact, the line would be completely cut once snow flew. Les and I and the Yagers were reluctant to make this final commitment.

It was an exhausting march in across the pass each day to cut, delimb and skin trees and drag the logs to the construction site, then tramp back out again that evening. Loni Yager often stayed behind to watch the younger children, but at times we all hiked in together. Les and Sid ranged ahead, chatting the way they did and growing close as father and son. They both loved Alaska. They seemed born for this life.

I had to stop frequently for Cara and Cora to rest. They fretted and complained all the way. After one rest break, they steadfastly refused to get up and go any farther.

"Too tired," Cara whined.

"Much too tired," Cora affirmed.

"Poor darlings," I sympathized. "It's only a little farther."

"No. Tired," said Cora.

"No," Cara echoed.

"I'll have to leave you behind."

"Okay," they readily agreed.

"What if a bear comes?"

Cara brandished her pink water pistol, scrunching her little face into a fierce scowl. "I protect us with this gun!"

I had to laugh, but we also had to go on. I couldn't carry them. I was already transporting a load of nails, tools, and other supplies. I couldn't leave them behind on the trail either. Too dangerous. Annoyed at their recalcitrance, I took off with Sean and Tommy, trusting the girls to eventually give in. They held out stubbornly until I disappeared around a bend in the trail and stopped to wait for them out of sight. A few minutes passed before I heard their shrill screams and they came running.

It was obvious the little girls couldn't continue to hike that long distance. We also wasted precious daylight walking in and out every day, time that might be better utilized finishing the cabin. It was June by now and the days were long and warm. But in Alaska, even in summer, the threat of the fierce winter remained omnipresent.

On one of his visits to the camp, Jeff Stoddard forced us to confront the decision we had been avoiding.

"Why do you walk in and out every day?" he asked. "You'll never get anything done and your cabin built unless you move in and live on your land."

Of course, he was right. The next morning the Cobbs began moving into the valley. We were committed. The Yagers remained behind at their blue bus. Loni looked haggard and worn; she sometimes yearned for a hot shower and a sit-down meal in a dining room.

Frontiers were hard on women. For the greater part of its history after contact with the outside world, Alaska had had the problem of men coming here without women. Adventurers, trappers, gold seekers, miners, missionaries, fugitives . . . All men. I read of how Nome during its gold rush turned out en masse and lined the streets in order to catch a glimpse of a new saloon girl coming to town. There were always forty or fifty men to every woman. Even today the ratio discrepancy between men and women runs about ten or fifteen to one.

"Few women survive the first winter," I learned people were saying in Manley when they spoke of me. "Neither will the Hatchet Lady."

Admittedly, I bore little resemblance to the big-boned, hard-handed, stalwart stereotype of a lady of the frontier. I was small in build and only a couple of inches over five feet tall. I looked very young, very unworldly. At twenty-nine years of age, I could pass as younger than Les's twenty-two. There were times, of course, when I missed putting on a pretty dress and going out to dinner and dancing. Men used to say I filled out a dress well. Male eyes turned when I walked into a room.

If these same men could only see me now in my old blue jeans and a flannel shirt, with my hair hanging around my face like wet black ropes. But I had endured too much getting this far to turn back now. I was determined to prove wrong the naysayers who thought this Kansas girl wouldn't last. After all, I *was* the last American woman pioneer. I was going to have my home.

16

On a Saturday afternoon Les and I were coming out of the trading post during one of our infrequent supply runs to Manley when I caught sight of Arnold Cranick emerging from the Roadhouse across from the end of the grass airstrip. He wore a pistol belt. He saw us at the same time. His hulking form swaggered out onto the dirt road, coming in our direction. I felt all blood drain from my cheeks; breath caught painfully in my throat.

"Let's go. Now," I begged Les.

We had spent the past two months trying to avoid Arnold, which wasn't difficult to do as long as we were in the bush and away from his easy liquor supply.

Les unhurriedly deposited the bag of staples in the back of our Ford Ranger and walked around to the driver's side. Jeff Stoddard happened to be in the store; he and another local stepped outside and stood silently on the porch to await developments. Tension was so thick it seemed to have descended over the settlement like molasses. Everyone in the territory knew of the bad blood between Arnold and Carl Nicholas on the one side and the Cobbs on the other.

"Lester, *let's go!*"

Arnold yelled from down the road, taunting, "Cobb! Cobb? You still hiding behind the woman and her hatchet?"

Les hesitated outside the pickup door. I was already inside and ready to leave. Les's dark beard seemed to bristle. He stood as still as one of the big granite stones that lined parts of Minook Creek, his narrowed eyes fixated on the pistol lying on the front seat.

"*Please,* Lester . . . ?" I cried desperately.

"Cobb?" Arnold sneered, playing to an audience now gathering outside the Roadhouse. He let loose a string of obscenities questioning the Cobb ancestry all the way back to Germany, the *least* offensive of which was *coward.*

Those blue-gray eyes of Les's turned to ice. I knew he had made up his mind and there was nothing I could do short of shooting him myself. Les was running no farther. He reached into the pickup cab without a word and picked up the holstered pistol. He turned slowly around in the wide dirt street to face Arnold as he calmly buckled the forty-four around his waist. He undid the hammer thong and made sure the revolver was loose. He adjusted the holster on his thigh so that it rode correctly.

Fear had turned me into the block of salt from which Lot's wife never recovered. I was mesmerized, like someone looking at the aftermath of a fatal car crash, wanting to turn away but unable to. This *couldn't* be happening. These things only happened in the movies to Gary Cooper or John Wayne. This was 1974—not 1874!

Down the road, Arnold hesitated as Les stepped away from the Ranger and started walking toward him, gun hand clawed and hovered above the butt of his pistol. Arnold suddenly appeared undecided. He stopped in the road and stood there, as though unsure of what to do next. I needed to take a breath, but it remained caught in my throat. I expected to hear gunfire at any instant.

Les's step never faltered. He continued walking in that slow, deliberate way until he stopped no more than twenty feet in front of the bully. He stood spread-legged in the road, crouching slightly, gun hand ready. The high sun cast twin shadows pooling at their feet.

"Go for your gun!" Les challenged, his voice clear and startling in the hush over the main street.

I suppose Arnold saw the same thing in Les's eyes that I had seen. Les intended to kill him in a duel, a showdown at High Noon. End everything right there.

The two men remained poised like that in confrontation for what seemed an eternity. I thought I was going to die as I waited for their hands to go for their guns, for the barking of the weapons, and for one or both of them to fall wounded or dead in the mud. It wasn't until later that I realized tears were streaming down my face.

Then, slowly, in order that Les would not misread it, Arnold lifted his hand away from his gun. Like most bullies, he was backing down when his bluff was finally called. Even from where I stood, I saw that he had turned the color of a peeled potato. He had lost his voice.

He carefully backed away, one step at a time.

"I *will* kill you, the next time I see you," Les said.

Arnold turned without a word and hurried back toward the Roadhouse, leaving my husband standing alone and safe in the road. Manley's tyrant had been faced down and humiliated in public. Chastised and ridiculed before those who had formerly feared and avoided his bluster and bad temper. He moved out of the area within the week, dragging his tail between his legs. We heard later that he robbed an elderly man in Anchorage and was being chased by police.

We certainly weren't back in Kansas anymore, Toto. I was receiving one rude awakening after another. On the frontier, if you were weak, the wolves started sniffing around to take you down. In order to survive, you had to prove you were as tough as the land and the people it attracted. I felt a surge of pride when I learned what other homesteaders were saying after Les ran Arnold out of the territory. If you had a choice, they said, between fighting an enraged grizzly or taking on Lester Cobb, you might be safer choosing the bear. He and his little wife, the Hatchet Lady, might be *chechakos*, but don't push 'em around.

17

For hundreds of thousands of years, bears and other wildlife had had free run of most of Alaska. By moving our tent into the valley and stretching it next to where we intended building our cabin, Les warned, we were encroaching upon the bears' territory, not they upon ours. This country was theirs first; we would simply have to learn to live with them. They left their sign everywhere—tracks along the creek, upstream and down; droppings; claw marks on trees, some of which were ten feet or more off the ground. Les identified the "big bear" sign as grizzly, the great brown behemoths of the North Country, the largest land predators on earth, unpredictable, aggressive, the sighting of which sent even a seasoned Alaska hand into a fit of terror. Out here, man was not necessarily at the top of the food chain.

There was something eerily discomforting about living among giant predators who might on a moment's notice take a whim to have human steaks for dinner. I kept a close and watchful eye on the children. I insisted Les or Sid accompany the younger ones with a gun even when they went to the outhouse. No one was to leave the tent alone at night; it would be too easy for the twins or Tommy, or even Sid or Sean for that matter, to be carried away. I assumed the personal duty of bear watch, maintaining constant vigil for the beasts and sniffing around for signs of their presence. I wondered nervously if I would ever grow accustomed to living with them.

Bears were most dangerous this time of year. They were fresh out of hibernation, skinny and feeling hungry and grumpy. Sows had cubs and hell hath no fury like that of a mama bear cut off from her baby. Throughout the bush, this time of year, talk went around of where bears had been seen lately and whom they'd attacked. These stories were passed on to us during those rare occasions when need for supplies forced us to climb out of Minook Valley and make the long trek to Manley.

We had met Rose Stowell and her husband, Charlie, in Eureka one day while they were washing clothes in a creek near their cabin. A pair of big grizzlies had paid them a visit, prowling around the cabin most of one night, peering in through the windows like King Kong on the Empire State Building and rearing up to place huge paws on the cabin's roof. They finally got tired and left before dawn, having kept Rose and Charlie awake and jittery all night.

"You always know where you stand with a griz," Jeff Stoddard said. "The guy is straightforward and pretty much always has a toothache. But a black bear now . . . You never know how he's going to behave. He's totally unpredictable. A grizzly kills you because he's mean. A black will often kill you because he wants to *eat* you."

"We eat them, so why shouldn't they eat us?" Les reasoned.

More people in Alaska were slain by black bears than by all other wilderness-type causes put together. We learned to our mounting distress that a man paying a visit to the cabin of a neighbor who happened to be away on a fishing trip had been attacked by blacks before he could get back to his pickup truck. The homesteader found his friend's body when he returned home; the guy was half-eaten.

It didn't take bears long to discover our invasion of Minook Valley. The dogs always knew it first when a bear lurked nearby. We had given the pups away in Manley, as we simply had insufficient food for them. That left us with Lady and Black, upon whose instincts we depended to warn us of danger. Black would bark at shadows and the wind whistling through willows. Lady seemed more dependable in her maturity. We let both sleep in the tent with us and Callie the cat, relying upon them to provide an early warning.

That proved to be misplaced trust. The first time a bear ventured into camp, neither Lady nor Black let out so much as a whimper. They were probably too scared. Black awoke me only because he was trying to crawl underneath the covers with Les and me.

"Cowards!" I admonished the dogs. They slunk off to a corner of the tent, properly chastised but obviously no more willing now than before to challenge the night visitor's right to go where he pleased.

We decided the next day that our caller was probably the big blackie that had been harassing the Westbrooks upvalley. Raiding their tent and larder obviously taught him there was an easier way to obtain food than working for it himself. Fortunately, the domestic rabbits we brought from Anchorage had long ago found their way to the cooking pot, we having discovered it to be more economical and convenient to hunt meat than to raise it. We kept all foodstuffs on a platform high in a tree too slender for most bears to climb. That left the dogs, Callie, and *us*.

It was Les's custom to rise early and build a fire to heat up coffee while he waited for me to come out and prepare breakfast before we started work on the cabin. He awoke us with a howl of outrage. Startled, expecting *anything*, the kids and I scrambled outside. Les stood pointing at the side of the tent, upon which was smeared a sticky-looking substance that resembled axle grease.

"Phew!" Sean puffed, pinching his nose. "It stinks like—"

"Because shit is what it is," Les snapped. He pointed to the bear's big tracks in the soft soil. "He came up while we slept and marked this tent as *his*."

A few days later, the Westbrooks' bear made another foray while we were all away working in the woods. We returned to camp to find the tent door claw-ripped open and the contents of our home demolished or strewn about. Even some of our few canned goods had been gnawed and tooth-punctured. Adding insult to injury, the creature had deposited a huge, stinking pile of bear dung right in the middle of the floor.

"Guess that shows what he thinks about us," Sid murmured.

"Lester!" I scolded. "We can't have this bear coming and going and doing as he pleases. What if the kids had been here by themselves?"

Les grabbed his rifle and grimly stalked away into the woods. He returned just as grimly, empty-handed.

The war was on. It became a personal grudge match between Lester and that bear. It was more than an even contest. The bear was smart. As the summer wore on and the construction of our cabin progressed, we sometimes glimpsed the animal in the woods, as dark and ominous as a moonless night, watching and waiting for us to leave our campsite unguarded. He would stand partially concealed by foliage watching us, snout lifted and sniffing, until Les made a move for his rifle. Then he glided silently away.

He sneaked in nights while we slept and left claw marks on trees. He never came in, however, when Les sat up with a rifle to ambush him. He waited until the next day when everyone left the tent. Then he took the opportunity to run down and create havoc, always leaving his calling card in a little odoriferous pile in the destruction so we would know who did it.

"I'm going to get that damned bear!" Les vowed, swearing roundly in front of the children so that I had to chastise him.

Les had grown up around the Colorado Rockies hunting and fishing, but never had he matched wits with an adversary quite as cunning and infuriating as the Westbrooks' bear. He constructed traps and snares and baited them with wild honey and spoiled meat. The bear, undoubtedly chuckling to himself, sprung the traps, destroyed the snares, and stole the bait.

Les and Sid waited in ambush along the trail; the bear never appeared.

They tracked him and hunted him all over the valley; he circled around and made another raid on the tent while everyone was away.

The contest would have been amusing, had not the bear held us in such a reign of terror.

"He's smart," Les grudgingly conceded, starting to admire and respect the big animal. "I'm still going to get him, sooner or later."

"What if you don't, Dad?" Sean asked. "What if he gets *us*?"

18

In wild places there may exist living things that cannot be explained. That, perhaps, we should not even try to explain. God does not have to ask man's permission for what he places upon the earth. Alaskan native peoples carried legends about such living creatures, talked about in smoky hovels at night and then not spoken of in the harsh reality of the sun. Of course, the Cobbs were not acquainted with the natives at this point in our homesteading and so we had not heard the stories. By the time we did become acquainted, we had encounters of our own to add to the legends. It seemed the Westbrooks' bear was not enough to add suspense, mystery, and fear to Minook Creek settlers; there was something else darker and more threatening living in the valley.

Although Sid, the elder of our brood, was only ten, almost eleven, he increasingly assumed the responsibilities and duties of an adult. He had muscled up during the summer's labors and his sharp face matured. Sometimes I accused Les of treating Sid like a man.

"A boy acts like a man, you treat him like a man," Les replied in that infuriating new bush manner of his.

Sid accompanied Les most everywhere to help with the work. The two of them were walking in on the trail one afternoon with their backpacks filled with supplies from Manley. They passed the Yagers' homestead; Roger and Loni and their four offspring had finally cut ties to their blue bus and moved onto their land. Roger asked Les to help him work on an engine.

After having supper with the Yagers, Les returned to work with Roger while Sid hoisted his backpack and left for home. It was an easy two-mile walk downhill. It was poor judgment on Les's part, allowing an unarmed kid to walk through two miles of bear country alone in the dusky dark.

The trail was one person wide and curled downward and around the low side of the mountain, following Minook Creek. That silvery light marking the nights of the Alaskan summer settled above the mountains while a purple hue oozed into the valley. Sid swung along the trail in his carefree manner, alert for bears and other dangers but at the same time not intimidated by them. Young Sid was as much in his element in the wilderness as Davy Crockett had been in his.

It wasn't something that happened suddenly. He simply felt hackles rising at the base of his neck. It was like someone had stuffed a snowball down the back of his shirt. He paused in the trail, reluctant at first to look around. What you *didn't* see wasn't there.

Someone, he thought, *someone* was watching him.

Slowly, he turned to look behind. His eyes scanned downhill toward the creek. He caught glimpses of Minook through the masking alders and willows that clogged its rocky banks. Uphill to his left were open stands of birch and spruce. He searched their shadows.

It must have been his imagination, his mind playing tricks on him because of the way shadow seeped and slithered around in the valley. He took a deep breath and continued walking, increasing his pace as one will passing a graveyard after nightfall.

He had walked only a short distance when he again experienced the feeling that he was being watched. Although he looked around a second time, he still saw nothing. He fairly flew down the trail. Not exactly running, as that would be admitting to childish panic, but certainly not out for a stroll through the park.

The next thing was a peculiar odor. It was indescribably rank, so strong and stenchy he tasted it as well as smelled it. It made him gag. It seemed to hang in the gloom all around, like the stink that hovered over rotted meat. It smelled like a bear that had rolled in the carcass of a two-week-old moose kill, only much more fetid.

He became aware of something even more chilling: Something heavy was walking through the trees uphill from him, keeping pace. When he stopped, it stopped. When he walked, it walked. He hurried on through the gloom, hearing the footsteps in the trees paralleling his progress, almost like an echo. Except he knew it was no echo. Panic congested inside his gut, like old grease.

A slight movement, darker among the straight pale birches, caught his eye. He froze in his tracks, momentarily paralyzed at the realization that he was seeing something for which his limited experience in the wilds offered no explanation.

It was an animal, but then again it *wasn't* an animal. At least no animal that the boy had ever seen. It stood upright like a man, only so much larger than any man he had ever run into. At first he thought it might be a gorilla; he had seen a gorilla once at the Denver zoo. Gorillas walked upright on their knuckles, but their legs were extremely short in comparison to their arms and the rest of their bulk. This creature stood erect on long legs, although it was seemingly covered with hair the hue of a cinnamon-colored bear. It stared down at him from the shadows with such intensity that it almost jolted him to his knees.

For more than thirty seconds the two confronted each other in that manner, the boy staring in awe and fear, the creature scrutinizing him with apparent curiosity. Then it turned suddenly and walked away, disappearing.

It must have been approximately that same moment, back in camp, that I experienced an alarming sensation that something was dreadfully amiss somewhere within my family. Call it what you will—mother's intuition, a sixth sense, extrasensory perception. I felt Sid's fear, ill-defined and amorphous though the feeling might be. Restless, uneasy, I finished stoking the campfire and went inside the tent to light the kerosene lantern. The feeling persisted. I came back outside and gazed intently into the surrounding forest and up the trail that led along the creek and around the mountain to Dead Horse Pass.

Sean was fishing in the creek and Tommy was playing cars and trucks next to the cabin. Cara and Cora hung onto my legs where my nervousness apparently transferred to them.

"What's wrong, Mommy? What is wrong? Bear coming to get us?"

"Everything's all right, girls. Your daddy and Sid will be home soon."

I felt as though I were taking a bath while someone, a stranger, peeped through the keyhole.

Lady lying nearby rose with a disturbing whimper. A steady low growl issued from deep inside her throat and the hair prickled along her spine. She glowered up the darkening trail, her fangs showing in a low snarl. Clearly she sensed the same thing I did—and it frightened her.

Black, being younger and less courageous, tried to wriggle in between the twins and me, seeking safety. The dogs had never behaved this way before. Generally when they smelled bear they took off to hide in the tent. This was obviously something new to them.

Suddenly, Lady charged off down the trail, barking fiercely. After a moment's hesitation, Black went with her, but kept back. Sean and Tommy ran up. I snatched the rifle Les had left for me, prepared to defend the homestead from attack no matter from which quarter it came. I was convinced that whatever was out there, even though I couldn't see it, posed a direct threat to my children and to our home.

We were still in a defensive posture when Sid bolted into view, casting wary glances back over his shoulder as he ran. He looked pale and his lips were dry and trembling. Incoherent words tumbled out.

"Mom . . . big thing, *big,* like a hairy man . . . ! I seen it in the woods . . . ! It . . . it *followed* me . . . It . . . it . . . it . . ."

WE HAD THE FIRE roaring to keep the night and its denizens at bay when Les came home. I jumped all over him.

"How could you let Sid go off by himself without even a gun? Lester, he's not a man, he's not even eleven yet. We can't be careless like this with our kids. This is a dangerous place if we start taking things for granted and not using common sense. Life is too precious to be careless with it. Lester, the Lord only knows what that . . . that *thing* is and what it wants from us!"

Les was understandably skeptical. "You sure it wasn't a bear, son?" he grilled Sid. "Bears'll stand up like that on their hind legs. It could have been a grizzly."

"Dad, it ain't no bear. I promise you it ain't no bear. I don't know what it is, but it ain't no bear. It's like a huge hairy man."

None of us had ever heard of such a thing. *Hairy man* was the only thing we knew to call it

"Lester, if Sid says he seen it, he *seen* it," I scolded. "He's just as reliable as you are. He don't spook easy. It came down around the camp too. The dogs and I all *felt* it."

Roger Yager was more skeptical than Les. He laughed heartily at his own explanation: "You say it was big and hairy and smelled bad? Sounds to me like you seen Les."

Roger changed his mind a few days later. He stopped laughing about it.

Loni, who smoked cigarettes like a stove smoked dead wood, ran out of Pall Malls and Roger hiked out to their stores in the blue bus to get more. On his way back down the trail, he came around a curve to confront a hairy manlike creature standing in the trail. He described it as nearly seven feet tall. He was too shocked to do anything except stare back at the creature.

"It . . . it was like his mind tapped into mine," he attempted to explain. "Through his mind, he told me to get out of here."

Les remained unconvinced. "I think Roger and Loni might be smoking too much wacky weed."

"Lester, there's *something* out there," I insisted.

For all we knew it could be Satan or one of his evil disciples. It wasn't like we didn't have enough to worry about with the bears. Now we had *this* to contend with. I had a feeling we hadn't seen the last of the hairy man.

"Whatever it is," I said, getting up to add wood to the fire that kept the shadows driven back, "it doesn't want us in the valley."

19

We tried not to let the presence of bears and the hairy man dictate our lives for us. We had too much work to do. The Westbrooks' bear still hung around getting into mischief and nettling Les. Occasionally, I caught a whiff of the hairy man and felt him watching us. I would look up real quick trying to catch him spying on us, but I never seemed to be quick enough.

Alaska during June and July was truly the "Land of the Midnight Sun." Days that were literally twenty-four hours long took some getting used to. Les never seemed to know when to quit work; he had more energy than any human being I had ever known. As for me, I could always tell when it was getting late and nearing quitting time by a bone-chilling dampness that settled in the air, and by the mosquitoes that swarmed with greater ferocity. The kids loved all that daylight. Alaska teenagers had a joke about it.

"Make sure you're home before dark, children."

"Okay, Pop. See you in August."

The walls of our cabin now stood upright and solid on the bank of the Minook, almost ready to be crowned with a roof. The Yagers and Westbrooks, being less skilled and industrious than Les, had sawed down a few logs but were not going to be able to complete their shelters before snow flew. It became more and more apparent we Cobbs were to be the only settlers in the valley to winter over.

Ray Yager's ninth birthday provided an excuse for a party and an afternoon off from our labors. Loni and I picked wild blueberries and made blueberry pancakes to celebrate. The two families sang "Happy Birthday" to Ray and and ate pancakes around a picnic table Les had built in the little clearing between our tent and cabin site until we were all stuffed. Afterward, the seven older children—the Yagers' brood of four plus Sid, Sean, and Tommy—wandered off downstream to fish for Dolly. I kept Cara and Cora near me after our bear trouble and the encounters with the hairy man. None of the kids were let out of our sight unless they were armed.

The Yagers' daughter, Chloe, now fourteen and the eldest of the children, was designated protectress and handed her father's forty-four, which she strapped around her waist gunfighter style. Sid rolled his eyes in chagrin, feeling it his duty as the *man* to be protector. He was at least a bit smitten, with his first attack of puppy love.

From the picnic table, we heard them laughing and talking, their voices diminishing in volume as they worked their way from fish hole to fish hole. Soon, they were out of sight. The discharge of Chloe's pistol clapping through the conifers, shattering the afternoon calm, shocked all four adults to our feet. The first thing that came to my mind was the image of Sean in Les's arms the day he was shot.

"Oh, my god!"

We soon learned what had happened.

As the children fished, Sean had leapfrogged on stones across the stream to the other side. He cast a grub on a hook into a pocket of smooth water protected by a large rock. He was concentrating so intently on the grayling he suspected hid there that he failed to see the little bundle of black fur that sauntered out of the forest behind him.

When he finally looked up and spotted the bear cub, it was sitting on its rump watching him with obvious curiosity. Sean giggled. The baby was so small and clownish with its hind legs spread in the grass that Sean forgot all our warnings that they should get as far away as they could, as fast as they could, from any chance encounters with bear cubs. Mama bears were fiercely protective.

That warning was about to be reinforced. A sharp, guttural bark came from the forest. The cub sprang to its feet and shimmered wild-eyed up the nearest spruce. At the same time, the kids on the other side of the creek spotted the sow darting through the trees toward Sean. They shouted in unison, a clamoring that failed to drown out the rapid, angry clacking of vicious teeth.

The mama bear charged out of the trees like a slab of greased night. She meant business. A bear at short distances can overtake the fastest moose and snap its neck or bite out its throat. Poor Sean once more confronted mortal danger.

"Run, Sean, run!"

Les was the first to recover. A gunshot meant trouble. He grabbed his own sidearm and led the frantic rush toward the fishing party. I thought I was going to vomit from fright and dread. Chloe was a mere girl and not practiced with firearms. Les should have given Sid his gun.

Pandemonium ruled when we four parents burst into the small clearing along the creek bank where the kids were fishing. My heart pounded as my eyes searched wildly for my sons. I saw them first. They were all jumping around with excitement and pointing to the other side of the creek. Then I counted the other four children. Loni Yager swooped them protectively into her arms. All seven tried to talk at once.

Only after we assured ourselves that no one was injured or missing were we able to listen. The kids shouted and pointed at a bear cub clinging to the top of a spruce on the other side of the creek. It regarded us with a combination of alarm and inquisitiveness. Sid and Chloe explained in feverish bursts what had occurred, each butting in, overrunning and finishing the other's sentences.

"—bear attacked Sean over there—"

"—and he ran on top of the water, Mom. He—"

"—almost got ate up by the bear—"

"—Chloe shot it—"

"—don't know if I hit it or not—"

"—it stopped at the water—"

"—then it turned and ran away—"

"I didn't want to shoot up the hide in case we wanted to use it," Chloe concluded.

"Chloe!" I shouted at that, grabbing my baby and clasping him to me. Sean's teeth chattered and he stuttered as if he had taken a tumble into ice water, which in effect he had. The stream was about thigh-deep at this point. "Chloe! You were thinking about that bear's hide when— Next time you just keep shooting. Loni, tell her!"

As usual, Les took control and restored order. "Everybody calm down. Nobody's hurt and there's no harm done."

The man could be so infuriating at times. He stood there grinning that grin of his while I needed to shout and rave and let it all out.

"Besides," he continued jovially, "we have us a baby bear for a pet."

That gave the kids permission to start laughing and teasing. I held on to Sean as long as I could. He looked okay. Color came back to his cheeks. He struggled now to escape and join the excitement around the bear tree.

"I'm okay, Mom," he said, racing off.

My mother's intuition told me differently.

Chloe's bullet had been more accurate than we first supposed. Les located a blood trail leading into the woods. He followed it some distance to make sure the sow wasn't lurking in the vicinity. He said he would have to hunt her down tomorrow.

"A wounded bear is very dangerous. We can't leave her alive."

Reinforced by the Westbrooks, we spent the rest of the afternoon and evening trying to get the bear cub down from the tree. It weighed no more than fifteen pounds and reminded me of a stuffed teddy I owned as a little girl. It *was* cute. It was also terrified.

The men intended to saw down the tree and throw a blanket over the cub when it hit the ground. The cub didn't fall for that. As soon as the tree started to topple, he leaped into adjacent branches. It took the deaths of three or four spruce before that tactic was discarded.

Next, Les shucked off his shoes and shinned up the spruce with the idea of lassoing the bear. That maneuver proved effective, with the exception of the part where the poor traumatized cub's bowels released a thick, black smelly stream directly into Les's face. Still undaunted, Les kept his hold on the lasso and jerked the baby bear out of the tree.

He made a leash for it and tied it to a tree near camp where he gave it water and attempted to feed it fresh fish from the creek. The little bruin refused all such attentions. It climbed up the tree to the end of its leash and clung there looking at us with a frightened and wistful expression. Les watched it back, fascinated, studying this first wild bear he had encountered at such close quarters.

"If we're going to live with the critters," he said, "we ought to get to know something about them."

I shuddered. What I knew of bears so far, I didn't particularly care for. Charming little animals such as this cub grew into raging monsters like its mother, who but for the grace of God and Chloe Yager's quick reaction would have mauled or killed my son. It seemed in Alaska there was always a challenge, whether in the form of a bloodthirsty swarm of mosquitoes, the weather, evildoers, a bear attack, or having a manlike giant stalk you from the shadows.

"You have to accept it," Jeff Stoddard liked to say. "It's part of the country."

20

During the night following the bear attack, Sean had nightmares, whimpering in his sleep and awaking with a start. "The bear was eating me," he fretted.

It broke my heart. I got up and went outside the tent into the night that was not a night and put more wood on the fire. I sat on a log and stared fixedly into the flames. Twice now since our arrival in Alaska, Sean could have been killed—first by the gun accident, now the bear. I was afraid this latest close call would provide more grist for the nightmares that haunted the little boy's sleep. He already had nightmares about guns; he trembled every time someone picked up one in his presence.

I shivered even though I sat next to the fire. *Was* I going to get our kids killed, as our parents warned before we left Colorado?

Les slipped down onto the log next to me. I felt his arms go around my shoulders. Tears welled in my eyes.

"Lester, I've grown to love it in this valley," I whispered. "I want it to be our home. But sometimes I have doubts . . ."

"Like today?" he said.

"The children are so young. I worry that we're cheating them—bringing them out here where it's so dangerous, away from other kids and everything."

"They have the Yager and Westbrook kids."

"You know what I mean. You said it yourself. The Yagers and Westbrooks are not going to last. Then it'll be only us. The kids isolated from a normal life. Oh, it's okay for Sid and you, but what about later when Cara and Cora want to be around girls their own age, when they want to go to parties and dancing and . . ."

My voice trailed off into more tears. Les gazed into the fire.

"And poor . . ." I choked up. "Poor Sean . . ."

Les's arm tightened around me. "Do you remember over two years ago when we made up the list of reasons why we should go homesteading and stuck it to the refrigerator door?" he asked.

"I still have it."

"Has anything on that list changed?"

I thought it over for a few minutes. "No," I finally admitted, and felt better immediately.

"The first thing we do when we get the cabin built," Les proposed, "is frame the list and hang it on the wall."

I laid my head on Les's shoulder. There were times when I loved this big, direct, no-nonsense man more than words could describe. We sat in companionable silence side by side on the log, isolated by a vast wilderness, gazing into the fire.

THE LITTLE BEAR CUB strangled itself to death on its leash overnight, all but breaking the hearts of Les and the children. Gary Westbrook and Roger Yager refused to accompany Les on his hunt to track down the wounded mama bear and finish her off.

"You're crazy!" they declared. "A wounded bear will kill you."

"It's suffering," Les argued. "I can't leave it like that. And we for sure don't want a wounded bear hanging around where the kids are."

Sid naturally volunteered to go, but Les reluctantly turned him down and took Lady instead. Lady seemed about as eager for the adventure as Gary and Roger. They were gone most of the day. I kept myself busy so my mind could not dwell on what could happen out there when Les met the bear. Relief swept over me like the hot, relaxing vortex of the hot springs in Manley when I saw Les returning, wet and exhausted. The sow hadn't been *that* wounded. Abandoning her treed cub, she cut a beeline out of the valley and kept going.

That left us with the Westbrooks' bear, who still continued to prowl about clacking his teeth, looking for ways to cause mischief while avoiding Les's traps. I sometimes felt the presence of the hairy man, but he kept out of sight. Neither appeared so threatening anymore as we grew accustomed to their presence. I imagined it was sort of like how people who lived in New York became hardened to traffic and muggers.

It was only a few weeks after the incident with the sow and her unfortunate cub that Minook Valley experienced a different kind of excitement. The temperature suddenly plummeted and a snowstorm—*in the middle of July*—filled the air with pale, blowing fury. We knew winters came early in the North Country—but *this* early? We later discovered even old-timers had never seen snow in July. Consternated and surprised by it, afraid winter was going to catch us without shelter, we attacked construction of the cabin with renewed vigor.

"We have to hurry," became Les's mantra.

21

Money was running low, and thus so were "town" supplies. We were learning to live off the land. Grayling and Dolly Varden from the creek, spruce hens, ptarmigan, snowshoe hares, an occasional duck, goose, beaver, or porcupine. Les planned on a big hunt for moose, caribou, and bear to fill our winter larder as soon as the weather remained cold enough that the meat would not spoil. The girls and I picked wild blueberries, raspberries, and cranberries and canned and preserved them as jellies or syrups. I also made syrup from rose hips, that portion left of the wild arctic rose after it has closed up to form seeds, and from the tender new growth of spruce tips, which were chock-full of needed vitamins. I was becoming quite the self-sufficient pioneer woman. When we celebrated the twins' third birthday on August 20, I griddled batches of pancakes filled with berries and dripping with rose hip syrup.

"I knew we'd eat good after we started homesteading," Sid sighed around his bulging belly.

Sometimes I made pancakes for an occasional Indian, trapper, or miner passing through the valley. In the bush it was considered insulting not to ask a wayfarer in to eat or to at least have a cup of coffee. Our most frequent caller turned out to be John Shilling, who had a prospecting site downvalley on Slate Creek, one apparently not too rich as he and his helper were barely making expenses. They had hope, however, and faith that the gold was there—but so did every other holes-in-his-jeans would-be miner in Alaska. Hope and little else was what sustained them.

John was an Ichabod Crane of a man, tall and stoop shouldered with hair almost white. We saw him three or four times that summer as he loped in or out on his tireless long legs or drove the trail downstream on an incredible tracked Caterpillar-like machine called a Bombardier. He hauled in building materials for us on his machine on occasion, a tremendous relief to Les's and Sid's backs.

His half-Indian camp helper confided that he, too, had encountered the hairy man, as had a number of the Indians and Eskimos around Rampart on the Yukon. In a way, it was a tremendous relief to know that we weren't simply imagining things.

In spite of the urgency to finish the cabin, we declared a holiday now and then and went exploring. There were several old miners' ruins downstream on the Minook left over from the last big gold boom right after the turn of the century. We dug up rusted horseshoes and old bottles, one dated 1836, but little else of interest. Jeff Stoddard had once unearthed a can full of gold dust from an old ruin. Sid expressed disappointment that we weren't so fortunate. Riches, I countered in a philosophical voice, were where you found them and how you recognized them, whether they be in the form of gold or in old bottles, nature, land, or family.

"Gold I recognize," Les teased.

IT GAVE ME great joy to watch the family working together for a common purpose. Even the younger children straightened nails or harvested tundra moss for chinking between the logs and layering on the ground as insulation between the cold earth and the split-log floor. After the cabin walls came the roof support beams. They were large spruce trees, between which would be placed lattice-worked smaller logs. On top of all that went a foot-deep layer of sod and tundra to form the roof itself.

Les, Sid, and I were toiling in a near-futile attempt to hoist roof timbers onto the cabin's walls one morning when two skinny, emaciated-looking characters with pimply faces and scraggly, greasy hair appeared walking down the trail. They looked so much alike they might have been interchangeable, hippies who hadn't heard the 1960s were over. Tweedledum and Tweedledee. I instantly thought of them as Heckle and Jeckle, a pair of identical prankster crows made famous by the comics.

They introduced themselves as Grey and Derek, our new neighbors who had moved onto land Grey homesteaded near Joseph Creek a couple of years ago. We had heard through the Westbrooks, whose homesite was nearest the trail up to the pass, that the neighborhood was filling up. The hippies were beginning construction on a tiny cabin sixteen feet wide by eighteen feet long.

"We need to borrow a saw," Grey ventured.

Les's brows lifted. "You're building a cabin and you don't even have a saw?"

Derek stubbed his toe in the sod. "We're gonna winter over," he said. "We have to get a cabin built, but we don't know how to build it."

The result of their unpreparedness and lack of skill was a trade. Bartering and labor exchange were more common among homesteaders than the use of cash, which was usually in chronically short supply anyhow. If Heckle and Jeckle would help Les put up our roof, he would in turn take the following week off with our tools to help them erect their small cabin. Deal sealed, the displaced hippies moved their tent down next to ours. It meant more cooking and cleanup for me, but it was worth it to have two pairs of strong hands to help Les with the heavy work of lifting the big beams to the walls of our cabin.

Something about Grey and Derek warned me to be cautious. I complained to Les that they were "sneaky acting."

"Didn't I warn you about Arnold Cranick?" I reminded him. "I didn't like him either and you saw how *that* turned out."

Les brushed it off. "You're too suspicious of people, Norma."

"You'll see I'm right, Lester."

"Keep your hatchet ready," he joked.

After our roof timbers were up, Les carried out his end of the barter and helped Heckle and Jeckle erect their shelter. He returned home to work on our cabin, but the cold fall rains came before we finished it. They drove us into the tent for days at a time as they slashed through the trees and hissed on the creek. Tempers frayed and our clothing mildewed. Fires were difficult to build and even more difficult to maintain.

Ravens huge and black as vultures perched in the trees like omens and taunted us.

" 'Nevermore,' quoth the raven. 'Nevermore.' "

That was all I remembered from the dark Edgar Allen Poe poem. The line juxtaposed against the constant presence of the ravens took on a menacing air.

For the Westbrooks and Yagers, rain proved the final straw.

"We've decided to winter over in Florida and try it again next spring," they said.

They were our nearest neighbors—only two miles away—and the only ones if you didn't count Grey and Derek at Joseph Creek and John Shilling at the Slate Creek Mine. John would likewise soon be leaving. Although I had expected the Westbrooks and Yagers to go, the prospect of being a family all but alone in the wilderness was a bit disconcerting.

The Westbrooks had dug a root cellar in which to store their belongings. The Yagers cached their stuff in a hole dug in the ground and covered. They made their farewell and in a small crowd trudged up and out of the valley toward Dead Horse Pass, leaving their half-finished cabins stuck in the forest like piles of bones. The forest seemed to whine with sudden desolation. Winds whispered in the trees and the trees seemed to murmur, *You'll be alone, alone. If the Arctic cold don't get you, the hairy man will* . . .

I shivered from the rain and the loneliness.

In between downpours, we worked on the cabin. Sodded and mossed the roof until the cabin interior was rainproof. Les cut doorways and windows into the log walls with a chain saw. He built a heavy front door and carried in two *real* glass-pane windows on his back.

Winter was on the way early. Rain wasn't the only sign of it. Ptarmigan and snowshoes were acquiring white spots by the end of August. Geese in honking vees passed low over the cabin, heading south. Pine squirrels became frenzied in their gathering. Birch leaves blazed with gold almost overnight, and the nights were markedly longer than the days. The Westbrooks' bear became more active in looking to steal food for a final layer of fat before hibernation.

Then, one day, the cabin was finished and in a delirium of excitement and joy we transferred everything unceremoniously from the tent to the cabin. It had taken us three months to build it. Its cost, other than our own labor and the free logs, came to less than two hundred dollars: four boxes of nails at seventeen dollars the box; three windows at twenty-seven dollars each; eighteen dollars for hinges . . . Henry David Thoreau at Walden Pond could have done no better.

We were proud of that cabin and thrilled to have it. Compared to the tent, it was a mansion. We stoked up the barrel woodstove, which soon emitted a thin comforting chimney of smoke into the air. What food staples we had gathered for the wintering over were stored in cupboard shelves in the kitchen area; the kitchen, living room, and master bedroom were a single room. A log stairway led to the children's bedroom in the loft. We were dry and safe at last from the Westbrooks' bear and the hairy man.

We had also amassed a supply of ammunition, medical supplies, fuel oil, batteries for our old car, an AM/FM radio, warm clothing, blankets, and other odds and ends. Once snow came, we would be trapped in Minook Valley without transportation and without communications to the outside world.

"Let us give thanks to the Lord for seeing us through," I proposed. We all clasped hands in a circle and bowed our heads in the little clearing in front of the cabin.

22

A few days after we moved into the cabin, John Shilling came out from his mine driving his Bombardier loaded down with gear. He was leaving the valley for the winter. He got off the tracked vehicle and walked around our cabin, looking it over with a critical eye.

"Why don't you come to Fairbanks to winter over?" he invited tentatively. "Just for this one year?"

Lester was a stubborn man. "This is our home," he said.

"Winters are harsh this far north. It's going to be an early season, seems like, and breakup may be late. Are you sure you have enough supplies to carry you through? You'll be in here alone for six or seven months."

He gave the roof closer scrutiny.

"Snowfall is awfully heavy," he went on. "If something happened out here, you'd have no way of getting out or of notifying anybody."

"We'll talk about it," I finally agreed, made anxious by his cautious appraisal. He moved on up the trail in his Bombardier and we were definitely alone. I almost heard the winds howling off the Bering Sea as they searched for crazy tenderfeet *chechakos* who dared challenge the fearful North Country in winter.

We hung on until mid-September, both Les and I made more anxious by the bite and snap of the Arctic winds growing colder, the increasing length of the darkness. It soon became apparent that the Cobbs, rough and pioneering though we might be, were still unprepared to survive an Alaskan winter alone. Finally, even Les conceded that it might be wiser if we moved south to Fairbanks where he could find a job to earn enough money to buy a Bombardier and other critical supplies for a fresh start come spring.

We stored most of our tools and provisions, boarded up the cabin, and hiked out to our parked vehicles. At Joseph Creek, Grey and Derek had a fire going and were still determined to see the year through.

"We've locked up everything out at our place," Les informed them. "There's nobody except you two left in the valley. Good luck. I guess we'll see you again come breakup."

PART II

And we are here as on a darkling plain
Swept with confused alarms of struggle and flight

—MATTHEW ARNOLD

23

Fairbanks was becoming a boomtown, transforming itself from a quiet pioneer town to a robust and exciting city. It reminded me of what I had read about Dawson and Skagway during the big gold rush of 1896. People—mostly men—were cutting deals, looking for jobs, hiring workers, or pulling scams on every street corner. The reason for all this activity was the new gold rush of the 1970s: *oil*.

With the discovery of oil at Prudhoe Bay in 1968, roustabouts from Oklahoma and Texas started flooding in to earn enormous salaries on the edge of the Beaufort Sea, a frozen arm of the Arctic Ocean. In 1973, President Nixon authorized the building of a gigantic pipeline from Prudhoe Bay to Valdez. Construction workers poured into Fairbanks, the hub city of the Alyeska pipeline, out of which they worked simultaneously erecting the pipeline north toward Prudhoe and south toward Valdez. Oil riggers, bulldozer drivers, welders for the pipeline, lawyers with vivid imaginations all continued the tradition of the goldfield immigrants, the daring men who built the first towns.

Alaska, as Les liked to say, was wide open with opportunity. Anybody with a frontier mentality willing to hustle and work hard could make it here. Alaska was a land for men—and especially for men like Les Cobb. He quickly landed a Teamsters Union job as a surveyors' helper. We rented a two-bedroom apartment on Old Nenana Road in Fairbanks and settled in to winter over. It would prove to be a productive if unsettling

time in our lives as homesteaders, a "trip sock" time again when we saved
money for the equipment we needed for homesteading and caught up on
repairing threads of our lives that had become worn and tattered during
the previous busy year. Although we were stuck in Fairbanks until
breakup, our thoughts and our hearts remained in Minook Valley.

Of us all, even Les, Sid most resented our return to civilization. Even
Sean, plagued as he was by nightmares of bears and guns, would rather
have wintered in the cabin; it offered the stability his fretting nature
craved. Although he missed home, Tommy was my in-between boy, ac-
commodating and simply going along for the ride. Cara and Cora, naturally, had that battling temperament that teamed them up against the
rest of the world, no matter where they were. They were so much like
their father.

Thank God for the Alyeska pipeline and the jobs and big money it
opened up. With Les working and earning good wages, our trip sock
soon bulged with money. We made purchases and stockpiled them in
hopes of being better prepared to construct two or three tourist cabins
on our land and perhaps a mechanic's garage and a trading post. All this
would go a long way toward proving out our claim.

We also bought a used red tracked Bombardier; a Honda three-wheel
ATV; and a 1969 orange GMC four-wheel-drive pickup to replace the
old white Ford Ranger clunker. Provisions for *next* winter stacked up in
the kitchen of our little apartment.

It was a time for other things too. All three boys attended school; next
year we would home-school them. Lady gave birth to another litter of
seven husky pups, two of which we kept to bring our future dog team
to four dogs, including Black. Sid and Sean attended an NRA-sponsored
rifleman's shooting class on Saturdays. Both did well with rifle and shot-
gun, but Sean panicked when it came time to fire pistols. Les had a talk
with him.

"Son, you've got to get over the fear. You can't go through the rest
of your life like this."

"Why can't I just shoot a rifle?"

Les patiently explained. I agreed with him after our experiences in the
bush with bears and the hairy man. After all, the bear at the creek had
almost gotten Sean. Once he knew how to use a pistol, he could always

depend on it for defense. A pistol was far more practical and easier to carry around and have near at hand than a rifle. It was important that men in the wilderness be comfortable with and confident in the use of any weapon.

"I'll try, Daddy," Sean promised bravely.

The little boy's hands shook violently when Les handed him his .44 Ruger at the firing range. He pulled back in stark terror. Les knelt to be on a level with him. He offered the pistol a second time.

"I can't . . ."

"You can, son. You have no choice. Take it."

The boy reached for it and held it gingerly in both hands, staring with widened eyes at one of the awful tools that had brought him such pain and fear. His lower lip trembled. He thrust it back at Les, then turned and fled. But at least he had touched it. That was a start.

"A little at a time," Les said. "We have to get him over this block."

Guns on the macho frontier equated with manhood. I might not agree with it, but that was the way things were. Guns were vital for survival and defense.

Wintering in Fairbanks also afforded me the time to read up on and absorb some of the history of this vast, wild land that had captivated my soul. I was in high school in 1959 when Alaska matured from a territory to a state. To a fifteen-year-old girl more interested in boys and sock hops than history and geography, the event hardly registered. I had rarely even thought of Alaska, in fact, until we were living in Seattle and saw the TV program that opened up for us the possibility of homesteading in the forty-ninth state of the Union. Now, I was fascinated by it. I brought home piles of books from the public library.

"The United States bought Alaska from Russia in 1867," I sprang on Les over pork chops and potatoes. "It was called 'Seward's Folly' and 'Seward's Icebox.' "

Les had not read a book since he dropped out of school to start working ranches. He was a practical man, good with practical things. A man tuned in to the world as it existed around him, living in the present. He only pretended to be interested in much of what I had to say that didn't concern engine repairs, construction, hunting, or fishing. I, in turn, pretended he *was* interested.

"One congressman said Alaska was an icebox that would never have enough people in it to make statehood. He said we should have just given Russia the seven million dollars it cost and told her to keep her darn colony."

"Shows how much a damned politician knows," Les grumped.

He paid more attention when I came across a history of the area around Minook Valley, which was inextricably entwined with the early Alaskan gold rush. In 1894, a Russian half-breed prospector by the name of John Mynook Pavaloff branched off the Yukon River and followed the creek upstream that would later bear his name, with a bastardized spelling. He struck pay dirt in the valley—$3,000 worth of gold, a good poke in those early times.

Thousands of gold rush pioneers beat a path from Eureka, which itself briefly supported a population of four thousand, across the pass that because of the toll it took became thereafter known as Dead Horse Pass, and spread out in the valley along Minook Creek. Fifteen hundred miners all grubbing in the earth for the elusive yellow metal, leaving ruins behind that Les and the kids and I had explored the previous summer. Jack London was only twenty-one years old and weak from scurvy when he settled temporarily in the valley and began writing some of his famous novels and Alaskan short stories. Tex Rickard ran a saloon along the trail; he later built Madison Square Garden.

Rampart, now a small Indian village of less than one hundred Athabaskans and Eskimos on the banks of the Yukon nineteen miles from our homestead, boomed with a population of over five thousand people. It had two newspapers, four saloons, a community dance hall, and a baseball field. In 1898, the stern-wheeler upon which Wyatt Earp and his wife, Josie, were passengers became frozen in at Rampart and couldn't get out again until July 1899. Earp took advantage of the inconvenience to open his own gambling establishment.

The gold rush ended shortly after the turn of the century. Eureka became little more than a ghost town, a status it retained into modern times. Manley Hot Springs and Rampart lost the majority of their populations. Miners abandoned Minook Valley, the trail in and out grew over again, and bears and the hairy man once more took control of it.

"I'll bet there's plenty of gold still in the valley if we could find it,"

Les said. In his eye I recognized the same glint that animated the eyes of prospectors Jeff Shoddard and Joe Pumper whenever they talked about the gold they expected to find *someday.*

"Lester!"

"Honey!" Les exclaimed. "All our money problems would be solved if we struck gold."

Looking for gold was a fool's pursuit.

"I was just talking, honey. Still, it wouldn't do no harm to kind of poke around."

As for the hairy man, I was embarrassed at first to ask the librarian if anything had ever been published about him. I was afraid she might think me daft. To my surprise and amazement, I discovered that entire books had been published about the legend of Sasquatch and Bigfoot, as he was called. He had been sighted many times not only in Alaska but also in other parts of the United States and the world. I showed artist's sketches of the manlike creature to Sid.

"That looks like what I seen!" he marveled.

"It *really* exists!" I cried, showing the drawing to Les.

Les remained unconvinced. "Fairies exist too, and ghosts and goblins and other things."

"Lester! Lots of people have seen it. Sid saw it. So did Roger Yager. I know now that we're not crazy. We've got a Sasquatch in Minook Valley."

"Live and let live," Les said, grinning. "As long as he leaves us alone . . ."

Les had hired on at the Teamsters Union until the end of March, after which we intended to move back to our valley. None of us knew how long the big oil boom would last. I convinced Les that we should take advantage of it while we could.

"You work this winter and I'll work the summer," I said, reasoning with my stubborn husband. "It'll give us the money to buy all the supplies we need for a new start."

He finally relented. Although I was a woman who would rather be a stay-at-home mom and homemaker, my life revolving around family instead of career, it nonetheless felt good to know that I might also contribute financially. In January I signed up with the Culinary Union to work at one of the pipeline camps over the summer. That meant moving into a workers' dorm if I was hired. Les would have to take care of the homestead and the children.

"Once we're all together again in Minook Valley at the end of the summer," I promised, "we're there to stay."

24

The Culinary Union still hadn't called by April to offer me a job. It appeared I might have the summer in Minook Valley after all. We needed the money, but I also missed our life in the valley. Bears, Sasquatch, and all. Les was so eager to try out our Bombardier that he couldn't wait for breakup and the snow to melt from Dead Horse Pass. Long before it was safe, we loaded the tracked vehicle with provisions, left the children for a few days with friends in Fairbanks, and chugged the trail over the pass. We hadn't seen Minook since the previous October.

We were so excited at returning *home* that the track seemed to creep along at an excruciatingly slow pace. But slow and grinding as it was, especially in the higher-elevation snow for which Bombardiers were not designed, it was certainly progress over carrying in supplies on our backs. Roaring past the little cabin at Joseph Creek, we observed that the walls were piled high with snowdrift and that the surrounding snow was untracked.

"I didn't think Grey and Derek would last the winter," Les commented. "Those hippies probably ran out of funny weed and couldn't stand it."

It was okay with me if they never came back.

We crept past the Westbrook and Yager homesteads with the top walls of their unfinished cabins sticking up out of the snow. Our eyes were riveted on the way ahead as we searched through the spruce for the first sign of our own little cabin. We expected to see the white of the snow-capped roof. It should be clearly visible through the green of the conifers, from whose branches the snow had been chased by wind and new spring sun. Instead, we were almost to the little clearing before we saw the cabin at all. Puzzled, Les swung out from behind the wheel of the Bombardier and stood on the cab roof to obtain a quicker, clearer view.

"Oh no!" he gasped. "It's caved in. The roof fell in from the weight of the snow."

He abandoned the track and dashed ahead to reach the cabin quicker. I followed. I saw the front wall, door, and window—but no roof. The door was sprung open and snow seemed just as deep inside the cabin as outside. It was a heartbreaking welcome home, and a little scary too.

"Lester! What if we had stayed the winter and were inside it when it collapsed? It would have killed us all—or else we would have frozen to death without shelter."

"Don't get excited, Norma. We could have kept the snow shoveled off if we'd been here."

All that work through the summer, to have the outcome demolished by the elements. We walked silently around the cabin to assess the damage, too stunned to speak. I was almost in tears. Sod, moss, timbers, and snow filled up most of the interior of the cabin, all of it on top of our furnishings and belongings.

As if that weren't bad enough, the Westbrooks' bear had apparently already ventured from hibernation and discovered the windfall. His distinctive huge paw prints were stamped everywhere in the snow. We found where he had entered the open door and tunneled through the snow to pillage for canned and packaged goods. He had had himself one fine spring-awakening meal. What he hadn't devoured, he destroyed by puncturing with his teeth or shitting on.

"I'm gonna get that bear," Les said, renewing his vow through clenched teeth.

"I'm beginning to think God doesn't want us here after all," I sniffled, feeling overwhelmed. "Or that the devil is trying to chase us out."

"We're staying," Les said.

He stood at the open door, pondering. "That bear is pretty damned smart," he mused, "but no matter how smart he is, he couldn't have opened that door."

"Maybe it was the wind."

Les shook his head slowly. "I don't know . . . It looks like we're back in the tent for a while."

He constructed a platform in the clearing high enough that a bear couldn't reach it. We began salvaging what we could. As we worked, it became more and more apparent that while the Westbrooks' bear may have contributed to the damage, he was a culprit only after the fact. Bears took food and destroyed things, but they didn't steal for profit or personal use. Our disappointment grew as we discovered that most of our pioneering stores were missing—a pair of twenty-two rifles; a crossbow used for hunting grouse and other small game; canning jars and lids; clothing; a saw, an axe, and other tools; a pair of boots; pots and pans; dishes . . . All gone, disappeared. All the things we needed to start the new homesteading year.

I recognized the grim look on Les's face, the way his chin thrust out and his shoulders rolled forward. He looked the way he had when he stepped out onto the main street of Manley to face down Arnold Cranick.

"The hippies!" he immediately declared. "You were right about them, Norma."

"We don't know that, Lester. There's no proof."

Secretly, I agreed with him. Heckle and Jeckle were sneaky varmints. This only proved it, but I didn't want Les getting into trouble by going after them.

"There wasn't nobody else in the valley," Les snapped. "Look at the way the snow is—and the front door left open. They broke in and ransacked the cabin *before* the roof fell in."

"Lester, we should let the law handle this."

"*Law!*" he roared. "Norma, what law are you talking about? There ain't no law out here. Haven't you seen that already?"

Fortunately, the hippies had already lit out of the country. Les glared at their cabin on our way back out to Fairbanks to pick up the kids. His rage exploded almost beyond containment when we reached the location where we'd left parked for the winter the two-ton Ford next to the Yagers' blue school bus. We had been in such a hurry to reach home on the trip in that we barely looked at the two-tonner. Now we saw that it had been vandalized. Windows and mirrors were shot out, tires flattened, the back door to the van bed wrenched off. There was no damage to the school bus. For some reason we had been singled out.

"Maybe Arnold's been around again?" I suggested.

"Arnold's too lazy to walk out here. Besides, the police are chasing him. It's Grey and Derek."

"Why would they do *this*? We helped them."

Les simply glared in the direction of their cabin. For their sakes, and for Les's, I hoped they never came back.

25

ITT, the food service group responsible for supplying cooks and maids and other domestic help for the oil pipeline camps, hired me to work at a camp called Cold Foot. The Culinary Union called and left the message in Fairbanks while Les and I were away. Les needed me in Minook Valley, but we needed the money even more now that most of our pioneering goods had been pilfered or destroyed. Les and the brood would have to return to the homestead and make do without me for the summer.

I flew in to Cold Foot with a company pilot in a Piper Cub. The camp lay three hundred miles north of Fairbanks in the Brooks Range of the Arctic Circle. The mountains in the south of Alaska—the Alaska Range, the Wrangells, the Aleutians—were imposing and majestic and made you believe in God even if you didn't. As you traveled north, the mountains shrank, became lower and rounder. Dukes and duchesses maybe, compared to the kings and queens of the south. By the time I reached the Arctic Circle, I gaped out the airplane windows onto country as flat as a table. It looked as if a giant had shook out a tablecloth and smoothed it out over the land. It was flat and gray and appeared as though no life had ever existed out there or would ever exist again. Even in the summer, you almost heard the frigid breath of the Arctic preparing to blow-howl across the flats, with nothing much to stop it until past Fairbanks. It was a land of such boundless emptiness, so lonely and forbidding, that the first time Les saw it, he murmured, "I bet there ain't even no mosquitoes out there."

I shivered involuntarily as the Piper Cub dropped altitude for landing. Everything was that same dismal color of gray. Cold Foot was the only sign of civilization within immediate sight. The pilot pointed it out, afraid I might mistake it for a great lichen parasite. The camp might be civilization, but it looked desperately temporary.

A fence on the flats surrounded a trailer park composed of approximately a hundred double-wide plain mobile homes sitting skirted to keep the wind out of their undersides. They still wore wheels and tires, as though prepared to be summoned elsewhere tomorrow. They were always referred to as "Atco," their brand name. "I have to get back to my Atco . . ." "Which Atco is yours . . . ?" Approximately one thousand five hundred people lived and worked here and on the giant pipe that stretched south like an artery and was pushing farther north day by day. Because of permafrost, the pipe was built aboveground and would have to be heated in the winter to keep the oil warm and prevent the interruption of flow. It was said there was enough oil on the North Slope to provide the needs of the United States into foreseeable centuries. First, Alaska had been about gold. Now, it was about oil.

When we landed, I was shown to the mess hall and kitchen—five Atcos melded together. A brusque woman with chronic PMS and work-reddened hands as large and powerful as a man's showed me to my dorm. Each dorm was a double-wide trailer with about twenty tiny cubicle rooms lining a hallway down the middle. Two people were assigned to each room, which was barely large enough for two single beds and two military-style wall lockers. Spartan, impersonal, cramped, and dark.

"It ain't much," my guide sourly admitted. "But up here you ain't needing nothing but a place to rest your bones at night. 'Cause all you're gonna be doing when you ain't working is sleeping, and when you wake up you go back to work again."

I fought back tears as I stood feeling alone and deserted in the middle of my tiny cubicle. This would be the first time I was away from Les and the kids for any length of time. I swallowed the painful knot in my throat.

"When . . . when do I start to work?"

"How fast can you change clothes?"

I started off as a pots 'n' pans dishwasher, being the newest flunky on the job. I worked a minimum of ten hours a day, seven days a week, for wages of nine dollars an hour, a tremendous salary in those days. The culture shock was worse than the long hours of labor. It was all a new experience for me, my first exposure to Alaska's boom world.

Call the camp a mixture of college campus, military boot camp, and prison. Keeping order seemed to be a constant challenge. Armed uniformed guards patrolled the fence lines and the hallways. They carried heavy wooden clubs and were prepared to use them when people worn out in body, soul, and nerves sometimes exploded into brawls and mini-riots. A mob attacked the airfield shortly after I arrived and set fire to a helicopter.

If the guards heard unnecessary noise inside a room, laughter, for example, they pounded on the door and demanded entrance. No vices were tolerated—no gambling, no sleeping around, no hooch. Alcoholic beverages of any kind, including beer, were forbidden north of the Yukon River by law, Prohibition having returned on a minor scale. Rooms and personal belongings were constantly searched for contraband.

In spite of all these precautions, however, the camp seemed virtually uncontrollable. Operators, welders, electricians, teamsters, all men, received top pay of up to thirty dollars an hour. Because of the wages, welder and pipefitter unions all over the Lower Forty-eight fought to get a toehold on the pipeline. Most of the men were lower-class laborers, rootless young males with a propensity for causing trouble. It was Pipeline Gomorrah. There were going to be pillars of salt. People fighting, cursing, sleeping around with whoever, guzzling smuggled booze. I would have cried myself to sleep at night during those first few weeks, except I was too exhausted for tears. I murmured my prayers, closed my eyes, and then awoke to more dirty pots and pans.

If the food was good and plentiful, it was supposed to compensate for lack of recreation and time off. A worker could have literally anything he wanted to eat. As much as he desired, and it was all free. Huge steaks, lobsters, shrimp. Five or six different salads for each meal. Four or five different main courses. Ice cream and uncountable desserts. Some of the men ate three or four thick steaks with all the trimmings at a single sitting. Yet, they *still* complained about the food and the cooking.

"Your wife or your mama would be ashamed of you," I scolded when I advanced out onto the floor as a kitchen helper and overheard all the groaning and griping. "Kings don't eat as good as you do. You never ate so good in your life. Why don't you grow up and stop acting like a baby?"

I was young and small and not unattractive. Men hit on me until I let it be known in uncompromising terms that I was a family woman. I had a man and we were homesteaders. The Hatchet Lady fought for what was hers and fought for what was morally right.

Norma, I admonished myself, *your mouth is going to get you fired. We need the money to replace what was stolen and destroyed at the cabin. Lord, give me patience.*

The longer and harder men worked without women and without outlets, the more difficult they became. One evening at suppertime, a teamster old enough to know better reached out and flipped up the skirt of a kitchen helper picking up food trays. I expected her to dump a tray of food in his lap. Instead, she broke down in tears and rushed toward the kitchen.

I had had it up to my eyebrows with rude, groping men and their nasty habits. I lit into the offender like Callie the cat with all claws bared.

"That was crude and uncouth and you had no right to do it," I tongue-lashed. "What would your wife say if she saw you do that? What would you say if that were your wife and some man did her that way? You should be so ashamed of yourself . . ."

I let him have it like that until I ran out of breath. His face paled, then reddened with embarrassment. He stopped eating and dropped his head like a chastised teen caught peeping through a hole into the girls' locker room.

"I'm so sorry," he murmured. "You're right and I was wrong."

He not only apologized to his victim, he continued to apologize every time he saw either her or me. He was never out of line again. He helped spread the word. "That Norma is a plucky gal. Hands off Norma Cobb. She don't play."

. . .

THE LONGER I WAS AWAY from Les and the kids, the more I missed them. I missed the valley. I had a favorite place by the pass where I imagined standing and looking out over Minook for most of its length and depth. Its beauty took my breath away. Birch and cottonwood would be spring-leafing now, making the earth reborn. The air would be clean and pure without smog and smoke, not air breathed so many times it tasted listless and manufactured. In my homesickness, I realized that in the short time I had known it the valley had become a part of me. Wherever I went from now on I would always miss it.

26

It was a summer during which it became clear to me that while Les, as a man, might be head of the Cobb family, I was its base, its foundation, the motivator who provided direction and purpose. I wanted a home for us, *our own home*; that was the family's focus. The damage to our cabin after the summer's hard work and the theft of most of our pioneering possessions left Les disheartened and temporarily discouraged. While I was away, he found it difficult renewing last year's momentum. I hadn't realized before how much he depended on me.

Rather than move into the valley near the cabin in order to start refurbishing it, Les, the five kids, Callie the cat, the two grown dogs, and Lady's two puppies took up residence in the Yagers' blue school bus, which was far more comfortable than a tent. Les's mind had a tendency to wander toward things other than homebuilding. The children loved it. They were all more apt to be out in the valley hunting grouse, fishing Minook Creek for grayling, pursuing the Westbrooks' bear, panning for gold, exploring, or visiting Ira Weisner's trading post in Rampart than they were to be cutting logs for a new cabin roof. Like grasshoppers fiddling all summer while the ant worked to provide for the coming winter.

Trouble followed Les. If it didn't find him, he would go looking to confront it in his own inimitable style. I served as governor over the most excessive of his impulsive nature. I was afraid, by leaving him alone with the children, that he might turn into Mr. Hyde as soon as my back was turned and the full moon rose. As it turned out, my fears were more than justified.

27

One Alaska trooper, *one,* served the law in all that vast territory north of Fairbanks, an area nearly twice the size of Kansas. Trooper Ross was a former homesteader himself who knew and understood the people. He was transferred out and replaced by a lawman who displayed the typical attitude of "civilization" toward the interior settlers. Because most settlers came to Alaska poor and seeking a new start, and because we lived literally from hand to mouth in the bush, it stood to follow therefore that we must be little more than barbarians. Typical stereotypes cast us as backwoods people, hillbillies, uncivilized, prone to violence, independent, and resentful of outside interference. The stereotype in fact held some large degree of truth; however, that the only constable in the entire territory should let it prejudice him assured that the bushers would be more prone than ever to handle their own problems. Bushers went armed not only to protect against bears but also against criminals and frontier bullies.

The new bush cop, Trooper Jones, soon received his first lesson in frontier justice. Not surprisingly, my husband was involved, if but in a minor way.

One night at three-thirty A.M. he was awakened by a noise outside the blue bus. He automatically reached for his forty-four as he sat up to look out the window. A shadow was prowling around the two-tonner. A man with a rifle braced over one shoulder.

"What do you want?" Les challenged.

"I'm hunting," the stranger replied.

"Step out where I can see you. Now."

The man was no hunter, that much was obvious when he moved out of the truck's shadow into view. He looked fresh off a disco floor in his high-heeled shoes and big-legged slacks. He was not from around these parts.

"It would be best to take your hunting to another valley," Les suggested, cocking his pistol for emphasis.

The intruder hesitated, as though weighing his chances. Then he turned back on the trail toward Eureka, where he later broke into Rose Stowell's cabin and lived there for several days undetected. Rose and Charlie were still in Fairbanks. While at Rose's, he ransacked several other cabins in the vicinity, causing a minor crime wave.

Gunslinger-miner Joe Pumper caught him walking along a trail wearing a pair of specially made mukluks belonging to local dog musher and racer Rick Swenson. Joe recognized them. His hand flashed to his low-slung forty-four.

"What are you doing here?" he demanded. "What are you doing with all that garb on? That stuff belongs to my friend."

Joe disarmed the thief at gunpoint and delivered him to Manley. He was obviously the cause of the local crime wave. Joe notified Trooper Jones only after the townspeople roughed up the thief pretty good. "Interrogation" by the angered populace resulted in recovery of most of the loot stolen from cabins around Eureka.

"What happened to him?" Trooper Jones inquired when he finally arrived. "He's all beat up."

"You handle crime your way, we'll handle it ours," the lawman was advised. "If he ever shows up around here again, we'll feed him to the bears."

He wouldn't be back. Turned out he was a fugitive serial killer fleeing arrest. He had been raping and butchering native women from Fairbanks to Minto. His stolen car had broken down on the Elliott Highway south of Manley. He continued on foot to what was, literally, the end of the trail.

"We *should* have fed him to the bears," Joe Pumper said. Bushers knew how to dispense justice.

. . .

A FEW DAYS AFTER the serial killer incident, Les spotted chimney smoke coming from the direction of Heckle and Jeckle's cabin. Grey and Derek must have unexpectedly reappeared. It was a windless day. Fire giving off smoke sent a signal high into the air, almost a half-mile straight upward, with never a waver in the column.

I had to hand it to Les. He at least *tried* the legal way first. He went to the new trooper and told him about the ransacking of our cabin.

"Do you have any proof they broke into your cabin?" Trooper Jones asked. "Maybe they thought it was abandoned."

"They knew better. What proof do I need? I *know* they did it."

Lester Cobb was never long on patience. His bearded jaw thrust out and his shoulders rolled forward.

"I'll take a report on it," the trooper said dismissively. "For insurance and tax purposes."

He knew bush people never had insurance.

"Besides," the trooper continued nonchalantly, as though he were too busy to be bothered, "I thought you bushers never wanted interference from the law."

Les glared at him, then turned and walked off. The law took reports for *insurance purposes*; if you wanted *justice* you had to render it yourself.

Les might be hotheaded, but he wasn't totally unreasonable. Trooper Jones made sense in one respect: Les had no convincing proof that Grey and Derek were our culprits, even though he might *know* they were. Using extraordinary restraint, Les confronted the hippies at their cabin.

"We swear we had nothing to do with it, Les," they protested. "It might have been some of the natives from Rampart. We don't know nothing about it."

"If you're both lying through your underwear..." The implication was clear.

"We swear, Les. We swear."

Things rode on like that for several days. Les began missing spare gasoline he kept stored in containers at the blue bus campsite. A gallon or two at a time vanished. Tired of the thefts, he set a trap for Heckle and Jeckle. They weren't nearly as smart as the Westbrooks' bear.

He poured a pound of sugar into a gallon of gasoline and left it out as an invitation for pilfering. Sure enough, it disappeared. Gray and Derek even had the gall to ask Les to repair their pickup for them. Its engine had seized. Sugar in gasoline did that to an engine.

Les roared his blasting laugh. "Get out of my sight!"

Suspicions confirmed that the hippies *were* thieves, Les set out to obtain proof that they were also responsible for the theft from our cabin. He launched a clandestine expedition to their cabin while they were away, nosed around, and was not particularly surprised to uncover some of our stolen goods. That was all he needed.

We had helped Heckle and Jeckle build their cabin, had lent them tools and fed them. Only to be repaid in this manner. There was no place in Minook Valley for thieves. In the valley, the way Les saw it, *he* was the law.

"You would have been proud of me, Norma," he exulted later. "I used patience and control just like you told me. I could have lynched them, but I didn't."

Some people might have called it patience and control, but certainly not restraint. Smoldering with slow anger mixed with his own brand of dark elfin humor, Les loaded a case of dynamite on the Bombardier and returned to the thieves' cabin. They were still not home. He planted sticks of dynamite at strategic sites underneath the cabin and linked their fuses so they would detonate simultaneously.

He was sitting on the doorstep wearing his forty-four, holding the end of the dynamite fuse in one hand, a cigarette lighter in the other, when Heckle and Jeckle came home. They grew quiet and approached cautiously.

"Howdy, boys," Les roared jovially.

"Les," Grey acknowledged. They still hadn't caught on.

Les slowly rose to his feet, a big, rough bearded man who had taken to the frontier life with enthusiasm and been driven too far. He snapped open the lid on the cigarette lighter. Blue flame appeared. Heckle and Jeckle watched the flame as though mesmerized by it.

"You are *thieves!*" Les charged with doomsday judgment. "There ain't room in this valley for you. You got two minutes of fuse to get down that trail and never come back. I'm gonna blow you out like the nest of rats you turned out to be."

He lit the fuse. Now they caught on. Grey's eyes bugged out. Derek dug a trench in the ground with his boots trying to obtain traction. Heckle and Jeckle tore off down the trail, long hippie hair flying, their screams of fear and outrage thudding flat in the forest. They were still running the last Les saw of them.

As Les knew little about the use of dynamite at the time, he had stoked the tiny cabin with enough explosives to bring down the Empire State Building. He nonchalantly walked down to Joseph Creek and took cover within its rocky banks. The blast that reverberated off the valley walls was enough to shake the top of Norky's Mountain. It knocked Les flat on his face. It was like the detonation of a bomb. He tried to burrow into the ground, hands clasped over his head, as the cabin hurtled by overhead in all its component parts.

He stood up slowly, amazed and wide-eyed, when the earth ceased shaking. The entire side of the hill was a gigantic cloud of smoke. As it cleared, he was left staring at a smoking crater where the cabin had once stood.

"Holy crim-i-ney . . . !"

Bushers knew how to dispense justice.

28

Les remained restless and unsettled while I was gone. The summer was passing and he still hadn't repaired the roof on our cabin. A lot of his torpor, I finally concluded, had to do with the macho bushman image he had assumed since our arrival in Alaska. Here I was working, earning money for the family, while he stayed home to *baby-sit*.

"I'm a house husband," he wryly commented when he visited me at Cold Foot.

Visits from the family, confined as I was to the oil camp, were welcome if brief respites. From Les I caught up on all the happenings in the valley and became even more homesick than usual after he left.

The Yagers and Westbrooks had returned, he said, but were not apt to stay long and were accomplishing even less this year than last. As Roger Yager needed to use the blue bus, Les and the kids moved into the tent again. It was uncomfortable in the tent and fraying on nerves. Plus, it was hard for Les to work on the homestead and look after the kids at the same time. He thought about returning to Fairbanks where he knew someone to take care of the brood while he obtained a summer job.

"If I could also get a job at Cold Foot or one of the other camps . . ." he suggested.

One bit of news from the valley I found particularly disturbing. Les and I must have been incredibly naïve to have missed all the little hints and signs thrown at us during our relationship with our neighbors, the

Yagers and Westbrooks. Looking back, however, I recalled the suggestive glances, the "accidental" brushing of one or the other of the four grown-ups against either Les or me, the veiled proposals that "maybe we should all move in together." It hadn't dawned on me that anything inappropriate had been going on until now when Les explained to me that Roger Yager and Gary Westbrook were engaged in wife swapping.

"What is *wife swapping?*" I asked.

It worked this way, he said: One man slept with the other man's wife, and vice versa.

"*No!*" I exclaimed, shocked and disbelieving. It was unreal what people did for entertainment when they had too much time on their hands.

Roger Yager had finally approached Les about our joining them in their bedroom capers.

"What did you say to him?" I demanded in a scandalized tone.

"I told him he didn't have anything worth swapping, so I thought I'd stick with what I had."

"*Lester!*"

I knew I would feel uncomfortable with our neighbors from now on. I felt a wedge driven between us and the only two other families in the valley.

"It's the Devil working," I declared. "The Devil is still trying to drive us out. He doesn't want us there. Lester, you stay away from Loni Yager and Hazel Westbrook. You hear me, Lester?"

DURING HIS TRIPS to Cold Foot, Les met another settler also looking for a job. He and Pete Pasquali took up together right away. They became like brothers, although about the only thing they seemed to have in common were their ages and their matching dark beards. Mutt and Jeff they were—Les tall and big, Pete short and stocky; Les talkative and outgoing, Pete quiet and rather withdrawn.

Les moved the kids, dogs, and cat back to Fairbanks where he found help with them. Pete and he scouted for jobs together at the oil camps. Cold Foot refused to hire either of them. It seemed like the "ol' boy" system in operation. A superintendent was hired from Texas or Oklahoma and he brought up his own crew, whose members had buddies of their own they wanted hired. Alaskans were left out in the cold, so to speak.

I kept checking on Les. If you didn't keep Dr. Jekyll with his incredible energy occupied and employed, chances were sooner or later the darker alter ego of Mr. Hyde would escape. Les was going to find trouble if trouble was around.

29

It all started innocently enough. People at Cold Foot got to know Les on his visits. He appeared in a room full of people and knew everyone in it by their first names within five minutes. Soon enough, someone asked him to bring back a bottle of booze, as a favor, which Les obligingly did. Others made the same request. Hooch was always being smuggled into the camps like this, a bottle or two at a time. Leave it to Les to see an opportunity.

Pete and he were driving past a liquor store in Fairbanks when Les slowed the pickup and whipped it to the curb. He sat there looking at the liquor store, in ponderous thought.

"You got a bellyache or something?" Pete asked.

"I got an idea."

"I knew you were in pain."

"I got five kids to feed, you got three," Les pointed out. "If I borrowed some money somewhere for our first load of whiskey, I'm sure we could sell it overnight at the oil camps."

Pete looked at Les and blinked. "That's called bootlegging. It's against the law."

"It's only against the law because the oil company says it is," Les countered.

"Al Capone probably said the same thing. He still ended up in jail."

"Al Capone had syphilis."

"What's that got to do with anything?"

"Nothing, but he still had syphilis. I say we buy a load and try it."

Les borrowed six hundred dollars and turned it all into booze through an acquaintance at a liquor distribution warehouse. He hauled the entire load to Cold Foot, without my knowledge, and sold it all within an hour, doubling his money. Surreptitiously peddling it out of the back of the truck, while word passed and men nonchalantly pretended to just wander by.

He sold three loads of hooch that same week before he went back home. He soon had a business going, making big money. Cold Foot no longer even pretended abstinence. It was as if a liquor store had opened up. Frustrated guards snooped around trying to find out how booze was entering the camp.

"It's somebody in an orange pickup," I overheard, but still failed to make the connection.

A day or so later, a lady I worked with in the mess hall took me aside and whispered, "I heard it's your husband."

"*What!*"

"The guy bringing in the whiskey. My boyfriend said his name was Cobb."

I flew at Lester the next time I saw him. "You'll go to jail. Then what will we do?"

"I got a family to feed," Les replied, as stubborn as always. "Pete has this old miner friend named Harry Leonard living at Wiseman. Harry used to run mules loaded with whiskey from Mexico to California during Prohibition."

"This isn't Prohibition, Lester."

"What else do you call it? It's the oil companies trying to tell people what they can and can't do."

He grinned that grin of his.

"At least if they put me in jail, they'll have to feed you and the kids. They're hiring fifty men a day at the oil camps, but they won't give me a job."

Bootlegging wasn't right and it was against the law, but only because the oil companies said it was. I neither approved of drinking nor of my husband being a rum runner, but I rationalized there were worse things in the world. Besides, trying to stop Les from doing something he wanted to do was like standing under a snow avalanche trying to stop it with upraised hands.

Business remained good, for a while. Some of the more conscientious guards continued efforts to identify and snare the mysterious bootlegger. But for every one of them, there was another guard who just as conscientiously worked to protect Les. Guards liked a drink now and then too. In addition to having a gift of gab that could have talked him past the gates of heaven, Les always brought along a few free bottles to keep his guard allies happy and the machine "greased."

It was only when state troopers were called in from around the Anchorage area that Les realized his bootlegging days were numbered. He could not evade them for long. There was only one road, the Alyeska Highway, in all of the country north of the Yukon River. It was a private road built by the oil companies to connect Prudhoe Bay and the oil slopes to the rest of Alaska. All the troopers had to do was blockade the road and stop everyone driving on it. It was not that there was ever a big traffic rush.

Les arrived at Cold Foot with a load before the road was blocked off. One of his regular customers scurried up before he alighted from the pickup.

"Troopers are watching!" he warned.

There was still an hour or so of darkness between sunset and sunrise. Les was in a quandary. He could neither peddle his wares without attracting the attention of the law, nor could he depart with his load intact. He already saw himself with a jailhouse tan. Worse than that, what was I going to say? What would the kids think? We were attempting to rear them as God-fearing, law-abiding citizens whether they were growing up in the bush or not.

Les was trying to make up his mind when one of the guards came out. "Follow me," he hissed from the corner of his mouth, barely moving his lips. Straight out of a Humphrey Bogart movie.

Les drove in the dark behind the guard's vehicle to a warehouselike building at the back of the camp. A window had been removed through which to unload the illicit cargo. When he drove back out a few minutes later and headed for Fairbanks, troopers pounced on him from everywhere. He was tempted to point out that a busher couldn't find a trooper anywhere to arrest a burglar who broke into his cabin, while troopers poured out of the woods to nab a bootlegger when the oil companies beckoned.

"Howdy, fellas," Les drawled innocently. "What can I do for you?"

"What do you have in the truck, Cobb?"

"Not a moose," Les cracked.

There wasn't even a bottle label. Nothing but the tarp used to cover the shipment.

"Next time, Cobb."

There might be only one road north, but a Bombardier didn't require a road.

One morning not long after this episode, I was cleaning up after breakfast in the kitchen at Cold Foot when Les unexpectedly strolled in wearing his bright grin.

"Howdy, honey. Here I am. Pete and me have got jobs here as flatbed drivers. I guess they figured if they couldn't catch us, they might as well hire us."

30

Les spoke to Pete Pasquali and his wife, Gloria, about combining our households and moving our five offspring in with their three. I liked Gloria. I took a couple of days off work to help Les transfer our family to a ghost-town settlement called Wiseman, where the Pasqualis lived. It was located about ten miles north of Cold Foot.

Sid especially was thrilled to be out of the city and back in the bush. I was even more thrilled to have Les working at the same camp as I and to have my family nearby where I could at least *visit*. Two families living together in one small house was by no means an ideal arrangement, but it would have to do until we Cobbs were back on our feet and able to return to homesteading. Les and I discussed it and resolved we might as well work the rest of the summer and all winter before returning to Minook Valley next spring. By that time we should have "trip-socked" a pretty good stake.

Wiseman was a cold and desolate place. In the 1920s it was an active little gold boomtown. Every stream and trickle of water anywhere near it was dredged up and the busted rock and gravel sifted for gold, leaving slag heaps in abundance and creating a moonscape appearance on the Arctic flats. With time, the gold played out. Boomers deserted their cabins and claims and chased their dreams elsewhere. Abandoned cabins were stripped and burned as firewood by those left behind. Now, only about ten cabins remained, most of which along with their adjacent gold claims had been bought up by old Harry Leonard. He patched up a few of the cabins enough to rent them out to workers at Cold Foot. The Pasqualis and Cobbs occupied the largest and best in "town."

At first I didn't like Harry. He was an odd-looking, ratty old man with his wiry, stooped frame and tangled gray beard. He had raced to the Klondike shortly after the beginning of the great gold rush of 1896, which put his age somewhere into the nineties. He had been pursuing rainbows ever since. He was convinced gold still hid beneath the tundra at Wiseman. Now that he owned all the claims, he was going to find it sooner or later.

Maybe part of the reason I failed to take to Harry right away was because he was part of the inspiration for my husband's having taken up bootlegging, as he himself had smuggled hooch from Mexico into California fifty years ago. Another part of the reason was because he was recalcitrant and brash and reminded me in a way both disturbing and comical of what my husband might be like within a half-century or so.

Should something happen to me, for example, I imagined Les with the same ratty gray beard going down to the creek for water, as Harry had done, and encountering the young geologist with his testing tubes.

"Are you going to drink this water, old-timer?"

" 'Course I am," says Harry, and so says Les.

"From all the gold mining, there's enough arsenic in it to kill you."

"Son, I been drinking this water for nigh on fifty years, and I ain't never had one bit of health problems."

Already, Les was every bit as irascible and bullheaded as Harry Leonard. As proprietor of most of Wiseman, landlord of its dozen or so residents, and therefore the town's de facto mayor, town council, and city administration, Harry had the duty of burying with his Caterpillar tractor whoever died. When an ancient enemy of his passed away, one of Wiseman's last permanent residents, Harry faced the unpleasant duty of planting him in the ground. He had sworn never to do a thing for the son of a bitch.

Nevertheless, he met his obligations and dug the grave, cursing and blackguarding the unfortunate deceased the entire time. As the mourners gathered at the open grave for last words, Harry revved up his Caterpillar engine.

"Pray quick, brothers and sisters," he shouted, " 'cause I'm comin' to cover up that son of a bitch and get rid of him as fast as I can."

With that, he roared down upon the mourners, scattering them, and filled in the hole, ready or not. Lester Cobb was capable of something like that.

Yet, the old man was hard *not* to like, another trait he and Les held in common. They were also both bullshitters who spun yarns one after the other until the rooster crowed. Harry loved women, *all* women, and went out of his way to please, amuse, and entertain. On account of our living at Wiseman with the Pasquali family, we were often treated to his wonderful tales of the Arctic and its characters, the most colorful of whom was old Harry himself.

"You ever have cabin fever out there in that cabin of yours in the valley, missus?" he would say, presaging one of his yarns. "Let me tell you about Jacob and Roy and cabin fever . . ."

Jacob and Roy, he began, were two prospectors who let isolation get to them. Both fervent poker players, they went into hibernation one winter to play cards until spring breakup. Only one of them, Roy, emerged from the cabin the following spring. As soon as he could travel, he dutifully reported to authorities the death of his partner, who died of natural causes during the winter and was placed in "cold storage" on the porch.

When the trooper investigated, he discovered a bullet hole square in the middle of the deceased's forehead. He promptly arrested Roy for Jacob's murder.

"I shot him for certain, the cheatin' scoundrel," Roy admitted. "But he still died of natural causes."

"How could that be?" the trooper demanded.

"Well, sir," said the accused, "Jacob truly did expire one night in bed."

When Roy found him the next morning, he placed him in a chair outside on the porch where the weather froze him solid, preserving him until spring when he could be given a proper funeral.

After a while, Roy got to missing the company of his old pal and poker partner. He started carrying his dead and stiff-frozen chum into the cabin every day, propping him in a chair at the table and playing cards with him. Each night Jacob was then expelled to the front porch to refreeze.

"I caught him cheatin'," Roy insisted of the corpse. "I got so mad I just drew my gun and shot him."

The medical examiner's autopsy report confirmed the old sourdough's story; his friend Jacob had been dead for weeks, even months, before the bullet drilled a hole through his deep-frozen brain.

Naturally, Les took to old Harry. With all his energy, the result we were to discover of an overactive thyroid, Les got off from a ten- or twelve-hour shift at work and still had daylight left to accompany Harry and Pete to learn about gold mining. I saw that gold fever was beginning to burn in his soul; it made me uneasy.

"He's teaching me things," Les explained defensively. "Harry has found things geologists say couldn't be found. Education only goes so far. He's teaching me how to read the lay of the land, to find where the gold is."

"How come he hasn't found it if he's so smart?" I asked.

"He will."

"He's ninety-something years old. He'd better hurry."

"There's gold there," Les stubbornly insisted.

We were *homesteaders,* I cautioned my husband, not prospectors itching to move on, forever move on, seeking rainbows over the next hilltop. We had a homestead in Minook Valley to prove out.

"There's gold there too," Les said.

31

At Harry's urging, Les and Pete Pasquali filed a prospecting claim in a canyon, a huge slit in the plain, near Wiseman. They built a tiny shack on its lip to be used whenever they had time to pound around looking for gold. They called it the Crow's Nest. One morning before going to work driving truck at Cold Foot, Les and a friend named Jeff King from the camp were puttering around in the canyon, preparing to climb out to the Crow's Nest. Plenty of daylight shone this time of year, more than twenty hours of it every day.

A thick twist of alders ringed a muddy creek seepage on the floor of the canyon. As the two men approached the alders, they were assailed by a powerful stench that seemed to emanate from the earth itself. It smelled like something large had died and rotted.

In the mud alongside the water seepage loomed a huge footprint so fresh the sides were still crumbling in. It resembled that of a man barefooted, except it was easily twice the size of any normal man's foot. Les placed his size twelve boot in the print and had plenty of room left over.

"What *is* it?" Jeff breathed.

Les was by no means a timid man, but the lingering stench and the size of the footprint sent hackles creeping up the nape of his neck. He drew his forty-four.

Jeff King pointed, his hand trembling.

"I—I think it's a bear," he stammered, as though hoping that *was* what it was.

It was four A.M. during that silvery half-light of an Alaskan summer night. An animal, a huge animal, was climbing the canyon wall. Climbing it hand over hand, as an ape would, or a man. It appeared to be covered with dark hair. A giant human wearing a heavy fur coat.

"That's no bear," Les murmured.

Awestruck, the two men watched the animal reach the top of the canyon. It stood up, glanced back down at them, then turned and walked away.

Les made a point of dropping by the mess hall where I worked before continuing to the truck garage.

"What did you say it's called, that hairy man thing Sid saw?" he asked, trying to sound casual.

"Sasquatch," I said. "Bigfoot. Why?"

He shrugged. "Maybe we oughta keep a closer watch on the kids when we go back to the valley."

32

Work on the oil pump stations and oil construction camps continued summer and winter. It was the decade of the oil crisis when the government warned we were running out of fossil fuels. Gasoline prices soared. Les contended that was because the oil companies were in a conspiracy to build the pipeline with no out-of-pocket expenditures of their own. Whether there was a conspiracy or not, we Cobbs owed our survival as homesteaders to the Alyeska pipeline. Our old trip sock bulged with savings to go toward repairs of our collapsed cabin in Minook Valley, the materials for a new modern roof that would not cave in again, and for improvements to the land to make it our own before the five-year time period expired for proving out on our homestead.

Pump stations and oil construction camps were different from each other in several ways. Pump stations were smaller and permanent in that they remained to service and maintain the line after it was completed. They were numbered in sequence, starting with number one in Prudhoe Bay and continuing on to the pipeline's end in Valdez. The camps were temporary and moved with the pipeline's advance.

I grew restive, impatient, and eager to return to Minook Valley. It was more than the result of confinement to my workplace and Atco cubicle, "cabin fever." I was a woman more comfortable being at home with my family than working away. The situation became even more unbearable when, with the approach of winter, I received transfer from

Cold Foot to Franklin Bluffs, while Les and the kids remained behind. I then transferred several more times as the winter progressed, working a number of pump stations and camps all up and down the line—Atigun, Toolik, Pump Stations 10 and 13. Working in kitchens and mess halls and as a bullcook whose duties were to clean the quarters of the other workers. After a while, one place merged into the other.

I missed seeing Les and the kids. Pipeline jobs with all their vices and temptations and long hours were for single people without other commitments.

The winter was harsh, dark, and long. Snow piled up eight to ten feet and pathways had to be cut through it from one building to the next. Lights blazed twenty-four hours a day in a feeble attempt to drive back the frozen eternal darkness. Although I worked seven days a week, ten hours a day, there were times when it was such an incredibly stunning world that I marveled at God's artistry.

Sometimes while walking back to my Atco, I paused to listen to the mournful yodel of wolves somewhere out there in dark space. There was breathtaking beauty in the howling of the wolves, the glisten and sparkle of new snow beneath lights, the splendid aurora borealis that never failed to fill me with wonder.

It was as though God hung the great curtains of fire to fill space with myriad colors of dancing forms and vast spears and shafts of light flashing from one horizon to the next in a dazzling display of His power and majesty. I held my breath and lifted my head to them and watched until I felt the air in my nose and throat freezing.

By the time the sun returned to the North Country, at first for only a few minutes a day, then rapidly expanding into hours, I was ready to quit and go home to our valley. We had so much to do there. I quit my job in May, with a great feeling of relief. I quit in a routine way by simply handing in my notice. Leave it to Lester to depart with drama.

33

Because of weather producing slick and dangerous conditions, Cold Foot faced the problem of recruiting bus drivers to ferry workers from camp to construction sites, then back again. Over ninety percent of the pipeline labor came from places like Texas and Louisiana that rarely saw much snow. Les volunteered to drive the pipeline welders' school bus for the extra pay. He got up at three-thirty each morning in time to load up the 798ers, as the welders were called, and drive them to work. He then did his regular job during the day and returned in the evening to bus the welders home again.

The 798ers proved to be a rude bunch who came to Alaska with one thought in mind—to rape the land and leave again with their money. Morning and evening when Les started up the bus and asked in a loud voice, "Is everybody on?," the welders responded with a cacophony of catcalls and insults questioning Les's intelligence, competence, upbringing, and breeding. Les, to his credit, put up with them all winter.

In May, 1976, when breakup started, an ancient grizzly emerged from hibernation in the low nearby hills. Les noticed him regularly lumbering around searching for something to eat. His coarse hair was falling out in wads and it was obvious he had worn out or lost most of his teeth. Unable to catch moose or caribou on his own, he had turned "garbage eater" and rummaged around the camp looking for food. If he were a human, he would have been using a walker, drawing Medicare and Social Security, and boring his grandchildren with long, pointless stories.

Les and Pete Pasquali, both of them equally full of mischief, devised a devilish scheme to foist revenge upon Les's 798er tormenters. One evening after dropping off the welders to the usual abuse, Les swiped a box of sandwiches from the mess hall. He and Pete left a trial of peanut-butter-and-jelly appetizers for the old bear to follow to the back of the school bus, the door of which they left open. They dumped the rest of the sandwiches on the back seats of the bus.

They expected the ancient and hungry grizzly to climb on the bus, gobble down the sandwiches, shit all over everything, and leave the mess behind to gag the welders when they got on the bus the next morning. The pranksters went home chuckling at the thought.

Instead, the old guy gobbled down the sandwiches and went to sleep at the back of the bus, sleeping soundly like hard-of-hearing old-timers will. Les and Pete stood outside in the morning chill. They looked at the slumbering bear. They looked at each other. Men were already coming out of the mess hall after breakfast and heading toward the bus, quiet and introspective as people often were at four in the morning when they hadn't been awake long.

"What are you going to do, Les?" Pete asked.

Les shrugged. "I'm going through with it."

They eased the back door closed on the old gentleman. Les went around and assumed his regular seat behind the wheel. The 798ers filed on and, as usual, crammed into seats at the front of the bus. Les called it the "Southern mentality" which asserted that gentlemen never went to the back of the bus. He could hardly wait to ask the usual question, which never failed to elicit the usual raucous response. Pete, wearing a sly grin, stood back a safe distance.

Finally, the time came. All was quiet on the bus, everybody anticipating the question. Les grinned.

"Is everybody on the bus?"

That triggered the hooting and yelling and questioning of Les's ancestry. It also startled awake the old griz, who must have thought he had fallen into a pit filled with demons. The giant spun over onto his haunches and sat up, banging his head on the roof.

Woof! Woof!

First, all sound ceased instantly. Heads craned in unison. Then, in less than three seconds, the 798ers totaled their own bus trying to get out of it.

Al Green, owner of transportation facilities at the camp, came running out. "What's going on? What is it?"

Tears of mirth rolled down into Les's and Pete's twin beards.

"Al, this is a good day to call it quits," Les announced, still laughing. "I couldn't top this one if I tried. Why don't you write me my check? It's time to go homesteading."

PART III

Not till the hours of light return,
All we have built do we discern.

—Matthew Arnold

34

I found it a bit depressing to return to the valley after so long away. Our poor little cabin sat as we had left it, roof collapsed, door sprung, with litter inside from where porcupines had gnawed. The trail from Dead Horse Pass had grown up some, and there were other indications that things had changed. Weeds sprouted around the topless walls of the Yager cabin; Roger and Loni had gotten divorced and would not be returning. The Westbrooks were back, but they seemed aloof, almost embarrassed, after the "wife swapping" incident. I suspected discomfort would drive a wedge between our two families. I knew I was uncomfortable and could hardly look at Gary Westbrook without blushing after the proposal he and Roger had made to my husband. How could Hazel and Loni, wives and mothers, have done such a thing?

Heckle and Jeckle, of course, would not be returning. They were probably still running from when Les blew up their cabin. I was unaware of that incident until we hiked past their site and I saw the big crater left in the ground.

"Lester?" I said sternly.

He confessed.

"*Lester!* How could you?"

He grinned.

John Shilling the miner would be back later to work his gold claim at Slate Creek. It looked like the entire thirty-three-mile length of the valley, until you reached Rampart on the Yukon, was occupied by only two families, the Westbrooks and the Cobbs, and one prospector. And, probably, the Sasquatch. I wondered if the Sasquatch had a family.

The long feud between Les and the Westbrooks' bear finally ended on an anticlimactic note. Les found him dead. Apparently, some time last autumn he had simply been too clever for his own good and caught his head in one of Les's snares. His body had frozen over the winter, then thawed out with breakup and begun to deteriorate. Les kept the skull. It was the width of two of his palms and would have been a Boone & Crockett record, he said, except the bear had not been taken in fair pursuit. I could care less about *fair* when it came to bears who might eat my kids.

I appropriated the animal's claws with which to make jewelry. My roommate at Pump Station 10 was an amateur jeweler who worked in gold, silver, and natural materials. She had taught me some fundamentals. I was eager to try my hand at it during the wintering over when outside activities became limited because of weather.

"I'm glad the bear's gone," I said. He would skulk in the woods no longer, clacking his teeth, shitting in camp, and waiting for the opportunity to snatch one of the children.

"In a funny way," Les mourned, "I'll miss him. He was just like me— trying to protect what was his."

My depression proved fleeting, soon succumbing to the joy of our being *home*. We returned more determined than ever to get on with our homesteading and get things done. Thanks to the pipeline and, coincidentally, to Les's bootlegging, we had the money in our trip sock to replace everything we lost and do it right. We had all the help we needed too, at least for the first part of the summer. Les's older brother Don and, a few days later, a childhood friend of mine from Kansas, Dee Russell, and her three urchins, Anthony, Kym, and Adrian, decided they wanted to experience homesteading and help us repair our cabin. None of them, I suspected, could take more than a summer's taste of it.

You looked at Don Cobb and saw a slightly older, skinnier version of Les, without the beard. He and Les and Sid went to Minook Valley in advance of the rest of us, hauling in a load of building supplies on the Bombardier and setting up camp in the clearing by the damaged cabin.

Dee was petite like me, with light brown hair pulled back into a ponytail and a way of screwing up her face whenever she lapsed into deep thought. She caught her breath in her throat when she first saw the valley laid out before her eyes at the top of Dead Horse Pass.

"It's beautiful!" she gasped.

She seemed less enthusiastic about the living facilities—two large tents, one for the adults and one for the kids; a tarped kitchen area; a log storage bin on stilts to keep food and supplies safe from bears. But the men had a homey fire crackling in the open area in front of the tents, and wild Arctic roses were gloriously blooming. The kids were already clamoring for pancakes and rose hip syrup. Dee laughed, accepting it, and everybody moved in. The Cobb clan now numbered an even dozen. I was truly happy to be home from the pipeline and to have around me so many of the people I loved.

Life quickly fell into a routine. Les, Don, and the older boys started work on the cabin. Les, naturally, did the work of three men. During the winter he had suffered heart problems, which were ultimately diagnosed as being the result of an overactive thyroid that kept him running at a hundred miles per hour. Medication for the rest of his life would keep it controlled, but he still ran at ninety and expected everyone else to keep up with him. He joked that an overactive thyroid was going to build our homestead.

The men cleaned out the cabin and began sawing, skinning, and notching trees for a new roof. The first roof had been one-way slanted and obviously insufficiently strengthened to withstand the weight of the winter's snowfall. The new roof resembled a barn roof from Kansas or Colorado, ballooning up in the center and slanting down front and back, providing a much larger loft sleeping area than the previous one. It was reinforced at every potential weak point. The roof was also of metal instead of sod and tundra moss.

"It won't fall in on us?" Sean worried.

"Never," his father promised.

While the men labored on the roof, Dee and I installed a plywood floor—just like a *real* house. In between that and maintaining camp, we cleared a small plot of ground for a garden. We planted tomatoes, peppers, onions, strawberries, and potatoes. We had no idea how they would grow, but we wouldn't find out unless we tried.

The men began laying in a plentiful supply of firewood. We were home to stay. In northern Alaska, winters were never far away, no matter what the season. Settlers were always either preparing for winter or recovering from it.

35

Dee sat next to me on a log by the campfire, chatting. Across from us, Sid worked with leather, building collars for Black, Lady, and Lady's two big rowdy pups. Les and Don were overnighting in Fairbanks to pick up more building materials. The rest of the clan romped around in the vicinity, creating din enough to repel even the most obnoxious bruin.

Dee's face was screwed up in thought. Clearly, she felt anxious about being left alone with another woman and children in the vastness of the northern wilderness.

"What if something were to happen out here, Norma?" she asked pensively, gazing into the fire.

"Like what?"

"Like if one of the kids were hurt or . . . *anything*? It's not like you can go to the telephone and call for help. It would take you a whole day to get to a doctor. Look at what happened to Sean."

I shuddered at the recollection. It was something you could not dwell on, however.

"And the bears?" she persisted. "The Bigfoot thing?"

Her eyes shifted uneasily toward the rifle leaning against a log within easy reach, and the holstered forty-four next to it. Pioneers a century ago lived like this, with a gun for protection always at hand. Les was teaching her and her kids to use weapons accurately and safely, but she was never at ease with them. People accustomed to policemen on the street corners and neighbors so near you heard them snoring found it difficult to visualize a wild world in which you either took care of yourself or perished. The vastness of so much space filled with wild animals and ravaged by fierce weather frightened people.

Dee hugged herself and shivered, even though the fire felt warm against our legs.

"I worry about you and the kids up here, Norma," she continued in the same vein. "I imagine you snowed in out here with a sick kid and unable to get out for months."

"We'll have dog teams soon, and maybe a sno-go machine someday."

"But *alone* out here . . ."

"I'm not alone. I have Les and the kids."

"What if something happened to Les?"

I looked into the fire. I looked across at the almost-finished cabin.

"Without Les," I finally admitted, "I'd be scared to death."

LATER IN THE NIGHT, after we had all turned in, noises outside the tent awoke me. I assumed it was the kids in their tent. I shouted at them to hush and go to sleep.

The sounds persisted. All four dogs and Callie the cat cowered in a corner of the tent, whimpering from fright. Bastions of courage they were not.

"What is it?" Dee whispered frantically.

"Shhhhh!"

Armed like Annie Oakley and feeling brave, pistol in one hand and rifle in the other, I crept to the tent flap and pushed it aside. It never got exactly dark this time of year. I blinked into the silvery near light that always reminded me of a black-and-white snapshot negative. Embers glowed from the firepit.

Dee's head poked out next to mine. She pointed suddenly and in a whispering near shriek stammered, *"B-b-b-bear!"*

Sight of the creature froze her in place.

A small black bear near the children's tent was attempting to claw his way up to the food bin. He cut a contemptuous glance in our direction before resuming his efforts to obtain easy food. I pictured him turning on the sleeping children. My knees went weak. I trembled so violently the barrel of the forty-four pistol banged against my knee. I had never shot an animal before, not even a rabbit or a pheasant. I recalled the sow Chloe shot that day at the creek when it attacked Sean and how dangerous Les said bears were when wounded.

"B-b-b-b-b . . . !" Dee said. It was one thing to see a bear in a zoo cage, quite another altogether to face one in the open with nothing between you and it except space.

"Bear!" I supplied, regaining my voice. I had to be brave.

I didn't want to chance wounding him and making him *really* mad. I inhaled deeply and shouted as loudly as I could: *"Get out of here!"* At the same time I fired the pistol in the air.

Pandemonium erupted. Dee screamed. Children screamed. The dogs yapped and gnashed their teeth, brave as long as they didn't have to face the intruder alone. Sid burst out of the children's tent, followed by Sean looking terrified and expecting the worst. Although he had recently started shooting a pistol under Les's tutelage, any unexpected gunshot was enough to cause him panic and nightmares for weeks thereafter.

As for the poor bear, he was more alarmed than anyone in camp. Gunfire, people screaming and stampeding, dogs barking . . . He woofed and shimmied up the nearest tree with the agility of a chased squirrel. The dogs, seeing his undignified retreat, darted out of the tent and raised a ruckus at the foot of the tree. The kids ran screaming for the adults' tent and huddled with Dee and me at the open doorway. We all stared at the bear. The bear stared back at us from the top of his spruce.

"Shoot him, Mom!" Sid encouraged.

"Definitely not! What if I just wound him?"

"What are you going to do with him, then?"

"Sid, I'm not going to do *anything* with him."

"We can't leave him up there all night."

That was exactly what we were going to do. Wait him out. He had to come down sooner or later, at which time I hoped he was thankful enough for his life to *get out of here*.

Dee and I quickly gathered the children, like two hens with their hatches of chicks, and hustled them into the tent with us. After some coaxing, Lady and the other dogs joined us. That left the bear plenty of room and opportunity to make his departure—which he seemed disinclined to do at the moment. I wanted him down from there and gone. At the same time I was afraid of what he might do when he did come down. I wished Les were home.

We took up vigil at the tent flap. There would be little further sleep tonight. Everyone watched the bear, silent and expectant and fearful. The bear watched us back, silent and expectant and fearful. We waited and waited. It was a standoff.

"Shoot again," Sid suggested. "Maybe it'll scare him down."

That seemed better than any idea I could come up with. I stepped cautiously outside the tent. Dee stuck to my side. Two women in long nightgowns and barefooted, eight kids' heads poking out the tent opening to watch.

"Don't go any closer, Norma," Dee whispered.

I shook her off so I could cock the rifle and fire it. I fumbled nervously with it and the pistol, attempting to juggle the two weapons. I was so nervous that when I cocked the rifle, I somehow accidentally discharged the pistol.

The report deafened me. The bullet blasted a hole in the earth between my feet, stinging my legs with a shower of dirt and rock. I sprang back with a yelp of surprise. I had almost blown off my own foot!

Any courage I might have possessed now disappeared, leaked out like air from a punctured tube. Blinded by tears, shaking all over, I retreated to the tent to be consoled by Dee while the children watched, hushed and tense.

The bear didn't budge.

"I think he's too scared to move," Sid opined.

Dee offered the next idea. "If we'll be real quiet, maybe he'll come down and leave on his own."

The plan worked—two hours later. Everyone emitted sighs of relief, but no one returned to bed.

"What if you had shot off your foot, Norma?" Dee exclaimed. "What would we have done way out here?"

But I *hadn't* shot it off. You could always play the "what if?" game. Some people played it to the point where they hardly dared leave home. Better to live a full life *your way* than to be afraid to live at all. I hoped the kids understood that.

· · ·

DEE PROMPTLY DECIDED it was time to head back to Wichita with her kids where large predators did not wake you in the middle of the night.

"Norma, I'll worry about you every day," she said. "I'll pray for you."

36

Bears, as Jeff Stoddard and Joe Pumper always liked to point out, were indeed a fact of life in the bush. A force of nature you learned to live with, as you learned to live with the changing of the seasons and the darkness of winter. Bears were Mother Nature's way of keeping man humble when he left his paved streets, blazing electrical lighting, fast vehicles, and burglar alarms and ventured back to his origins. I always thought it would be a good thing to take politicians, celebrities, and others bloated with their own self-importance and throw them into the bush with bears in order for them to regain touch with man's true place in the universe. I imagined man still living in caves huddling around his fire while casting fearful glances into the surrounding darkness.

After the harrowing episode of the bear in the tree, I was more apprehensive than ever about being left alone in the valley with the children. Tents could never keep out a bear if it decided to make itself at home. Dee and her offspring departed with enough tales to horrify Wichita for the next decade. Don's girlfriend Debi came out for a week's visit, then Les and Don drove her to Fairbanks to catch her flight back. There wasn't enough room in the truck for all of us; the kids and I remained behind overnight.

It was a long wakeful night during which I winced at every sound, cringed at any strange scent that might warn of the hairy man's proximity. Sid and I gathered his younger siblings into the adults' tent for safety, then I lay with my eyes open listening to the breeze hissing through the spruce and cottonwoods and the nervous stammer of the nearby creek. I would no longer be afraid, I assured myself, once we completed the cabin and could escape behind stout log walls.

I listened for the noise, and when I first heard it—rustling, scuffing, snuffing—I thought I might be listening too hard and imagining it. My heart leaped into my throat when it persisted. The brave dogs cringed; bears ate dogs. Sid touched my shoulder to let me know he was going to peek out through the tent flap to check it out.

"The bear's back," he reported, returning for his rifle.

"Sid, why did you leave the door open?"

"Shhh, Mom."

Why did these things always happen when Les was gone?

Stiffening my resolve, I reached for my own rifle. Sid jacked a round into the .308 his dad had bought for him used. In that action, even in the darkness of the tent, I recognized something new and different in my son. Les was right. My little boy, only eleven years old, had become a man.

It would have required a chisel to pry me off his side as the two of us moved toward the door. Cara and Cora, fortunately, were already asleep. Sean and Tommy sat straight up in their night bags, holding their collective breath. The noise outside seemed to cease.

"Maybe he's gone," I hoped.

We cautiously peered out into the near twilight. Sid jumped back a step. I froze.

The bear lurked directly outside the tent, not twenty feet away. As startled by us as we were by him, he rose to his hind legs like a snake uncoiling. While he was not an exceptionally large bear, he seemed at the time to be a giant who towered above our heads and even above the tent. Teeth and splayed claws and baleful pig eyes filled my vision. I almost choked on his musky dog-cave odor.

Sid reacted. He swung his rifle to his shoulder and fired. Cara and Cora bolted awake, shrieking.

The bear dropped.

An expectant hush enveloped the little forest glade. No one moved. We remained frozen in place for what seemed an eternity, our eyes glued on the still intruder. I half thought he might sit up again and charge us, like the monster in some horror movie. Instead, he lay where he fell. His muscles continued twitching for a few more seconds. Then he became still in a silky black fat heap.

Sid started toward him. I grabbed his arm.

"Shoot it again to make sure."

He did. There was no need. His first shot had proved incredibly accurate. A brain shot. Everybody gathered around the dead bear. Suddenly, we were all laughing and jubilant. Sid's bony chest seemed to stick out a foot more than it had yesterday. I was so proud of us. Left alone, we proved we could take care of ourselves. We killed a bear without Les. The Cobbs' first bear, if you didn't count the Westbrooks' bear Les caught in a snare and the cub who strangled on his leash—and a Kernel had taken it.

"Wait'll Dad sees *this*," Sid boasted, swaggering a little.

Now we were confronted with what to do with the carcass. In the bush, you wasted nothing. Les was the only one of us experienced in skinning and butchering big game. Sid and I managed to gut the beast, but then we weren't sure how to skin it in order to best preserve the hide. We finally decided to tether it in the creek to keep it cool, clean, and free of flies. That turned out to be the worst mistake we could have made. By the time Les and Don returned from Fairbanks, the hair was starting to slip and water had ruined the meat.

"It's too bad about the meat," Les commented, then followed up with that grin of his. "But you all did good. You're real pioneers."

"Real pioneers who still live in a tent," I reminded him. "If we had our cabin, this wouldn't have happened."

37

Sean's bear nightmares doubled up on him. I wanted to get him out of that tent and into the cabin where he might feel safe. For the next couple of weeks, all of us labored exceptionally hard to complete the log house. Soon, we had a roof of metal to shed the rain and slip the winter snows. We rechinked between the logs with fiberglass insulation rather than with the moss we previously used. We laid linoleum on the plywood floor.

There were actually two rooms—downstairs and upstairs. Downstairs consisted of the long kitchen area on one side, whose height extended all the way to the roof. The rest of downstairs, all open except for the partial wall formed by the steep log stairs leading to the loft, was the "master bedroom" with a window overlooking the junction of Minook Creek and Lost Creek. There were two other windows, one near the door in front and a second upstairs at the end of the loft. The children's sleeping loft took up only half of upstairs, with the other half open above the kitchen area.

Les and Don built most of the furnishings out of natural woods readily available—bedsteads, rough-hewn dining table and chairs, shelves, a sofa of sorts. They went to Fairbanks and brought back a propane cookstove, a small gas-engine wringer washing machine, and propane and kerosene lamps. It was like Christmas in July.

Of course, the cabin was no longer a two-hundred-dollar structure. Insulation and linoleum alone cost us over one thousand dollars, and the roof almost that much. What with these expenses, coupled with the costs of a few "conveniences" and the stocking of foodstuffs and other supplies for the coming winter, our trip sock was growing uncomfortably lean.

First thing after moving in and tacking our "Homesteading Incentives" on the wall, Callie christened the new cabin by giving birth to a litter of four kittens in a box of clothing stored in the loft. The father had to be the Westbrooks' tom. I stood in the cabin hand in hand with my rough husband. My eyes filled and overflowed along with my heart. This time the cabin would stand. *This* was what I had dreamed of those nights back in Colorado. This was the fulfillment of God's promise of a new start. He had found us worthy. I already felt warm and safe.

"Welcome home, honey," Les said.

"Welcome home, Les."

38

The symbol of Alaska is the Yukon River. Draining the heart of a great continent, 1,979 miles in length with much of its course running close to the Arctic, it had for centuries provided a highway into and out of the interior. Frozen in winter, it became a wide expressway, first for dogsleds, then later for snowmobiles, called "sno-goes" by Alaskans. Canoes and boats took to it during the summer months. Many Indian villages along its length could only be reached by the river. Rampart nineteen miles downcreek from the Cobb homestead was one of these.

The trail that gold seekers tramped from Eureka across Dead Horse Pass, and which we few Minook homesteaders were improving upon, became an Indian trapline trail along Minook Creek. It followed the creek downvalley until the valley opened wide where it encountered the Yukon. There on the flats lay Rampart. No roads other than the trail and the river led to it. Gradually, the Cobbs became acquainted with some of the local townspeople. Although Rampart was the nearest settlement to our home, the trek to reach it by foot was more challenging than hiking out over Dead Horse Pass to our vehicles and then drivng to Manley Hot Springs.

By any definition, the village was a messy affair, slung like a giant collection of antiques on a low flat bluff overlooking the river. About a hundred and fifty people, mostly Eskimos and Athabascan fishers and trappers, lived there in little frame shacks whose yards were perpetually littered with parts of old dogsleds, rusted animal traps, boats with holes in them, fish nets, and other debris from a harsh frontier life. The natives were small, dark-skinned people with hair as black as an Arctic night and eyes genetically slitted to withstand snow glare and freezing winds. They were standoffish when it came to whites and outsiders, but became as friendly as family when they finally warmed up.

Old Alaska hands claimed the natives came in one of two varieties—either they were the teetotaling minority when it came to booze, or they drank like fish. Both the Russians and early Americans banned the sale of alcohol to natives, but by then it was already too late. The Indians had already learned to make *hoochinoo,* from which the slang word *hooch* was derived. We had heard stories of how no Indians could stay sober more than three weeks in a row, of how Indian men mistreated their women, and of how if you took a hundred miners—be they Indian or white—ninety-six of them never amounted to a thing.

Setting out from the homestead for either Manley or Rampart was no casual undertaking, not like a city family jumping into the sedan and shooting down to the corner convenience store when it needed a loaf of bread. Trips were planned days or even weeks in advance. To Manley, it was a shorter trek out of the valley to where we kept our vehicles parked at trail's end. However, there were certain conditions of weather and season when the vehicles couldn't be used at all. Mud and snow, for example. Then it was closer and easier to follow the Minook Trail along the creek to Rampart. At first Les and Sid and Don, before he went home, made the expedition to become acquainted; later, the younger kids and I accompanied them riding the slow-going Bombardier. The journey generally required a camp-over en route.

The tallest building in the village was Ira Weisner's general store and trading post. It was the first thing you saw coming out of the bush. It rose two stories tall and seemed to dominate Rampart. Simply entering it became an education in North Country living. It smelled of cured leather and gun oil, whiskey and onions, cotton cloth and fur. It seemed anything could be purchased there, or exchanged there if you had the right trade goods.

Walls and ceilings were cluttered with steel traps hanging by their chains, pelt stretchers, saws, axes, hoes, and other tools; mounted moose heads and bears and giant salmon; mukluks, dog harnesses, sled runners . . . There were cases of ammunition, shotguns and rifles, booze, snow tires, although there wasn't a single vehicle in town, canned peaches or sardines, open barrels of pinto beans and potatoes and onions sold by the pound . . .

In the back part of the trading post were clothing, caps, parkas, boots and shoes, bolts of cloth, wood-burning stoves, and the Rampart post office. To the left was hardware, to the right notions and luxuries. At one time a female mannequin dressed only in bra and panties stood at the bottom of the stairs leading up to Ira's second-floor living quarters. Someone broke into the store and stole it. Rumors for years afterward traced the fickle mannequin's progress from cabin to cabin among the region's lonely bachelors.

Ira was a giant of an old man, white-haired and white-bearded, shrewd in business and so tight, it was whispered, he still carried in his pocket the first penny he ever pinched. As virtually the only white man along this part of the Yukon, not counting half-breeds, he often suffered the ire of the natives who claimed, rightfully or not, that he took advantage of them.

As with Harry Leonard the Wiseman miner and any number of other characters of the North County, Ira was believed to possess a shady past. Rumors had it that he was running from the law when he came to Rampart in the 1920s and that he had shot and killed several enemies and thieves since his arrival. A black man who once worked for him— and attempted to embezzle money—simply vanished and was never heard of again.

Ira was the core of the regional literati, having published a book about Alaska two decades earlier. He and Rampart would eventually become important to the Cobbs because of his death and the fact that he owned a number of gold claims in Minook Valley.

"The Cobbs from Cobbsville!" he boomed in his great voice when he came to know us. "The Cobbs and the Kernels!"

Until Rampart, I had never met anyone other than Les and Sid and Roger Yager who admitted to having actually seen a Sasquatch with his own eyes. We never mentioned our encounters. After the "Hatchet Lady" episode, Les's "gunfight" in Manley, and his *alleged* dynamiting of Heckle and Jeckle's cabin, our consorting with legendary woodland creatures was all we needed to *really* cement our reputation.

It was different among the natives. Down through the generations had passed tales of the notorious hairy being known to the Indians as "Bushman." He had become a sort of bogeyman evoked to frighten children into being good. When the Indians realized I was being neither condescending nor patronizing, they readily opened up.

"The Bushman clan is so small," confided one woman, "that they steal our children to raise as their own. See that woman, the ancient one?"

She pointed to an old squaw as dark as spruce bark in the rain and as twisted, wizened, and shrunken as a fairy-tale gnome. She wore a full dress trimmed in greasy bits of fur, an equally filthy fur cap of mink, and summer mukluks.

"Bush People kidnapped her when she was small. She lived among them until she escaped."

Primarily because of that one near-supernatural experience, the crone became a sort of medicine woman in the village with access to spirits and beings that rarely visited lesser mortals. She regarded me with her rheumy suspicious eyes before concluding I sought serious knowledge.

"Yes," she admitted at last. "A Bushman captured me when I was a young girl and away from the others picking blueberries. He did not harm me. He had his own clan that consisted of females and other males and a very few young ones. One of the babies was very ill. I was kidnapped to make him well because they thought we had magical powers."

The Bush People clan lived all together in a cave, she said. They wore no clothing and they smelled bad because their fur was dirty and they did not bathe. They were dying off gradually because humans kept pushing them deeper into dwindling wilderness. They dared not show themselves because humans shot at them and chased them. Due to their diminishing numbers, they sometimes captured human children in an attempt to fight extinction.

"How did you talk to them?" I asked in astonishment.

She touched a forefinger to her temple. "It is like their mind felt mine," she explained. Roger Yager had tried to explain how the mind of the creature he met "tapped" into his.

"How did you escape?" I asked.

"They let me go because they thought I helped their ill child. They said they would take me back to the village as long as I never told anybody where they were."

It was an incredible story, but one related in dead earnestness. Whatever had happened, it was obvious the old woman believed she had experienced *something* extraordinary.

Her eyes slowly roamed to where Cora and Cara and Tommy were laughing and running with some of the Indian children. Her voice rose a slight octave, sounding thin and strained with a note in it so ominous that it was like an icicle falling down my back.

"You are alone in the valley," she warned. "Bushman will steal your children."

39

Adaptation was the key to survival in the North Country. Snowshoe hares and ptarmigan changed colors to blend into the seasonal landscapes, both becoming pure white in winter. Lynxes and wolves relied on massive padded feet to carry them over winter snows. Beaver occupied most of their summers "managing" the forest by cutting down trees for food and shelter, damming streams, and constructing enormous lodges, some of which reached heights of fifteen feet. Otter, mink, marten, and other fur bearers grew fat on various stream fish like grayling and Dolly Varden, building up insulating fat layers against the inevitable approach of cold. Moose, bear, and caribou did the same thing. Most of Alaska's large numbers of geese, cranes, and ducks survived winter by simply packing up in autumn and, like our neighbors the Westbrooks, going to Florida or Texas or somewhere else warm.

Summer was a time of heightened activity for everything that inhabited the North, including people. Although long summer days intensified growth and turned the North interior into a rich boreal forest teeming with uniquely adapted plants and animals, winter's short snow-filled days were never far away. Cold or the threat of cold remained the predominant factor of life in the North. The short growing season at 65 degrees latitude was prone to both late and early frost.

Like the Alaskan plants and animals, we were also learning to adapt for survival, to live in and off the wilderness.

My dad had owned a small farm in Kansas. I remembered the feel of warm summer soil on bare feet after a fresh ploughing, the smell of the rich dark sod turned belly up to the sun, the sight of first sprigs of corn or wheat gowning the naked earth in transparent green veils. Alaska was no cultivated land of wheat and corn and would never be. My garden sprouted, but the soil was cold and acidic and none of the plants did well.

However, Minook Valley offered a myriad of flowers, medicinal plants, berries, and shrubs that rose above the thick ground cover to provide sustenance for many forest dwellers, including humans. In season, I made syrups and desserts of blueberries, high bush cranberries, spruce tips, and, of course, rose hips. I prepared and canned the surplus for our first wintering over. I also learned the utility of chewing inner birch bark, a natural aspirin, for headaches. A silvery-green bush with tiny thin needles that smelled minty and good, and that locals called a "Labrador Tree," provided from the same plant both a laxative tea and a cure for diarrhea.

The foundation for North Country sustenance was built on meat. Meat and only meat ensured survival. By the time the cabin was finished, firewood stacked, and goods stored for the wintering over, the days were rapidly shrinking and a sharp edge of frost crept into the night air. The men began serious efforts to fill our meat larder.

Les and Don were hunting a moose pasture in the bog upvalley on Minook Creek when they spotted a fine bull moose feeding off the tender tips of a willow thicket. He wasn't a hundred yards away, an easy shot for Les with his .308. Les lifted the rifle, took aim at the moose's head to prevent damage to the meat, and fired. He was a crack shot.

The moose neither bolted nor fell. He froze in his tracks, looking straight ahead.

"What the hell . . . ?"

Les took more careful aim and fired. The moose didn't even flinch. He behaved totally unnaturally for a wild animal.

"You missed him," Don surmised, whispering, "and he doesn't know where the shot came from."

Puzzled, Les cranked in another cartridge. There was no wind to affect the bullet's trajectory, no foliage between him and the target to deflect it. He took careful bead on the lung area directly behind the big animal's shoulder. He followed the principles of marksmanship—suck in a deep breath, exhale half of it, hold . . . hold . . . Trigger squeeze, let the discharge be a surprise . . .

The rifle stock recoiled smoothly into his shoulder.

The bull remained stationary, unmoving.

Les blinked. Don gave him a confused look.

"I *couldn't* have missed," Les stammered. "Not unless the sights are completely off. They look okay."

"Maybe we need to move a little closer," Don suggested.

"If we get any closer, I can ram the barrel up his butt and pull the trigger."

"It looks like that's the only way you're ever going to hit him."

Les glared at his brother. Using available cover, they stalked to within fifty yards of the bull. The moose stood as still as a statue.

"Wave your arms at him," Les said, taking aim just in case the moose decided it *would* flee.

Don waved one arm. He waved both arms. He jumped up and down and waved both arms and hopped about and shouted. Completely befuddled, Les lowered his rifle and stared.

"He's gotta be blind and deaf both."

Marveling at it, they walked up to the creature, who stood nearly seven feet tall at the shoulders. He was *dead*. Dead while standing, propped up on four stiffened legs like a sawhorse. Don laughed nervously.

"You must have scared him to death, Les," he accused.

The only explanation they had for the most freakish phenomenon either man had seen during their years of hunting was that Les's first shot to the brain, instantly mortal, caused the animal's legs to lock in place. They had to take a rope and topple him onto his side in order to butcher out the meat.

Butchering out a beast as large as a moose, nearly a ton on the hoof, was an all-day chore from start to finish, longer if you worked in a bathtub as we had in Anchorage when Les shot the old bull with his .22 rabbit rifle. The men gutted the animal and dragged the offal aside to be left for bears and wolves. They skinned it and used the hide as a sort of blanket to lay the meat on, being careful not to contaminate it with sticks, dirt, and grass. They separated the legs, called "quarters," and deboned them. All the "loose meat" was then sliced away from the back, rib cage, and neck. After the butchering, they stuffed the meat in gunny sacks and made several trips back and forth to the site to transport it all. The weather was cool enough that the meat stored in our bearproof log "smokehouse" would not spoil.

"We can probably use one more moose," Les decided. "Breakup is still over nine months away."

To run out of food in January or February and not be able to get out of the valley invited disaster. Bushers had been known to boil their muk-luks and eat their dogs, only to starve to death anyhow.

40

Weather descended like a feathery blanket, thick and hanging but a few feet above the earth, creating one of those foggy surrealistic mornings best populated by ghosts indistinct and flitting. Les and Sid were hunting winter meat together on the other side of Dead Horse Pass after Don left Alaska to return to Colorado. They were working from the Bombardier off the trail, sweeping out on foot to flush out swampy draws of the sort moose inhabited.

Through a shredded break in the fog, they spotted a bull ambling downhill away from them in that disjointed walk of a creature who seemed constructed of various leftover animal parts. He was about a quarter mile away, moving slowly as though winter were still a summer away instead of mere weeks. Les grabbed his .308 when the animal stopped to feed along a stream, giving him and Sid the opportunity for a stalk.

They cut swiftly into the draw on a course designed to intersect the moose's projected path should he decide to move on. They lost sight of him in the heavy fog that clung in the spruce forest like cotton to the teeth of a gin. They found the stream and followed it, unable to see more than a few feet ahead. Alaska's vast silence became even more pronounced; the cloud-on-earth absorbed sound like a sponge soaked up water.

The fog lifted suddenly to reveal the moose less than twenty yards away. He raised his great rack of horns and stared directly at the hunters. Fog eddied around his knees and seemed caught in the spades of his antlers. Before he realized he was even threatened, Les placed a bullet crashing through his chest. No locked legs on this guy. He went down hard and stayed. Les walked up and finished him with a second shot.

The two hunters ripped out their skinning knives, rolled up their sleeves, and went to work. So intent were they on their task that they neglected to remain aware of their immediate environment. The Alaskan wilds, as we were discovering, could be a dangerous place, made only less so by constant vigilance.

The moose had dropped on muskeg moss in a tiny clearing surrounded by that thick, stunted conifer timber so common near the Arctic Circle. The first indication the hunters received that something was wrong came when Sid caught a flash of movement from the forest on the other side of the small stream. It snapped him erect, poised with knife in hand and blood smeared up to his bare elbows. He looked all around, seeing nothing but fog slowly percolating in the trees. He bent and wrestled up a hind quarter for his dad to dissect from the carcass.

Les came erect and squinted into the fog.

"Dad?" Sid said in a low, tense voice. "I thought I saw something too."

A moment later, a huge head emerged from the dirty-white shroud at the edge of the stream. Yellow eyes glowered. A slight breeze sighed through the trees, thinning out the fog a little so that other shapes appeared, disappeared, and reappeared amid the trees surrounding the small clearing.

Les murmured, "Wolves!"

Mere utterance of the name was enough to evoke chills. The Alaskan timber wolf is an immense, magnificent beast with thick fur ranging from almost white to black, long legs, wide head, and a bushy tail. An adult male may weigh a hundred and fifty pounds or more and measure seven feet from nose to tail tip. Although we occasionally heard them howling in the valley when a pack gathered for a hunt, we had not until now encountered them. It was generally assumed wolves did not attack people, a fact passionately disputed by miners and trappers.

"They've smelled the blood," Les said.

In Alaska as elsewhere wherever wolf and man existed side by side, folktales evolved concerning the animal's cunning, patience, and savagery. Wolves were so populous in our region of the interior that we had heard of incidents in which they invaded cabin yards to snatch sled dogs off chains in order to carry them off and devour them. Hunters told stories of how wolf packs crowded in on a shooter's fresh kill and attempted to intimidate and drive the hunter off. How hard they pushed depended upon how hungry they were.

This bunch seemed awfully hungry. It was a large pack. Les estimated ten or more animals. They made little noise as they slunk about, often pausing at the edge of the clearing to stare at the butchered moose, salivating and licking their powerful jaws. Although they appeared more curious than aggressive at first, their mere presence, the way they seemed to glide about within the fog carried threat, a certain undeniable menace.

"They're trying to scare us off," Les said calmly. "They want the bones and guts. Ignore them."

Sid tried to ignore them, as his father did, but it became increasingly hard to do as the wolves grew bolder. Individual animals ventured nearer, slinking bellies low to the ground. They bound away growling whenever Les or Sid threw them a warning look. Even Les found himself unnerved by the beasts' belligerence.

A huge male whose wicked fangs shone bright and deadly-looking against an almost-black coat stalked to within a dozen feet of the hunters. He stood spread-legged with his broad head lowered almost to the ground, lips curled back in a low bullying snarl. He eyed the moose carcass. Hunger appeared to have overcome the wild beast's natural aversion to humans. This one seemed primed to charge in and appropriate the moose for himself and his voracious comrades—and to take down anything that stood in his way.

"Dad!" Sid cried. "Shoot him!"

"I can't," Les confessed.

His rifle had contained only two cartridges when he jumped off the Bombardier with it. He had failed to reload after he and the boys had done some target practicing a few days earlier. His first bullet brought down the moose. He used the second to finish the animal. Now they were corralled by a crazed pack of wolves that seemed to sense their vulnerability—and their only defense was an empty rifle and two skinning knives. Les had even left his .44 pistol at the Bombardier.

"Let them have the moose," Sid said, frantically seeking a solution.

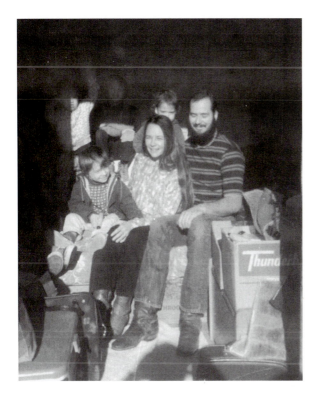

The Cobbs on their way to Alaska in 1973, living in the back of their two-ton truck. Les and Norma with Tommy in front; Cara behind them; Cora and Sean from left to right in back. Sid was taking the photo.

The Cobb family in the spring of 1974 when they first arrived in Alaska and were still living in a tent. Les and Norma are in back with (from left to right) Sean, Cara, Sid, Cora, and Tommy.

The cabin is still under construction as the children play on the bank of Minook Creek.

A winter scene of the Cobbs' cabin in which Norma spent a winter alone with the children while Les went outside to work.

Norma while working on the Alaska pipeline. September 1975.

Les while working on the pipeline as a truck driver. September 1975.

Rebuilding the cabin in June 1976.

The Cobb family: (front, left to right) Cora, Tommy, Cara; (second row) Les, Sean, Norma, and Sid.

Minook Valley; the homestead is directly in the middle of the valley in this scene.

Les and Pete Pasquali on a fishing trip; Pete has been Les's friend from our first days in Alaska.

Norma and Les in July 1978 while building the mechanics garage.

Minook Creek during the spring breakup from glacier build up.

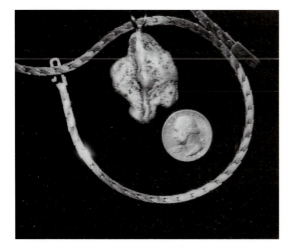

The gold nugget Les discovered in Minook Creek while dredging. It was his first major find.

Les shown working his placer gold mine on Hoosier Creek during the beginning stages.

Minook Valley, with Elephant Mountain in the background.

This is the house the Cobbs reside in today. It is on ground about 100 yards higher than where the original cabin was built.

"They ain't getting it," Les declared. "It's ours and we ain't giving up what's ours to no mangy bunch of curs."

If the Devil ever tried to lay claim to Les's soul, I'm convinced he would battle the horned one all the way to hell and back.

There was a spruce deadfall within a step or two of the moose. Les grabbed a snag off it and charged the black wolf, flailing the stick and shouting. The animal sprang back into the trees, then held his ground as though daring the puny human to push his luck.

A second animal darted toward the moose from the opposite side. It was a common pack trick for wolves to divert their prey while others charged in from the rear. Sid shouted and waved his arms. The wolf leaped back to the edge of the timber.

The pack circled ominously in the fog, snarling and growling. Two of them got into an argument and fought hellishly. The smell of blood was driving them into a frenzy. If even one became bold enough to charge, the entire pack would attack. Les and Sid, unarmed, stood little chance against them. They would be ripped to shreds.

Wolves were single-minded beasts when they sighted prey. Hunting, they traveled into the wind to prevent their target smelling them. They quietly approached their prey, perhaps in single file. When they cornered their quarry, they attacked the rump or sides of the animal, trying to wound it and make it bleed until it weakened. They grabbed the defenseless victim by the throat or snout. They usually killed even a very large animal within only a few minutes after their final charge. Until then, they were patient animals. An entire hunt could take several hours.

Les recognized the routine. This pack gradually lost all residual fear of these particular humans, whom they somehow sensed were unable to either harm them or resist their efforts to steal the partially butchered moose. Blood smell made them reckless and daring. Les and Sid fought back, bombarding the wolves with shouts and sticks from the deadfall.

"Quick! Gather some dead wood!" Les ordered his son as the situation degenerated into desperation.

He stood guard with a sturdy tree limb in each fist while Sid stripped the deadfall.

"Put it right next to the moose," his dad instructed.

They might not have had bullets, but they had matches. Sid soon had a fire crackling and roaring. They made firebrands and waved them at the wolves. The beasts lost some of their aggressiveness. They retreated to a safe distance and regarded the humans with renewed respect.

"They're fussing with us over the moose," Les said. "There's no way they'll attack a man if we aren't near the meat. Sid, I'll stay here and keep them back. You run up to the Bombardier and get some more shells for the rifle. I think they'll leave if we shoot a couple of them."

Sid's twelve-year-old face sharpened. His dad was asking him to go out into the woods, alone in the fog, with a pack of starved wolves!

"The wolves won't hurt you," Les insisted. "They'll stay here around me and the meat."

"What if they don't?"

"They will."

"But what if they *don't*?"

Les thought about it. Sooner or later the fire would consume all the wood in the deadfall. The wolves seemed prepared to wait them out.

"Okay," Les said. "Build up the fire real high and I'll go."

"Don't take the rifle," Sid protested. "Leave it with me."

"It don't have any bullets, son. If I take it, I can shoot them from away out there."

"I don't want you to take the rifle."

Irrationally, the boy assumed he was safe as long as he had the weapon, however useless it might be. Les gave up the argument. Father and son were about evenly matched when it came to stubbornness.

Les prepared to make a run for the Bombardier *without* the rifle. Just as he was about to take off, he noticed the fire seemed to be working. The wolves withdrew inch by inch, sensing that their easy meal wasn't going to be that easy after all. Then, to the hunters' relief, the pack vanished into the fog as silently as it arrived, like smoke dissipating. Sid blinked. He hardly believed it.

When Les and Sid returned to the cabin that afternoon with winter meat intact, they were as proud as a pair of mating grouse cocks. They had fought for their rights against incredible odds—and won. They were on such a high. I watched them walk off together, laughing and talking over their adventure, with Les's arm thrown around the boy's shoulders. Those two . . . If ever anyone had found his element, those two had.

41

Drafts of cold wind from the north carried a sharp threat of what was to be our first winter in the Alaskan wilderness. By October, the hands of our windup clock showed ten A.M. before daylight arrived seeping gray into Minook Valley. It was dark again by three P.M. Daylight was not *real* daylight. Not until March would we actually see the sun again. For a Kansas girl accustomed to lots of sunshine, getting used to living without the sun in my daily life was a major adjustment.

Nonetheless, I was content that summer and fall. We were finally in our own home, homesteaders building a life. Everything was turning out exactly as I dreamed it. God tested us, found us worthy, and was now blessing us. The cabin proved a bit cramped for a growing, rambunctious family, but the glory and spread of the valley more than compensated. During Indian summer, the mountains glowed with color and beauty. I took short walks sometimes to be alone, to sit on a log by the creek and bask in the wonders of this splendid land and of my God who seemed to have created it especially for us.

Only one cloud hovered on the horizon of my total happiness. During the summer, Les continued to disappear periodically for a day or two at a time to get together with his buddy Pete Pasquali and Harry Leonard, the old sourdough at Wiseman, to prospect a little and learn more about the science and techniques of gold mining. I thought I should indulge him that much, since he worked so hard otherwise. I might not have been so indulgent had I known about Gary Streicher, an ambitious, energetic man in his fifties, who was putting together an oil-field service company. Gary became impressed with Les's brash, macho can-do attitude and offered him a job at $5,000 *a week* to ramrod the construction of oil-field derricks—iron islands—in Prudhoe Bay. The job began as soon as the bay iced over in October and had to be completed by April Fool's Day. If Les accepted the job, it meant he would be gone the entire winter. The kids and I would have to winter over in Minook Valley alone.

"Honey, I don't see how I can turn down that kind of money," Les argued. "We're almost broke again. It's better I work in the winter than in the summer when I'm needed here to start building our tourist and hunter cabins."

"Lester, the kids and I can't stay out here by ourselves."

We left it at that. Even though $5,000 a week was an unimaginable amount of money to turn down, I thought—or perhaps I only *hoped*—that Les was giving it up. I should have known better; perhaps I did know better. Although we never talked of Gary Streicher again that summer, every now and then I felt dark clouds edging closer from the horizon. I ignored them.

I was heartened and encouraged when Les and Sid talked about how they were going to train our dogs for sledding as soon as there was enough snow. We had bred Lady to a good Alaskan husky before returning to the homestead; she gave birth to six beautiful masked puppies in the early spring. That brought us up to eight dogs and the making of a sled-dog team. Sid chattered to Les incessantly about the great Iditarod dog race across Alaska and, at every opportunity, threw questions at our Eureka neighbors, Susan Butcher and Rick Swenson, both of whom were racers and mushers. He read everything he could find on mushing.

"You'll have plenty to keep you busy this winter," I casually mentioned to Les when I noticed his restlessness growing. "There's the dogs to train, trapping . . ."

Les looked at me, nodded, and walked off. My heart raced with unspoken dread.

Gary and Hazel Westbrook and their brood of three secured their cabin upvalley and left, departing for Florida. They bade us a cool farewell. Even though they were our only neighbors, we rarely saw them all summer. As I predicted, relations with them turned chilly after Les undiplomatically rebuffed Gary's and Roger Yager's overtures for swapping mates. We weren't sure if the Westbrooks would return or not.

John Shilling, the miner from Slate Creek, left next. He stopped to look over our cabin, as he did the first cabin two years ago. This time he nodded his approval. In his opinion, it would do for wintering over.

With his departure for the safety and comfort of Fairbanks, things became quiet and lonely in the valley. We Cobbs were the only family remaining from Rampart to Eureka, a distance of nearly forty miles.

Our last visitors of the fall were Ted and Steve, roving young schoolteachers from the Yukon-Koyukuk School District out of Nenana. Each year they traveled to busher cabins all over the district delivering homeschooling books and materials for the coming school year. They made at least three regular rounds a year—once in September to drop off materials and do testing, another time around the holidays if they were able to get in by snowshoes or sno-go, and then again in the spring for final testing. I doubted we would see them again until after breakup.

All the Kernels were in school this year: Cara and Cora turning five and in kindergarten; Tommy, second grade; Sean, fifth grade; and Sid, eighth grade.

"Who's gonna be our teacher?" Sean asked.

"I will be."

"*You,* Mom? Are you going to be mean?"

"What if we play hooky?" Tommy teased. "Will you send us to the office?"

"Yes. Your dad is the office."

Except, Dad wasn't going to be here.

There came that evening of the first snowfall when Les pushed back his plate and looked at me across what remained of supper's black bear roast.

"Norma . . . ?"

Fire in the wood-burning oil-drum stove roared like a grizzly coming down the stovepipe and the whisper of snow on the black windows of the cabin became as ominous as gossip at a funeral wake. The next morning my husband hiked out of the valley through the blurring snow, abandoning me and our five small ones in the middle of the northern wilds with wolves literally at the cabin door and snow bringing the long darkness of the Arctic winter.

42

I was scared. I was angry. I was resentful of Lester's leaving us out here completely on our own, as alone as if we had been rocketed into space. I was afraid things were never going to be the same between Les and me again. We had lost something. It was hard to say exactly what it was we lost, but I felt sorrow at losing it. It was replaced by a persistent fear that chilled me even in the middle of the day with the fire in the barrel stove roaring.

Our only communication with the outside world was an old car AM/FM radio that operated on a twelve-volt battery. Messages came in, but we could transmit none out. Twice each day, once in the morning and again in the evening, KIAK-FM Radio in Fairbanks broadcast *Pipeline of the North* as a service to people in the bush. Travelers on the outside called messages in to the station. The messages were then relayed on the air to be picked up in isolated cabins whose inhabitants clustered religiously around radios waiting for news from husbands, fathers, and friends.

"This is a message to Eileen and kids in Minto from Dad: 'I made it out. I'll be starting back tomorrow . . .' "

"To the Cantrells on the Yukon . . . Your mother in Abilene, Texas, is ill . . . Call home if you can . . ."

I listened to *Pipeline*'s morning half-hour only, then turned off the radio in order to save the battery. Two days after Les departed, his message came through: *"To the Cobbs at Minook and Lost Creek: 'This is Les Cobb. Have arrived at Prudhoe and start work tomorrow. Good luck, Norma . . .' "*

Good luck, Norma! I touched the radio with the palm of my hand, as though hoping to make more intimate contact with my husband. *Good luck* was what you said to an acquaintance before he set off in a canoe down the Yukon, or to a hunter before he left for the tundra on a caribou hunt. *Good luck* was not what you said to your wife. Tears brimmed in my eyes. I felt so sorry for myself I could have burst into loud wet sobs, except I didn't want to alarm the children. Little Sean noticed my distress nonetheless and ran to hug me.

"Mama, are we going to be all right?" he inquired in a hushed voice.

To Sid, all puffed up over his new responsibilities as "man of the house," it was all a wonderful new adventure. I depended on him. But Sean, Tommy, and the twins depended on me. I snuffled back tears, wiped my eyes, and rose from my chair.

"Of course we're going to be all right," I declared as confidently as possible. "I was only missing your father."

WINTER CAME SWIFTLY. The thermometer started its steady and sometimes precipitous descent. Weather at such temperatures had real power in the way icy air sped down into the lungs and almost froze them, in the curious manner in which your face was comfortable one minute and frozen the next. Bitter cold moved up and down the Yukon as if propelled by some strong wind, then oozed out, spreading away from the river and into the valleys and lowlands. More snow came and would not melt again until breakup in the spring. It accumulated in a drift that almost reached the cabin's eaves on the northern exposure and piled up in the woods, measured in feet rather than in the inches I was accustomed to in Kansas. Smoke from the cabin chimney rose and, on still days, hung motionless and frozen in the air until it gradually dispersed.

Having nowhere else to turn, I had to face myself that long winter and sort out priorities. I would suggest being snowed in during an Alaskan winter as a catalyst for the longest journey to search one's own soul. Many people go through their entire lives without ever looking very deeply into themselves. I prayed I had the courage to pass the test, and if I lacked it, that I would acquire it.

I was raised and baptized Lutheran, but became "reborn" as an adult. I grew up at different stages on a small farm or in the suburbs of Wichita with a brother and two younger sisters. My parents divorced shortly after I graduated from high school. Average modern American family. Little house in the suburbs, well-behaved children, divorce . . . Spirituality was what saw me through. I depended upon it even more in the bush country.

However much I loved my home in Minook Valley, I was lonely and devastated at being left so far away and isolated from the outside world. Since I had no adults to talk to, I talked to God as if He were a person. Whenever I felt afraid or sad or angry during the day, I paused long enough to say a prayer. I praised Him, scolded Him, yelled at Him, and asked questions.

"God, I want you to listen to me. What *are* Your intentions for us?"

Jesus had wandered the wilderness for forty days and nights, seeking. I was to have six months of it, roughly one hundred and eighty days! Jesus had had his doubts, crying out to God to ask Him why he had been forsaken. I experienced my own doubts, starting with Sean's gunshot wound, followed by all the other hardships and trials—Arnold Cranick, Heckle and Jeckle, the collapsing of our first cabin, bears, Bushman, lack of money . . . Now *this*. Alone with my kids in the woods. It was almost as if the Devil were trying to run us out of Alaska—and God permitted him to keep trying in order to test our mettle.

In the evenings, I ended each night by gathering the children around me in the warmth of the wood-burning stove and reading from the Bible.

And thou shalt remember all the way which the Lord thy
God led thee these forty years in the wilderness, to humble
thee, and to prove thee, to know what was in thine heart,
whether thou wouldest keep his commandments, or no.

Then we discussed it. "How does this pertain to our lives?" I asked.

"Mama, is it like us?" Sean blurted out. "Ain't we in the wilderness? Ain't God trying to teach us something?"

I kept the door locked and the fire going. I often rushed to the window to peer into the dark shadows of the surrounding forest. Whenever Lady and Black and the six pups burst out of their little houses and hit the ends of their chains clamoring and raising a furious racket, I grabbed the rifle by the door and breathlessly searched the trees for imminent threat. Shadows flitted, but as it was always night in the trees it was hard to tell if wolves were approaching or the Bushman was skulking about.

Yet, there was another side to the winter. It seemed God was always there to open my eyes to the beauty of His creation whenever I thought I would fall into the depths of a despair from which I might never return. In isolation, you learned to cherish and appreciate the little things that enriched life. There were many fine and beautiful things, I discovered, that only darkness can bring. Among these were the northern lights and moonlight on snow.

During a full moon with the night still and the kids and cats safely in their loft, I dressed in furs, slung a rifle across my shoulder, and skied along the trail we had made next to the creek. The dry snow sparkled and shimmered under the moon as though nature's diamonds had been cast all afire with inner life and beauty. Such awesome nights crackled with the excitement of freedom, mystery, and danger. There was the crisp chatter of the skis on snow, the wide panorama of a land where even sound froze, the play of light and shadow, black and white, where the moon reflecting on the snow cast almost as much light as the sun, only a colder, more lovely light.

On nights when the skies were clear but there was not much moon, the aurora borealis began its heaven-encompassing dance with the great ebb and flow of the colored lights as they pranced across the darkened sky and filled it with fantastic performances. The sky shimmered. Breathtakingly brilliant light darted here and there, snaking back and forth and playing tag among the snow-coned mountaintops. Our cabin was like a precious jewel set in a priceless mounting.

On such nights I had no doubts about God's intentions for us. Feeling rejuvenated and full of the land, I skied back to the little cabin whose windows filled with lamp glow beckoned me home.

43

I had nightmares that we might run out of food and starve to death or out of firewood and freeze. We had meat from a bear and the two moose cached in the smokehouse, a natural deep freeze, and rice, beans, flour, dried milk, and other dehydrated foods stored tightly in the built-in pantry. I utilized our food carefully and completely, wasting nothing. I tried to calculate how long it would last and if it was sufficient. The building-sized pile of firewood outside the door seemed to be depleting itself far too rapidly.

"We could always eat the dogs and burn the furniture," Sid joked. He was so much like Les.

We organized our lives around the dwindling number of daylight hours. By noon in January and February, what day remained was only a dim twilight. The air was almost the color left by a full eclipse of the sun, even darker when the skies were cloudy. By two in the afternoon, darkness was again settled upon the land.

We utilized mornings inside the cabin to do domestic chores such as cleaning up after breakfast, sweeping and dusting and washing clothes in melted snow water. I often baked bread or put on beans to boil for lunch and dinner.

Outside chores consumed the few hours of daylight. Feeding and watering the dogs and cleaning their area; dumping the honey pot as we had no indoor plumbing and it was cold, and sometimes even dangerous, to traipse to the outhouse; bringing in moose meat from the smokehouse; burning trash; shoveling snow off the roof to keep it from sagging and perhaps buckling from the weight; hauling in wood and water.

Unlike the Yukon River, which always had a core of running water, the shallows of Minook Creek froze solid. Only a few of the deeper, protected holes remained available. Each day the boys and I loaded up on buckets and made the one-mile trek through snow to fetch water from one of the nearest holes. The twins accompanied the expedition, but were too small to carry buckets. Sid brought his rifle.

At the beginning of the winter, Sid chopped a hole through the surface ice to get to the water below. We tried to maintain the opening by covering it after each use with a sheet of plywood and a foot or two of snow. It still froze to some degree, making it necessary to chip through the previous day's freeze with axes in order to dip out water.

"Mama, didn't we use to have running water right inside the house when we were in town?" either Cora or Cara inquired.

"Yes, dear. Don't you remember?"

"Mama, how come we can't have water in the house out here?"

"Foolish girl," Sean teased. "We *do* have running water."

"We do, Sean?"

An impish grin. "When I open the door, you run in with it. *Running* water."

"*Mama!* Sean's being mean."

Sid was protective of the younger children, especially of the girls. "Stop teasing them, Sean."

"Who died and made you boss, Sid-ney?"

The kids poked and teased and argued with each other more and more as the winter wore on, the cabin walls closed in on them, and cabin fever began to set in.

Sid eventually devised a way of putting the dogs to work and easing our burden of bringing in water and wood. During the summer, Les had traded Rick Swenson out of a broken-down dogsled and a dog harness. The runners on the sled were wooden and worn. Some of the thong bindings had rotted off. Sid spent much of his summer's free time repairing it; it turned out to be a productive investment.

He constructed a second harness from scraps of webbed nylon. He then lashed Lady and Black to the sled; the pups were still too young and undisciplined to take to harness.

"It's time the dogs started earning their keep," Sid declared.

Black was a stout malamute of about one hundred and twenty pounds, all big bones and sinew and muscle. Lady was a silver-gray husky with a white mask. At a distance she resembled a timber wolf, until you saw the gentle warmth in her eyes. Both dogs were willing but unschooled in the art and science of pulling a sled.

Sid was patient with animals and younger children. At first he led the two dogs pulling the sled to the water hole, filled up five-gallon cans of water, then led the dogs pulling their load back to the house. By the end of winter he had taught the dogs to mush in proper style. He either ran alongside the sled then or rode on the rear extended runners while the two big canines yapped and grinned and threw their chests into their work. No more hauling water by hand with buckets.

Lady and Black more than proved their worth when we ran low on firewood, having misjudged the amount we required. We took to the woods to saw and chop more, using a hand crosscut saw and axes. Les had left a chain saw, but I was afraid to use it lest someone get hurt with no way to get to a doctor. The dogs hauled all the wood to the house in the sled.

By two P.M. when the long night began and outside chores were completed, it was time to come inside and start school. At first, all five children appeared enthused about home schooling. I doubted their enthusiasm would last. As for me, I felt nervous and anxious about the responsibility. I had only completed high school, but I was determined that, bushers or not, my kids would grow up with the best education I could provide. Teaching turned out to be the most demanding job I ever undertook.

When they came out in the fall, Ted and Steve had carefully gone over the materials with me. The courses, they promised, were largely self-explanatory. Nothing to worry about. Simply follow the guidelines. Anybody could do it.

"If it's so simple," I wondered aloud, "why do we bother hiring teachers and spending millions of dollars on public schools? Why don't we just pay parents to stay home and school their own children?"

Steve laughed. "I think you'll find out before spring why most parents wouldn't do it for any amount of money."

Five hours a day, five days a week, we hit the books. The cabin hummed with debate, questions, explanations, shouting, pleading, scolding, and sometimes tears. All of us crowded at the table around the kerosene lamp. Books and papers were scattered everywhere. Twins coloring or working kindergarten puzzles. Sid having trouble with math. Tommy taking a spelling test. Sean deep into a Hawthorne novel. Keeping the stove fed with firewood. Sometimes taking a break to look out the window at the snow, eyes scanning the shadows in the woods for wolves or Bushman.

The two older boys, Sid and Sean, readily picked up the self-paced routine and required little supervision. Sean was my bookish, sensitive one. Sid was bright and inquiring and mature, but at nearly thirteen his interests ran more toward hunting, fishing, trapping, dogs, and the freedom they offered than they did toward book learning. Fortunately, he received Physical Education credit for a number of normal homesteading activities, such as skiing, snowshoeing, dog mushing, and fur trapping. His favorite subject, of course, was the trapline he set along Minook Creek where he caught a few marten. He and I were both learning to tan skins into soft furs and turn the furs into warm caps, gloves, and parkas.

Tommy needed help, but the girls received the most attention simply because they demanded it. At first they enjoyed learning. Then they rebelled at the required discipline. It was a fight from then on to keep them at it. I often went to bed at night twisted into knots of discouragement and frustration. Angry with the kids, angry with myself, with Les, and with the entire world. No wonder so many settler parents failed at home schooling and their children grew up uneducated bush dummies.

I vowed not to quit, or to let the kids quit. I met each school day with renewed determination that my bunch would be schooled. One day they would have to go out into society on their own. They would not always be bushers. I wanted them to be prepared.

I STOKED THE STOVE with firewood to maintain the cabin's warmth while the kids and I congregated at the table to begin our daily chores.

Snow fell lightly in a murmuring whisper. Windows were frosted over in dazzling patterns. The stove glowed red while the sound of wood burning and the aroma of baking homemade bread filled the cabin with hominess. There were times like this when life seemed incredible and just right.

A knock at the door! The six of us went stiff, staring at each other in astonishment. We had been alone so long in the valley that the appearance of another human being startled us. It was a little scary. Who could possibly be knocking on our door in the middle of a snowstorm? The Bushman?

"Ain't we gonna answer it?" Sean whispered.

Sid dashed for his rifle. Cara and Cora puckered up to cry; Tommy attempted to comfort them and keep them quiet. How could a mere knock at the door cause such alarm?

I stood up, squared my shoulders, and started to the door. "Naturally I'm going to answer it," I said as bravely as I could.

I cracked open the door and peered out. The smaller children cowered behind, staring past me with widened eyes. Sid stayed farther back with the rifle. Swirling snow blew a soft voice through the crack.

"H'lo?"

The visitor's appearance so dumfounded me that I simply stared, like a bear cub run up a tree. There stood a medium-sized fella wearing furs from his Eskimo mukluks to the heavy wolf fur hood of his parka. The only thing human in all that fur was the face. It was a long, slender Eskimo face brushed ruddy by the freezing temperature. The eyes gleamed black through narrow folds. Rime ice crusted his eyebrows. From a distance, with all that fur, he might well have been mistaken for Bushman, although a much miniaturized version. He carried a rifle slung barrel down over his left shoulder.

"H'lo?" the Eskimo repeated. "My name is Bony Newman. I am from Rampart."

I found my voice. "Hello. We're the Cobbs."

"I know. I am out trapping and I see your cabin and smoke."

He tilted his head suggestively toward the door. It was customary in the northern wilderness to invite travelers inside for coffee and a meal. A form of simple hospitality that under the right conditions meant the traveler's survival. I wasn't yet comfortable with that particular code of the wild. Here was a stranger, a native Eskimo packing a gun, wanting to come inside the house of a woman alone with her children.

"My husband will be home any time now," I warned.

"That is good. You will perhaps have coffee for him," he hinted.

"It'll be a little while yet."

I braced my foot against the back of the door, afraid he might attempt to force his way inside. There was a long awkward standoff. Bony Newman shuffled snow off his mukluks and cleared his throat.

"Will you tell your man that Bony Newman came to visit and that he did not mean to frighten?"

He turned and stepped off the little porch. He went into the forest and melted silently away. I was immediately ashamed of myself and my fears that had turned a neighbor away from warmth, nourishment, and safety.

"Mr. Newman?" I called after him, but I heard his dog team and knew he was gone.

I forged myself a promise at that very moment that no traveler passing through Minook Valley would ever again be turned away, that our home, humble though it may be, would be offered to all in honoring the Northern code of friendliness and hospitality. I hoped I received another chance sometime to make it up to Bony Newman.

It was only later that I discovered to my surprise that winter, if not too severe, was the best time for traveling. Frozen streams made ideal highways for dog sleds and sno-gos. Tundra, so difficult for walking in the summer, became easily negotiable on skis and snowshoes once it was covered with snow. As our cabin was the only one occupied between Eureka and Rampart, an occasional night rider mushing his dogs might stop by at any hour. I never turned away another wayfarer. The coffeepot was always on. The kids and I enjoyed the break in routine whenever a musher stopped by with news from other places.

44

We hardly expected to see Les again until Christmas, and then only if weather permitted. I missed him, especially at night after the day's routine was finished and I had time to lie in bed and think. A woman was never meant to be without her man. Especially not out here.

One night, for no reason, my loneliness seemed particularly acute. I went to bed thinking of Les. Once or twice, my eyes popped wide open; I actually expected to see him walk into the cabin. The way that macho man could grin, how his blue-gray eyes sparkled with mischief . . .

I listened to snow falling on the roof and filling up the spruce woods in the night. Listened to the silence interrupted only by the reassuring crack of wood burning in the stove and the distant not-reassuring howl of wolves starting a hunt. I drifted off, to be awakened by pounding on our thick wooden door.

I jumped out of bed and grabbed the rifle. Although I was accustomed to night riders by this time, it always paid to be prepared.

"Who is it?"

"It's me. Les."

"Les!" My heart pounded, but I controlled it. "Les who?" I asked.

He swore. "Norma! Les. Your husband, Les."

He was in no mood for teasing, having tramped in through the snow from Eureka. I still resented his having left us.

"I don't know any Les."

"Norma, let me in. I'm freezing my ass off."

"I haven't seen my husband in a long time. How do I know you're my husband?"

"Look out the window."

"Well . . . You look like my husband, but I can't be sure. Take off all your clothes so I know it's really you."

"Norma!"

"I'm not letting you in until you take them off."

And I didn't. A woman has her ways of getting even.

45

Les's visit proved a short one; he promised to be home for Christmas, God willing. He would let us know the date on *Pipeline of the North*. From December 1, it became a Cobb cabin ritual for the kids and I to gather at eight-thirty mornings and turn on the old car radio. It was always tuned to KIAK's *Pipeline*. Finally the message came:

"To the Cobbs in Minook Valley, from Les Cobb: 'I'll be home for Christmas on December 20.' Merry Christmas out there to the Cobbs . . ."

There followed a savage chain of days in which the thermometer dropped to thirty and forty below. The skies were clear and the northern lights actually crackled like static electricity. Starting two weeks before Christmas, the cabin became a whirlwind of excitement and activity. Sid cut a tree and we strung popcorn strings for it; we made molasses candy, taffy, and cookies. The kids created gifts for each other, hiding in corners and upstairs in the loft behind blankets to keep them secret until they could be wrapped in old newspaper or whatever paper we had and placed underneath the tree.

Cara and Cora crayoned paper strips and glued them into long chains for cabin decorations. We constructed homemade Christmas cards and the girls drew big Santas and stick-figure reindeer that resembled scarecrows with red suits and sawhorses with antlers. But we all knew they were Santa Claus and his reindeer, and that was what mattered.

It warmed up some on the nineteenth and a snowstorm blew in. The poet Robert Frost would have been astonished had he been there to watch how quickly these woods filled up with snow. We rushed to complete the outdoor chores on December 20. We cleaned the cabin thoroughly and I cooked a special homecoming dinner—a roast of moose with some of the last fresh potatoes and carrots, which I had saved for the holidays. The twins glued their little noses to the window and kept a rag handy to wipe the frost and fog clear. Classes were suspended in honor of the day. Everyone was too excited to study anyhow.

By early afternoon it was already completely dark. No Les appeared grinning and waving through the storm. It grew late. Cara, wrapped in a blanket, nodded off in a chair and Cora was about to give up her own vigil at the blackened window. Sid carried Tommy upstairs to bed. Sean paced.

"Why ain't he here?" he fretted.

"He'll be here," I said cheerfully, attempting to bolster morale and quell our fears.

Sean tortured himself as well as everyone else by putting terrifying possibilities into words. "What if he hurt himself? Maybe he's freezing to death? The wolves could get him! He had a fight with the Bushman! He fell off the mountain!"

I tried to make light of it. "It looks like you've covered every angle, worrywart. He probably got started later than he intended. He'll be here tomorrow."

I fell asleep at the table on my crossed arms. The guttering of the lamp getting low on fuel awoke me. I replenished the oil. Sid and Cora had pulled a blanket over themselves on the makeshift sofa and were snuggled underneath it. I stood at the window in the morning silence for a long time, mesmerized by the heavy sighing of snow against the window. Two or three feet of new snow covered the porch and banked against the door. Blackness as dark as outer space, and just as scary, loomed beyond the outer edge of the porch. The cabin was a spaceship lost somewhere between Earth and Mars.

My emotions swung from being furious at Les for worrying us like this to a deep and cold near panic that he was out there somewhere. Alone. Freezing . . . I prayed that my husband was all right.

At eight-thirty we gathered around the car radio and held our breath all through *Pipeline*. Finally it was over. There was no message. We stood in stunned silence looking at each other.

"What date is it?" Sid asked for the first time on that interminable day.

"He'll be here," I said, hoping.

We went through the routine of another day, and we waited. I sat at the cabin window staring out without really seeing. Polar winds cold enough to freeze a ptarmigan in flight drove the snowfall into a crazed frenzy and gnawed at the eaves of the cabin. Snowflakes as big as snow-balls bashed themselves in suicidal dementia against the windowpanes. From the forest came the mourning call of an owl, a sound that steepened the melancholy into which I felt myself driven.

Sid stood beside me. I hadn't noticed his approach.

"What date is it?"

"I've told you twice before. December 21."

"I know, but . . . He was supposed to be here yesterday."

Unlike Sean, Sid was not normally the worrying type. Concern now sharpened his face. He looked out the window past me, as though half expecting to see his father ploughing through the snow coming home.

"But he *said* . . ." Sean whimpered from across the room.

Anxiety caused me to snap back at him. "I know what he said, Sean."

I dabbed away tears before the children saw. I had to be strong for them. I prayed silently and hard. How many times was God going to test us?

Les was over twenty-four hours late. No one caught out in a storm like this survived without food and shelter. Temperatures hovered around twenty below. You couldn't see more than a few feet through the swirling snow. It would be easy to wander off the path and get lost. I imagined all sorts of fates for my tardy husband, each more dreadful than the last. If Les wasn't already dead and was simply being inconsiderate, I was going to kill him when he got here for putting us through such torment.

I COULDN'T SLEEP and I couldn't *not* sleep. It was like I was in a waking nightmare. A zombielike coma. I got out of bed at five A.M., having made a decision.

"Mom?"

Sid had slept little himself.

"I'm going out to look for Les, son. He'd come for any one of us if we were out there."

"Let me go instead, Mom."

"I need you to stay and take care of the young ones in case—"

I started to say, *in case something happened to me.* Sid understood without my saying it. He bit his lower lip and said nothing.

I waited until after eight-thirty. When nothing came up on *Pipeline* from Les, I layered out warm with boots and furs, thinking that if I ever showed up on someone's doorstep looking like this I would be about as welcome as Bony Newman the Eskimo was on my doorstep.

With a last glance at Sid, I opened the door, letting in a hard cold breath of nature filled with snow. I stepped into darkness in motion. Visibility reached about as far as I could hold my hand out in front of my face. I didn't think of *how* I hoped to find Les, only that I had to *try.* I found my way to the doghouses and loosed Lady to go with me. I felt safe from predators as long as I had my rifle and Lady to warn me.

I thought I couldn't get lost on the trail if I kept the rise of mountains to my right and the valley to my left. Even though I couldn't make out terrain features, I sensed them enough to keep my bearings. After all, how many times had we tramped back and forth this way to Dead Horse Pass and Eureka?

Skis were impossible to use in such deep snowfall and under conditions of near blindness. I promised myself to have snowshoes by next winter. I sank up to my waist and chest in drifts and had to physically plough my way through. Lady followed in my beaten path, whimpering.

My face instantly froze. It felt like I wore a mask of numbed flesh. It was hard going. Fifty feet from the cabin and for all I could tell I may as well have been with Admiral Byrd at the North Pole. I beat down an attack of panic and kept going.

Action was better than inaction. That was Les's motto. Better to do *something* than to do nothing, he was always saying. But then, of course, I didn't have his overactive thyroid.

Exhausted from the struggle, I had to rest every few minutes. The length of time between rest stops shortened until I had to stop and gasp for breath after every few steps. Then it was only one step at a time. Flail at the snow, lunge into it like a horse caught in a bog, pause while I sucked in cold air that ached in my lungs and marshaled the courage and strength for another step.

My husband was out there somewhere. I had to find him. *Please, God . . . ?*

Tears of frustration froze on my cheeks. How would I ever find him? If he collapsed, snow would soon cover his body. We wouldn't find him until after breakup in the spring.

They wouldn't find my body either until after breakup.

I felt like looking for a big log somewhere, sitting down on it, and bawling my heart out while I shouted at God.

46

There was a saying in the North Country that Mother Nature was unforgiving; she killed you if you made a mistake. Les's first mistake was in not taking food and water with him when he parked our pickup at Minto, sixty miles away, which was as close as he could get because of closed roads, and set out for the cabin on a borrowed SkiDo 440, a fast snowmobile that should have had him home in time for supper on the twentieth.

He raced the machine across the Top of the World with Minto behind and Eureka and Manley Hot Springs to the west. He knew he was in serious trouble when he blew a piston. Within minutes, fresh snowfall filled up his tracks and he could barely make out the nearest horizon. It would be dark soon.

He estimated his position as about equidistant between Minto to the southeast, Eureka to the west, and home straight ahead. Whichever direction he chose, he would have about thirty miles of rough terrain to negotiate before reaching shelter. No snowshoes, no food and water, no compass. Only his indomitable will, his stubbornness, and that macho Alaskan pioneer attitude of his that assumed Lester Cobb could do anything he wanted to do or had to do.

He abandoned the sno-go and started trudging homeward, head bowed against the developing storm, gloved hands thrust deep into the pockets of his parka, beating a path through powder only knee-deep up here close to the wind. Fresh on his mind was a story old Harry Leonard told about a miner who got lost in a blizzard only a mile away from his cabin and wandered around lost until he froze to death.

That couldn't happen to Lester Cobb, grandson of a Colorado pioneer homesteader and heir to the Cobb mountain man legacy.

The bleak twilight of day turned to the blackness of a moonless and starless night. The mercury plummeted to forty below. Les kept walking, pacing himself to prevent sweating underneath his layers of arctic clothing; dehydration almost always preceded hypothermia. A pack of wolves yapped and howled on the high tundra to his rear quarter flank, reminding him that he was unarmed.

After the first few hours, the journey turned into a kind of surreal nightmare. One of those in which you confronted some danger and tried to run but could muster nothing beyond a plodding slow-motion shamble. The moaning of the wind and the hypnotic, monotonous swirl of snow in his face dragged him into a daze as he plunged along, head bowed. After a while, he lost all track of time.

His thoughts turned inward, as though to wall themselves off against the reality of a predicament that grew more perilous with the falling temperature, his inability to distinguish landmarks, and the gradual expenditure of his great strength and energy. Occasionally, he shook himself alert and looked numbly about, searching for something familiar. Finding only snow and stunted spruce like battalions of ghosts rendering judgment over him. A hundred feet behind, snow filled in his tracks and it was as if no one had ever come this way before.

He depended on one thing, and to that he desperately clung; he would eventually reach Minook Valley if he stayed to the more open high country and kept the north wind blizzard in his face.

Progress under such conditions was restricted to less than a mile per hour. That meant, say, thirty hours to reach home if he traveled as straight as the raven flew. More likely, it meant forty-eight to fifty hours with the twists and turns and confusion of hiking under adverse circumstances.

He trudged on. He walked through the night and into the gray twilight of a day so thick with snow that he barely distinguished it from the night it futilely attempted to supplant.

Hypothermia crept insidiously into his limbs. First his toes were cold and biting, then his fingers. He shivered with chill and suppressed the urge to pick up his pace to let the activity of his muscles warm him. He battled the urge for hours—he had to conserve his strength—before lack of energy more than willpower conquered it.

He chanted through lips cracking and freezing and crusted with his own blood, exhorting himself to keep going: "Don't stop! Don't stop! One more step . . . one more step. Hut-two-three-four! Hut-two-three-four . . . !"

He stopped. He looked around in a daze, his thoughts disorganized and scrambled. How much time had passed? Hours? Days? He couldn't figure out where he was or why he was here. It was like waking from a dream in a strange place and attempting to determine which was more real, the dream or *this*? He stood there in the cold and blowing snow for a long while, like an old man with Alzheimer's who has run away from the nursing home and doesn't understand who he is or where he is. Delirium was setting in. A first marked sign that the body was shutting down.

He no longer shivered. Instead, he felt warm and drowsy. He looked around for a sheltered log upon which to stop and rest. Only for a minute or two.

His mantra kicked back in; it had worn a groove through his brain, like a broken record that played the same thing over and over again: "Don't stop! Don't sit down! Hut-two-three-four . . . !"

His worn body continued to seduce him, tempting him with sleep and rest.

"Hut-two-three-four . . . !"

Somewhere deep inside his befuddled mind he realized that if he sat down he might never get up again. He slapped his face hard with mittened hands. He grabbed snow and mashed it into his face.

"Wake up in there! You wanna *die* out here?"

His tracks zigzagged erratically. He stumbled forward, kept stumbling onward toward Minook Valley. It had to be up ahead somewhere. He attempted to concentrate on a picture of a hot stove full of blazing firewood, imagined pulling up a chair before it, with me and the children gathered around. . . . Sometimes he almost heard our laughter. He had to stop and focus to convince himself that it was only the wind.

Staggering, fighting delirium, sustained only by that unconquerable Les Cobb willpower, he continued his lone struggle through the heart of darkness so cold it froze thought. He sang, muttering an old Johnnie and Jack tune he remembered his mother listening to: "Poison Love." He smiled to himself, remembering.

He stumbled and fell, rolling in the deepening snow. He was tempted to lie there. It felt like the feather mattress his granny used to own. All he had to do was pull up the heavy warm comforter and close his eyes . . .

47

Les was not coming home. If he was still in Prudhoe or if he was safe somewhere, he would have let us know by *Pipeline*. Alaska had claimed another *chechako* who underestimated the country's fierce power. I *knew* he was out there somewhere buried in snow.

In a state of complete mental and physical exhaustion, defeated by the elements, I turned back to the cabin. Sid knew by the look on my face that it was hopeless.

Inertia claimed the Cobb cabin. I kept hoping Les had had a change of plans at the last moment because of the storm or that something unanticipated had occurred to keep him at Prudhoe Bay. We tuned in *Pipeline of the North* that afternoon and again the next morning, huddled around the radio hushed and white-faced, hoping but already privately mourning. It was now December 23; Les was supposed to be home on December 20.

There were no messages.

Accept it, Norma . . .

I had to decide what to do. One thing was certain, we were stuck in the cabin until after breakup. A man like Les might walk in and out of the winter valley—obviously not without a final penalty—but a woman and kids had no chance of doing so. We had to continue to survive. Keep on keeping on. Once we got out in the spring, we would have to pack up what few things we could and return to Kansas. Our parents' misgivings were proving prophetic. Sean had almost been killed, *twice*. Now it seemed Les . . .

There was no question now about our future as homesteaders. Without Les, there was no homestead. I found it excruciating to think of the valley without Les in it, of life without Les. I felt deadened inside.

Get yourself together, Norma. What happened to your faith in God?

Not a dozen words were exchanged in the cabin throughout the day.

That afternoon the wake for Les Cobb was interrupted by a feeble knock at the door. My heart leaped into my throat. I ran to the door, not knowing what to expect. I flung it open.

An apparition stumbled into the cabin. It was caked with snow, the beard stiff with ice, like a snowman dying on its feet. It slowly sank to its knees. Les's eyes burned up at me out of the snowman.

"Lester!"

I had seldom experienced such relief, such joy. I instantly forgave him everything just for coming back when I thought, when I *knew*, he was gone. I sank to the floor with him, holding him, trying to warm his poor face with kisses.

"Honey," came a hoarse, broken whisper. "Honey, I'm home for Christmas."

48

After surviving that first wintering over, I felt I had gained the confidence to survive *anything*. Most fear lies in what is unknown. The fear goes away once the unknown is confronted. Les grinned when I shared that with him.

Oil job over, Les returned home in April 1977 to stuff enough cash in our trip sock that we wouldn't have to worry about his getting another outside job for at least a year or so, if we were prudent. Which we were. By that time, hopefully, we would have our tourist business going and Les would be earning money as a big-game guide. The way we mapped it out it seemed easy enough.

Naturally, nothing was ever that easy in the North Country, where nature was always a formidable adversary poised to strike the unwary. Like everything about homesteading, we *chechakos* had a lot to learn—and most of it, as we constantly discovered, had to be learned the hard way. I understood why pioneers of the Old West wrote in their diaries about how life on the frontier was a constant struggle against the elements. Against winds and storms and drought and heat and cold and floods and . . .

Unknown to us, natives in Rampart commented among themselves about how near Minook Creek the crazy white greenhorns at "Cobbsville" had built their cabin. It was on a high bank, but it was still right next to the stream. The Indians and Eskimos were too shy and polite to say anything to us. By the time we became acquainted well enough with Bony Newman, my first fur-covered Eskimo visitor, for him to warn us, it was already too late.

Sid noticed first that something was wrong. He ran into the cabin shouting, "The creek's coming through the house!"

Les sprang up from the breakfast table, knocking his chair spinning across the floor. The entire clan rushed outside to see what Sid was talking about. The twins brought up the rear in a howl of excitement.

Sid was right. Ice in the creek was diverting the main channel as it melted out of its banks. A small torrent of water chuckled past the outside back wall of our cabin. It was easy enough to see what was going to happen when another sunny day produced even quicker melt-off. We were going to have a river rising all around the cabin. The yard and garden would become a lake, the cabin roof an island.

It was a phenomenon with which we were to become familiar and against which we had to battle during every spring breakup. It began when the creek started to freeze in the autumn. Edges next to the banks froze first, then the surface of the stream by degrees. Layers of ice gradually formed and built up from underneath, pushing the ice higher and higher, a process called glaciering. Freezing rain and sleet and snow added more layers until even a small creek like Minook built up fifteen to twenty feet of ice.

The problem began in late April and early May when all that accumulation started to melt and added to the snow melt-off pouring down from the mountains. It either melted slowly, in which case it caused little concern, or it melted quickly and caused flooding. It all depended on the weather and temperature as the long spring and summer days arrived.

"Get some picks and shovels!" Les shouted.

The battle was engaged. Les, Sid, and Sean attacked the icy heart of Minook Creek to open a water channel while the rest of us frantically shoveled ice to open a path at the cabin for the water to return to the creek. It was an all-day fight, the outcome of which, as in most battles of equal adversaries, remained uncertain.

We succeeded in saving the cabin, at least for the day. Freezing set in once the sun went down and temperatures dropped, providing both sides a much needed respite.

We reengaged the following morning as melt-off resumed pouring water down the creek, which again threatened to twist out of its banks and destroy all we had worked for. It continued like that for the next three days. Hack at the ice all day until the creek froze at night. Rest, start all over again the next morning. Nip and tuck, ebb and flow. A battle that left the entire family speechless with exhaustion by the time evening brought about refreezing and slowed the enemy's advance.

The outcome of the war remained so in question that Les and Sid continued to labor long after the rest of us collapsed. They cut and sawed logs to build a barricade, like a fort, around the cabin to cut the strong flow of the creek in case it managed to escape from its banks in spite of all our efforts. When they came inside, they were too tired to eat.

Les on the sofa stretched out his long legs toward the fire and was soon snoring. I looked down at Sid's thin features reposed in sleep at the table. He had shoved his plate aside to make room for his crossed arms, which he used as a pillow. I brushed the straight unruly mop of hair away from his eyes. Sid was twelve years old, but he had become a man almost overnight, right before my eyes. I bent and kissed him softly on the forehead, a liberty he would never have accepted had he been awake.

Les and he. So much alike not to be of the same blood. I felt a sudden overwhelming tenderness for the two of them.

I went and kissed Les on the forehead. He stirred slightly, then continued snoring. This man, this rough, brash, sometimes thoughtless, often infuriating man. For all his faults, I could never have chosen a better father for my sons. Nor could I have selected a better mate. We were the Cobbs, and we were the Kernels, and we were of the same stalk.

I covered Sid at the table with a blanket. I brought another blanket and, snuggling up next to my husband, covered us with it together and immediately went to sleep with him.

I KNEW WE were winning the glacier wars when the channel we cleared down the center of Minook Creek remained open and running overnight. It gradually widened on its own. Water ate away at its ice banks and grew into a raging white chute of fury. Whereas in the summertime the creek was gentle and wadable for most of its length, except in the deeper pools, it was now a raging torrent ten feet deep rumbling like the hungry innards of the mountains. A dangerous ungentle force of nature determined to return to the sea as fast as it could get there.

At least it had spared our cabin. This season.

49

Most of the snow melted in the clearing around the cabin, leaving an accumulation of winter's debris—sawdust, wood chips, trash from the cabin, dog droppings, all concealed by the snow until now. We made a family project of cleaning up. Tommy was carrying wood chips to the creek to dump them into the current when he screamed.

I jerked up in time to see his little body devoured by the violent froth of Minook Creek. A jagged tooth of ice upon which he stood had given way beneath his weight. His head bobbed to the surface once or twice as the icy current swept him downstream. I was so jarred I couldn't have moved even if a stick of dynamite went off in my shoes.

Thank God Les wasn't affected the same way. In one heartbeat, he assessed the situation and went into action.

During our first summer in the valley, Les constructed a log bridge across Minook to allow us easy access to both banks. It was about thirty yards downstream from the cabin. Les made a dash for it. If he could get out on the bridge before Tommy swept underneath it, he had a good chance of snagging the boy out of the deadly water.

Later, I discovered I had held my breath the entire time without even knowing it; my chest and lungs were sore for days afterward. Frozen in place, mesmerized by the terrifying sight of Les sprinting along the bank, head turned toward Tommy who was being hurtled through the water at about an equal pace. The scene engraved itself into my memory to become part of my personal horror movie that included snippets of Sean being shot, of Sean chased by a bear, of Les lost in the snowstorm . . .

If Les failed to reach the bridge in time, my Tommy would ride Minook Creek to his death. We might never find his body as it tumbled down the creek to its junction with the Yukon River, then on into the Bering Sea.

All that passed through my thoughts in an instant.

Sometimes Les seemed as big and clumsy as a bear, but he also possessed the bear's surprising agility and speed. He was within three steps of the bridge and an equal distance ahead of Tommy barreling after him in the white water when what hope I retained dissolved.

The bridge was a single gigantic log with hand railings. When Les felled it across the stream during the summer, there was a spread of approximately fifteen feet from the surface of the creek to the bottom of the bridge. Even at flood stage, the spread from water to bridge was still over four feet, far too great a reach for even a tall man like Les to snatch Tommy from the creek as he sped underneath it at twenty miles an hour.

My Tommy was gone!

Les had already considered the bridge and rejected it. Instead, he flung his two hundred pounds sailing through the air toward a jagged shard of ice stretching out into the stream from the bank directly underneath the bridge, like a small pier. With luck, Tommy would sweep within arm's reach of it.

Les landed solid on the frozen pier. One leg drove all the way through. Water and ice exploded. The pier was breaking up.

Les reached for a brace that kept the log bridge solid and in place. With the other hand, he grabbed for Tommy as the boy came sweeping within range. Hand and arm disappeared into the white froth. I thought he missed.

Tommy reappeared, stopped against the current like a salmon at the foot of a waterfall. Les had him firmly by one arm. As he attempted to swing the boy out of the current's grip, the ice in which he was rooted disintegrated from underneath him, sweeping his feet out into the stream.

Man and boy were both now caught in the unrelenting current. The only thing that kept them anchored was Les's one hand gripping the bridge support.

"Norma!"

His shout above the roar of the creek jolted me out of my trance. I ran toward the bridge, shouting back and praying at the same time.

"Norma, take Tommy! Quick!"

I dropped belly-down on the bridge and braced my feet against the hand railing. Using all his strength, Les one-handed the boy up to me. I grabbed him soaked and freezing.

"I got him! I got him, Les!"

Struggling, Les pulled himself out of the water. He lay on the log to catch his breath. I hugged Tommy so hard that not all his coughing and spluttering was due to water in his lungs. The three of us huddled on the bridge while the Minook howled its disappointment underneath. I whispered over and over: "Les . . . Tommy . . . Les . . ."

50

During later years, I often shook my head uncomprehendingly as I watched society in the Lower Forty-eight degenerate into a bunch of whining, sniveling crybabies. America was turning into a land of *victims* who blamed everyone and everything except themselves for how their lives turned out. They expected government to take care of them from cradle to grave, to cushion and protect them against the consequences of their own choices. Little by little, in the name of security, they were relinquishing our personal liberty. I always remembered a quote explaining the fall of Rome, how the Romans gave up liberty in exchange for security and ultimately had neither security nor liberty.

Homesteading offered no promises. We could be wiped out by floods or forest fires, lose our lives to bears, accidents, and the environment. Those were hazards we had to accept in order to enjoy that greatest gift of all from God to man—*freedom*. The right to live our lives according to our own dreams. If we failed, we blamed no one but ourselves for not working hard enough.

Les and I were survivors. Dominating people. We would never have made it this far otherwise. Only an average of two out of every hundred would-be Alaskan homesteaders had ever proved out their claims. One or the other, husband or wife, simply lacked the steel for it, that good old-fashioned true grit.

I want to throw up when I hear people whining of being *disadvantaged* and therefore helpless. The relationship Les and I started in Colorado hadn't even jelled properly before we quit our jobs and took off north on our adventure. We had five kids and little money. What sustained us was a dream. It took us over a year just to *get* to Alaska. By necessity, we built a strong marriage that required us to depend upon each other and work together for a common goal and basic survival. Even the children, who had to pull their own weight, were bound to grow up tough, dominating, and strong-willed. Survivors.

"This year," Les chafed, "we've got to get our business going."

We were already more than halfway through the five-year period during which we either proved progress or lost our homestead—except for the five acres upon which our cabin sat. A trade and manufacturing site like our eighty acres had to *manufacture* something, had to be involved in *trade* within the less than three years remaining. Tourists were Alaska's number one cash crop. But it wasn't as if you put in a gas station or a motel and expected travelers to hike up the Yukon to reach a better mousetrap. What did we have to entice tourists to tramp across a mountain range and down into a valley full of bears and a frightful legend known as Bushman?

Two things, Les pointed out with enthusiasm.

"Wilderness! A chance for them to see Alaska the way it originally was. They'll come once we clear that muskeg swamp in the middle of the property and build an airstrip, then add a bunch of isolated cabins for them to stay in. Maybe even a small trading post."

And the second thing?

Bear, caribou, Dall sheep, wolves, and moose. Alaska's big game. Alaskan law required that a prospective big-game guide serve an apprenticeship of five years under a licensed guide in order to obtain his own license. Pete Pasquali from Wiseman and Les were going into the guiding business together for the spring and fall hunting seasons; Les had already acquired a guide sponsor to start his apprenticeship. He would begin guiding in the fall.

In the meantime, over the summer, we had a lot of work to do; we were young and strong and had our lives ahead of us to build. Les and Sid tore into the woods with chain saws and axes. The growl of the saw and ringing of axe blades filled the valley during the long days of summer sunlight. The walls of the first tourist cabin slowly grew. A new outhouse, sturdy and blond with fresh logs, became for me a symbol of the advancing of civilization.

Preparing for the Arctic winter that never seemed to be far off fell mostly to the two younger boys, the twins, and me. We hauled firewood to a stack the size of a house. Fresh in our memories was how we had almost run out of fuel during the winter and had had to fight our way into the snow-filled woods to cut more.

My first vegetable garden last year did not do well. Frost descended just as my tomatoes, green peppers, squash, and beans were blooming. Unlike the Darts in Manley who owned the natural hot springs and had built a greenhouse over them in which they raised melons, fruit trees, cucumbers as big as squash, zucchini four times normal size, and tomatoes as big as cantaloupes, everything extra large, succulent, and perpetually growing, I had to look for new methods of gardening if I expected the family to enjoy fresh vegetables.

I turned to artist Rose Stowell and a native Indian friend in Manley, Vera Strack, to help me plan a garden using organic methods. I even coaxed Les into building us a small greenhouse. Under Rose's and Vera's tutelage, I used ashes from the woodstove to neutralize the soil's natural acidity and dog dung as fertilizer. Mulching and composting were difficult because of the cool climate and permafrost being so near the surface.

I managed to coax up small yields of onions, radishes, lettuce, cabbage, carrots, turnips, green beans, and potatoes. Enough to feed the family during the growing season and a welcome respite from wild game, berries, mushrooms, sourdough biscuits, and dried or canned foods. Sometimes I complained that mosquitoes harvested a richer crop from my blood than what I harvested from the soil.

Together as the family was for twenty-four hours a day, there were times when we got on each other's nerves. Clashes, arguments, the banging of stubborn heads together. Les ran roughshod over me if I permitted it, turning me into a mouse. I fought back and the partnership we built was one of equals.

Generally when tempers flared, I took a walk along the creek and talked to God. There were other times, however, when my reaction to stress was less than exemplary. Once when the children were especially unruly at supper, complaining of what I had prepared, I grabbed their plates and thrust them at Les, who sat at table grinning in confusion.

"Here, give it all to Lester. He has no taste buds. He'll eat anything."

I ran everyone out of the cabin and locked the door. Les knocked.

"Go away!" I shouted. "You're just like your damned insensitive children."

Wash out my mouth. After the first tourist cabin was finished, it gave me a refuge where I could go, lock the door, and read or sew in peace.

When I carried things too far, Les brought me back down by grabbing my shoulders and shaking me. He never shook me hard.

"Knock it off, Norma!"

"Okay, okay. I'm knocking it off."

It didn't always work. On one occasion as he let me go and turned away, I grabbed the broom and broke it over his shoulders.

Included on my next shopping list when Les went to Fairbanks were *two* brooms. Les looked at the list and gave me that grin.

"What's this? His and her brooms—one to use and one to knock over my head?

He bought me two brooms anyhow.

By July it was obvious that Les and twelve-year-old Sid, with what help I offered in between maintaining the family, were not making sufficient progress on the tourist cabin. Hunting season was coming, winter would be upon us, and another year gone before we even started on the second tourist cabin. We had to have full-time help; we could not afford to hire it. Our homestead and our dreams for it were at stake.

51

Along came Andrew Farnsworth. During a rare family day off when we had gone to Fairbanks for more supplies unobtainable in Manley, we were having a real supper treat at Kentucky Fried Chicken when Andrew and a friend came in and took the table next to ours. Les never met a stranger; he talked to fence posts. Before long, he was chatting it up with Andrew like they were old pals. Andrew confided how he was from California and had always dreamed of coming to Alaska to homestead in a cabin in the wilderness.

"Yeah?" Les said. I saw his mind working. "You don't look like the busher type to me."

He was about twenty-eight years old, short and rather plump. Scholarly looking in his rimless glasses and stylish haircut. A nerd unfamiliar with labor. He might once have repaired his own flat tire when he had no other choice, but certainly he had never repaired more than one. Turned out he had a Ph.D. in sociology or something and was taking some time off from the *real* world before settling down.

"You can't homestead in Alaska anymore," Les pointed out. "They've closed down homesteading. Norma was the last homesteader."

"That's what I've discovered," Andrew said. "Most land is government land, and what isn't is prohibitively expensive."

Les thought it over. The guy seemed eager.

"Andrew, if you're really serious about this, we may be able to strike a deal. I need some help building cabins. You come out to Minook Creek and take a look. If you still want to stay, we might work out something."

Andrew beamed. "I'm strong!" he exclaimed. "I can work hard. You won't be sorry."

I hoped not.

A FEW DAYS LATER Andrew came walking across Dead Horse Pass with his Irish setter Zack, a sissy city dog if I ever saw one. The Westbrooks, who had returned for the summer but were still standoffish, directed him on down the creek. He looked a bit anxious and weary from his jaunt through the wilds. He brightened when he spotted the cabin and everyone busily going about their tasks. He wiped sweat from his rimless glasses using his shirttail and grabbed Zack before the dog rushed among our chained sled dogs and got his butt soundly whipped.

He sighed with relief. "I thought I had taken the wrong path."

"I told you it was isolated," Les said.

"It's like *The Lost World.* I thought I saw a bear."

"Maybe you saw Bushman," Tommy blurted out.

"Bushman?"

"He steals kids," Sean explained. "You're probably safe."

In spite of Bushman tales delivered with relish once the brood discovered our city visitor susceptible, Andrew entered an agreement with Les to stay on at the homestead and help construct an airfield and all the cabins we needed. In exchange he received one acre of our land a short distance downcreek. Les would help build him a cabin to live in before winter so they could get on with the homestead work next summer. It sounded like a good deal for everyone. Andrew and Zack moved into the one tourist cabin that was already finished until their own cabin was up.

I doubted Andrew realized what he had let himself in for. Felling logs, stripping them, dragging them to the desired site, notching them, and then erecting them Lincoln Logs style was backbreaking labor. Unlike Les, who had grown up working hard on ranches and farms and who had acquired his education in the practical world, Andrew had acquired his learning secondhand, from books, and he had done virtually no physical labor. He might spout the formula for πr^2—"No, dummy," Les retorted, "pie 'r' round"—but a saw and how to use it without a detailed demonstration might as well have been the Rosetta Stone.

For all Andrew's immense education, I would rather be stuck on a desert island, or in Minook Valley, with a man like Les and his less-than-high-school education than a brain like Andrew with his Ph.D. Quoting Shakespeare failed to put meat in the larder or fur on your back. If he were ever stranded in a snowstorm such as the one Les went through, the odds were strongly against his survival. The more I saw of sensitive Alan Alda guys like Andrew, the more I appreciated my practical husband with his big hands and macho can-do attitude. I wondered if practical, competent men were becoming extinct because of schools and universities.

Andrew always seemed more comfortable with women than with men, especially with rough-shod men like my husband. He was almost bursting with pride over the bed, table, and cabinets he built on his own. Like a child.

"Norma! I want you to come look at what I've made!"

"Haven't you ever done anything like this before, Andrew?"

"Well . . . I built a birdhouse once. Birds wouldn't live in it."

"What did you *do*? I mean, in your life?"

"I went to school. Then I went to the university."

Les's patience with him gradually wore thin. *Next* summer, he hoped, we might finally get our money's worth out of Andrew's labor.

"I would have done better hiring Sid," he complained in exasperation.

"You already had Sid for free," I pointed out, a little too smugly.

The two men finally completed the cabin and Andrew and Zack moved in. It was low-profile and snug and sat inside a copse of spruce about a hundred yards downstream of our cabin. As fall hunting season and winter approached, Andrew seemed to grow increasingly tense and uncertain. He asked a lot of questions about what winter was like.

"It's a lot of snow and it's cold," Les said in characteristic understatement.

"What do you do when you have all that snow?"

Sid had an answer. "You go dogsledding and trapping."

"For *furs*? Ugh! Don't you get tired of being snowed in and it being dark all the time?"

Les grinned. "If you get cabin fever too bad, we'll lock you in your cabin and unlock you come spring breakup."

52

Les received his first grizzly hunting clients that fall. He was under apprenticeship to the licensed guide, but hunters were still assigned to him or to Pete Pasquali. As with homesteading, bootlegging, or whatever else received Les's attention, he went into professional big-game hunting with passion, excitement, and total commitment. Partly for effect and partly because it was practical, he took to strapping his six-inch .44 Ruger Blackhawk Magnum revolver across his chest in a quick-draw holster. He looked impressive, tough, and prepared.

"What makes grizzly hunting the hairiest shooting in the world," he lectured novice and experienced hunters alike, "is that on any given day chasing him, the bear ends up with a fifty-fifty chance of getting *you*. Most emergency shots will be taken at twenty-five feet or less. That's *seven steps* away from his jaws. At that range, your margin for human or mechanical error is zero, zilch. Everything had better work the way it's supposed to."

Andrew Farnsworth shuddered at the thought of confronting such a fearsome quarry—and he stayed home in his cabin when the men went hunting.

From the first day we arrived in the valley, and especially after his feud with the wily Westbrooks' bear, Les had been fascinated by the big creatures. He read everything he found about bears, their habits and nature, diet, temperament, *everything* . . . Not only that, but every chance he had he was out in the bush with them, stalking them, observing them, testing theories. I knew it wouldn't be long before he knew as much about Alaska's grizzlies, browns, and blacks as any guide or hunter north of the Canadian border.

Prior to the opening of hunting season, Les and Pete took a three-day scouting hike up around the Sawtooths to check grizzly range. They spotted a large sow griz ambling across an expanse of rolling, open tundra. Whereas black bears were creatures of the deep woods, grizzlies could be found anywhere. At the top of the food chain, they went where they pleased. They feared absolutely nothing.

The two men watched the sow as she shambled along, as big as a cow but behaving more like a hog by rooting around underneath rocks, checking roots for larvae, tarrying to harvest a patch of blueberries, completely oblivious and uncaring about what the rest of the world might be doing around her.

"I read in *Field & Stream,*" Pete said musingly, "that if you came upon a grizzly and two of you got side by side, held hands, and ran at the bear, you could scare it off."

Les looked over at Pete. "Hold hands?" Les said, suppressing a grin. "Pete, is there something you ain't told me?"

"You hold hands to make you look like one massive critter."

Les nodded. "You game to try it?"

A griz under most circumstances was virtually fearless and would not back down from a cement truck. Along with a perpetually bad temper came power to overturn and maul a pickup truck, the speed to outrun a horse for short distances, a terrifying set of claws like sharpened steel hinges, and fearsome teeth in a mighty jaw.

"Why not?" Pete said.

By this time the sow was cutting across directly in front of them. The tall bearded man and the short bearded man stepped out from cover, clasped hands, and charged the bear, shouting and waving their free arms.

For an instant, but only for an instant, it looked as though it might work. The surprised bear woofed and jumped back in surprise. You could almost read the expression on her face: What the hell is *this?*

It didn't take her long to recover. She spat and screamed back at her attackers. She reared up like a horse coming out of a starting gate. Then *she* charged.

"Oh, *shit*!" In unison.

Fortunately, there was a rock pinnacle rising up out of the tundra nearby. Les and Pete reached it ahead of the bear. It was like a rock needle, affording few handholds. Both men somehow scrambled to the top of it and huddled together on its point while the sow screamed and stood up and scratched at the pinnacle as though to bring it tumbling down.

She complained and paced around the base of the needle for several hours. Sometimes she sat on her haunches and craned her head and glowered at her cornered prey, daring them to come down, link hands, and try that stunt again.

"Pete, the next time you read something stupid like this from *Field & Stream*," Les said, "leave me out of it."

NEAR THE BASE of a jagged mountain called Ragged Top, Les and his hunting client glassed a blond boar grizzly stalking big-humped across a blueberry field about three hundred yards away. He looked as big as a Hereford bull. Swaggering casually, he had his head down as if he knew he was the meanest creature south of the Arctic Circle. He seemed evil-tempered and spoiling for a fight.

A wide alder thicket about thirty-five feet in front of the hunters separated them from the blueberry field and the bear. Les's nervous client, Tom Sheldon, inadvertently banged the stock of his rifle against a tree trunk. That was all it took. The boar's head shot up, instantly alert. He stood high on his hind legs, nearsighted but depending on his keen sense of smell to locate the enemy. He whiffed the wind, homing in on the intruders.

Without further hesitation, he dropped back to all fours and charged like a dragster taking off from a starting line. He disappeared into the far side of the alder patch. He would reappear, soon, and with terrifying presence.

"He's coming!" Les said. "Get ready, Tom. Do you hear me? Get ready."

All they saw of the bear was the rapid parting of the alders as the beast blazed a trail directly at them with amazing speed. An attacking grizzly bear was a terrifying sight to behold, even for an experienced bear man. Tom Sheldon trembled so hard he had trouble releasing the safety on his rifle. He appeared ready to start spraying the bushes, hoping for a lucky shot.

"Steady, Tom. Steady."

You could not shoot what you could not see. There was no retreat within reach, no pinnacle rising out of the tundra this time. Les accepted that their only chance depended on waiting until the attacking bruin broke out of the thicket in front of them—thirty-five feet away, ten steps, one second away from impact—and then opening up on him. He would be on top of them faster than party crashers on free booze.

The client might get off one shot. Certainly no more. He was so excited, so *scared*, he was lucky if he even squeezed his trigger. Les drew his forty-four for close-in shooting. It was a guide's duty, his moral obligation, to protect his client, even if it meant losing his own life. Les intended to go down shooting.

Still at a dead run, the griz broke free of the alders with a final unnerving crash of brush and a low, cavernous growl. His huge head rode low and thrust forward, teeth bared.

A bear had such a low pulse rate that even if a bullet pulverized his heart he still might complete his charge and maul his victim. That eliminated the heart as a close-in target.

A brain shot even on a stationary animal was iffy. Les therefore went for a spinal shot. He lined up the Blackhawk on the blond flash of the bear's rising hump. The hammer was already cocked. There was no time for a second bullet.

The crash of the big forty-four, the most powerful handgun ever made at the time, merged with the report from the client's rifle. Sheldon missed; Les didn't.

The bear dropped and skidded in the tundra, his back broken. Four-inch claws clacked against my husband's boots. Les hammered a second round into the grizzly's brain to finish him off.

"Thank you, Lord. Thank you, Lord," the client chanted in a breathless whisper. "I'm getting out of this country—and I'm *never* coming back."

LES BROUGHT HOME a small cinnamon grizzly hide for me to tan. It was beautiful clean fur. It looked as though the bear had just finished taking a bath before he was shot.

Bear hides were big and heavy and an ordeal to work with. Sid and I kept busy for days fleshing the hide, soaking it in alum to set the hair, then cleaning and rinsing it. I left it on the porch to dry, then nailed it to a large board and soap-pasted it. After it dried thoroughly, I scraped off the soap paste and worked the hide by hand to soften it. Les said I should chew it to make it pliable, like the natives did. They didn't chew them with the hair on! When I finished with the pelt, it looked quite impressive hanging on our cabin wall.

Grizzly meat was rank. Black bear was good. It was very sweet meat if the bear had fed mostly on blueberries and not fish. It could be very foul if the bear had gorged on rotten fish during the salmon migrations. Like the old saying went, we were what we ate.

From a black bear, I charcoaled steaks, made roasts, cooked it into bear goulash. The family's favorite method of preparation was to cut it into thin strips and smoke it in our crude makeshift smoker constructed of a barrel Les hauled in for the purpose. Later I learned that bears, like swine, sometimes carried trichinosis, and that smoking the meat was not a thorough way to cook it. You had to cook it well, the same as pork. Nonetheless, smoked bear was much better tasting than smoked strips of caribou or moose.

53

Townspeople and visitors from outside often asked settlers how we prepared for winter, stocking food and supplies for those seven to nine months when it was either difficult or impossible to get out for resupply. Most normal people had trouble stocking up for a week. But it wasn't like we could run down to the nearest Quik-Trip for a loaf of bread and a gallon of milk.

Eating was a big part of a winter's pastime in maintaining sanity. Meat, especially, contributed to the good mood of a winter's isolation. That was why it was so important that the larder be stocked with a couple of moose or a moose and a caribou, along with a bear or two. Of course, when weather permitted, a grouse or a ptarmigan or a snowshoe became a welcome addition to the season's pot.

This year we expected to have beaver as well. During the summer, I had managed to make up to Bony Newman the Eskimo for my rudeness when he paid his call to our cabin last winter. He and his Indian wife, Liz, and their dozen children became our best friends at Rampart and adopted us as their white family. Bony's son, Boots, who was about Sid's age, and Sid became buddies. As time passed, Sid turned to Rampart as his social center and Boots as his best friend. The village readily adopted him.

"Get ready for it," Les cautioned, teasing. "Our son is gonna bring home a pretty squaw."

"Lester! What difference does it make as long as she's decent, clean, God-fearing, and good?"

Bony and Boots Newman taught Les and Sid how to trap beaver and the best way to prepare the pelts. Beaver were hard to skin and difficult to tan because they were so greasy. The natives taught my men how to dry the pelt into large circles, which they then tanned or sold to furriers in Fairbanks. Liz instructed me on how to prepare the meat. She loved eating the tail. Nothing was ever wasted. I made knife sheaths from the skin of the tails.

We caught on to living off nature as much as possible. There were a variety of wild berries for canning and jelling—cranberries, blueberries, raspberries, tundra berries, salmon berries, blackberries . . . Rose Stowell showed me at least twenty different varieties of eatable mushrooms, my favorites of which were the orange delicious, puffballs, and boletus. They turned out to be part of nature's treasures. I experimented with different ways to cook, preserve, and eat them.

We bought those other staples not reproduced in the wild. It was important that we hauled these in before snow filled Dead Horse Pass. The depth of snow made travel across the pass extremely difficult and hazardous from October to May.

We used dehydrated goods as much as possible since they were easier to haul in and to store and lasted longer without waste. They were also simple to cook with once you learned the tricks. The most common dehydrated foods were mashed potatoes, hash browns, sliced potatoes, sliced onions, bell peppers, powdered milk, buttermilk, cheese, sour cream, eggs, Dream Whip, and even powdered butter and peanut butter. Just add water. If we were low on meat, which we seldom were, we utilized dehydrated soy beans.

Main staples included beans, rice, flour, sugar, oatmeal, noodles, coffee, tea, dried milk, along with canned vegetables and fruits, which we bought in case lots of number ten cans. Sometimes we splurged on canned bacon, which could be preserved for years and taken out of the can and fried. Wild animals did not produce bacon.

For a winter we bought eight hundred pounds of sugar and one thousand pounds of flour. I made lots of bread, rolls, pizza, and cakes, pies, and cookies. It was always better to have more than enough food-stuffs.

I helped Andrew Farnsworth stock his cabin. He continued to be anxious about the coming winter.

"Are you sure this is enough?" he asked. "Are you sure?"

Firewood, more than ten cords of which we stacked, was the next necessity, followed in order of importance by medical supplies. Treatments for colds, bronchial conditions, and fevers were our main concerns, along with the means to treat accident injuries. That included a suture kit I hoped I would never have to use.

During the summer we acquired in various ways several more sled dogs, in addition to Lady's spring litter of pups. Twenty-five or more dogs ate a few barrels of feed themselves, making it prohibitively expensive to feed them if nature hadn't helped provide.

Sid contracted a deal with Bony Newman for Sean and him to help clean fish during the salmon fishing season. Natives were permitted to use net and wheel traps to harvest migrating salmon, which they cleaned, cut up, and sun-dried or smoked on wooden racks. In return for their labors, the boys received poor-quality "dog salmon" as dog feed. Native mushers kept up their dogs on cooked fish and rice.

Sid drove the Bombardier to Rampart to bring back his fish, which had frozen because the temperature was already hovering around or below freezing in September. He piled the load in the shade and kept it covered to maintain its low temperature. He cooked fish for use in a barrel cut in half. He and Sean built a fire under the barrel half, put in salmon, rice, water, and a little used Kentucky Fried Chicken grease salvaged from KFC in Fairbanks and boiled it. The dogs lapped it up. All that grease provided oils their systems required against the winter cold, plus it helped keep their feet lubricated against snow and ice.

Cooking dog feed led to another of the accidents to which little Sean seemed prone. The grease caught fire and blazed up in the makeshift kettle. Too young to know that you never tossed water on a grease fire, Sean did just that. The flame burned his face badly. He ran to the cabin screaming in pain. I cleaned the burn carefully and applied Vitamin E gel to it two or three times a day for the next two weeks. He healed properly with no scars or other permanent signs of yet another close call.

Since we rarely enjoyed fresh foods except during the summer, and since sunlight remained scarce or absent for months at a time, I grew to depend upon vitamins to help prevent poor health conditions. Sleep, exercise, work, and play were also important in maintaining health in a cold, dark wintery environment. Between vitamins, prevention, common sense, and prayer, I doctored my family the best way I could. The physical, mental, emotional, and spiritual had to be attended to as a whole. The open country with its natural surroundings added to the peace and tranquility of one's soul and therefore to one's health. God wanted us to be happy, healthy, loving, and whole. Even in the winter.

54

Accidents happened in the bush, as they must on the frontier with people outdoors so much working, fishing, hunting . . . The possibility of being injured or becoming ill made Andrew Farnsworth fret constantly. *What if?* was a major part of his vocabulary. I tried to reassure him by explaining that you kept a well-stocked first-aid box—and a Bible. Prayer saw Sean through his gunshot wound; God guided Les home through the blizzard. God had not failed us so far.

Andrew stared at me. He said nothing, but I knew from his blank expression that he thought my faith incredibly naïve. So be it. I felt sorry for him, his having no Higher Power to believe in. He was so lacking in competence and ability that it must have been difficult for him to even believe in himself. I wondered if he were becoming the norm in the modern outside world.

When Cora and Tommy decided to have a regular brother-sister row, as siblings will, Cora fell and gashed open her forehead. Blood streamed. I grabbed her and washed the wound. It required stitches. I gulped. It seemed I was about to perform my first surgical procedure.

I compressed a bandage to Cora's little towhead to stem the bleeding, then went for the suture kit, which had sat all this time in a corner of the cabin, like some sort of shrine or threat. Cora screeched when she saw it.

"Are you gonna *sew* me up, Mama? You gonna *sew me up?*"

The other kids and Andrew, attracted by the commotion, gathered to watch around the dining table turned operating table. Les had gone hunting. I took a deep breath to stop my hands from shaking.

"Mama, sew her mouth up too," Sean suggested.

"Hush now," I warned. I was nervous enough about it already.

Cora continued to wail. "*Don't* sew me, Mama! It'll *hurt!*"

I thought Sid would have to hold her down. Andrew looked queasy. Worthless as always. Cara the twin wailed in sympathy.

My own stomach roiled at the prospect of taking one of those curved, wicked-looking needles and puncturing my little girl's flesh with it. I tried to appear outwardly composed in spite of my turmoil inside. I went to the cupboard and fixed Cora a hot whiskey toddy and had her drink it. It always worked for the cowboys in the movies when John Wayne or Gary Cooper had to remove a bullet or chop off a leg gangrenous because of an Indian arrowhead. John would say, "Here, slug down the whole bottle," then whip out his Bowie knife and start to work.

I thought about a toddy for myself, only I would probably throw it back up. Cora was starting to look a little dreamy and had stopped screaming. I didn't want to set her off again by letting her see the doctor vomit before the operation.

I sucked in a few more deep breaths, squared my shoulders, thought about doing some deep knee bends or other exercises to loosen up, decided that would be more procrastination than warm-up, and went instead for the needle.

My poor little Cora. Five years old and her mother had gotten her *drunk*.

It seemed to take me forever to place two stitches in her forehead. Cora cried, Tommy and Cara cried. I postponed my own tears until it was all over and done. First, you had to react to the crisis. Then you broke down. That was what it took to be a pioneer.

"I don't know if I could have done it," Andrew confessed.

"If you think you can't, you can't."

CUTS AND BRUISES and minor illnesses and even burns like Sean suffered from the dog food grease fire. Those we took care of at home. After hunting season ended, Les got metal shavings in his eye while working on the Bombardier. I did everything I could, but it wasn't enough. He remained in such agony that he and Andrew finally hiked out to the vehicles and Andrew drove him to the hospital in Fairbanks. The eye was severely damaged.

"It should be removed," the doctor advised.

"No!" Les was adamant about it.

"It's getting infected and could be fatal. It may infect the remaining eye. At best you may go blind. Mr. Cobb, I'm trying to get you to see how serious this is."

Les's shoulders rolled forward and he thrust out his bearded jaw. He could be a stubborn man. "I'm not giving up my eye."

He finally consented to see a specialist in the Lower Forty-eight. Since we hadn't the funds for all of us to travel, Les flew by himself to Colorado where he lived with his parents while being treated. I stayed behind with the kids to worry about my husband and pray to God that everything turned out all right. By this time, the Westbrooks had returned to Florida for the winter. They were barely speaking to us anyhow. Anxious and upset by Les's condition to begin with, I now confronted the prospect of wintering over a second year without my husband, with only the kids and a quackish hired hand for company.

55

Cabin fever, more so than bears or blizzards, was the scourge of the North Country. Months of isolation and confinement to small spaces, living without sunshine, often produced unexpected and bizarre consequences. Murder, suicide, divorce, child abuse, wife beating, and insanity were all common.

"Judge, you don't know what it's like," lamented a busher charged with beating his wife to death with a steel fur trap. "You are stuck in a cabin and all you see is that mouth of hers flapping. Judge, she complained and bitched until I couldn't take it no more. Judge, you would have did the same thing."

There was another story of how a homesteader came out of the bush that fall in a state of apparent shock. He explained to Trooper Jones how he and his wife were trapped inside their cabin for three days by a pair of marauding grizzlies. They finally saw an opportunity to escape and made a run for it. He made it. His wife didn't.

Trooper Jones organized a rescue party to go in for the body, or what remained of it. Sure enough, she was mangled and partly consumed by bears. However, an autopsy revealed that while bears may have eaten her, they hadn't killed her. She had been stabbed to death with a skinning knife, then tossed into the woods for the bears to enjoy while they destroyed evidence of murder. The bears hadn't eaten enough of her.

"Ol' Joe, I guess," went the general consensus, voiced in the rough humor of the bush, "just couldn't face another winter locked in a cabin with that woman."

Shortly after Les left for Colorado to have his eye treated, snow came and the weather closed in. The prospect of wintering over now that I was a veteran wasn't nearly as scary as it had been last fall. We were much better prepared. Besides, there was always Andrew Farnsworth, even though it was *I* who would probably have to take care of him. I already noticed initial signs of cabin fever in his behavior.

I invited him often for supper. I felt sorry for him, stuck down there in his cabin alone except for his sissy dog Zack. He looked so lonely and lost as he fought the snowdrifts between his cabin and ours.

The kids and I were often busy and hadn't the time to sit around with Andrew and chat. We had home schooling, plus all the outside chores of hauling wood and water and tending to a pack of dogs that had grown fourfold in numbers from last year. Sid went out trapping for marten, fox, lynx, and beaver, an activity that seemed to offend Andrew's finer Ph.D. sensitivities. At other times, training his dogs to the sled, Sid mushed over to Rampart to chum with his friend Boots Newman. Andrew was afraid to venture that far away from the safety of his cabin.

Bony Newman's wife, Liz, gave me good tips on sewing furs into useful items and doing beadwork. I utilized the long winter darkness, what time I escaped home schooling and my other chores, to crochet and make hats, mittens, and mukluks out of Sid's furs. Handcrafted fur items brought three times the prices of raw furs alone when peddled through tourist outlets in Anchorage and Fairbanks. Sid and I split the profits.

"I see you're too busy for company," Andrew whined.

"I can talk and work at the same time."

"No. No. I don't want to be in the way."

"Andrew! Get in here."

"I'm going back to my cabin. It seems like I'm always in the way. You never come to visit me."

He sounded like a silly, petulant woman with too much time on his hands. He came over even less frequently. He stopped shaving and cutting his hair. He no longer melted snow or hauled water for bathing. An offensive odor clung to his body. His eyes turned red-rimmed and became encased in dark folds, as if he had trouble sleeping.

"He's flipping his lid," Sid diagnosed.

I ordered the kids to stay away from his cabin. Then I felt guilty about it and broke a trail through the snow.

"Andrew, are you okay?"

"Don't I look okay?"

"You look awful."

"Norma, I'm too busy right now. Come back some other time."

I was too worried about Les and his eye to play this game. I turned around and went home. Still, I couldn't simply leave him down there to stew in his own bad juices.

The next time I checked on him, I found him sitting in a chair in the middle of the floor with a .44 revolver in his hands. Sitting there with his disheveled hair falling over his burning eyes, watching the door as though about to defend himself against demons.

"Andrew!" I cried in alarm. "What are you doing?"

He seemed to shake himself mentally. He got up and put the gun away. He turned and glared at me. His mind, tormented by isolation—a severe punishment for some people—had obviously taken hold of some imagined slight on my part and turned it into a major grudge.

"Why don't you mind your own business?" he snapped.

Things between his cabin and ours grew worse as the winter progressed—with the coldest, darkest part yet to come. When Callie my cat disappeared, I found other huge cat paw prints coming up to the edge of our clearing and became afraid that a lynx had gotten her. She was only a calico tabby, but she was a great source of comfort and pleasure to the family while Les was away and we were socked in by weather. We had already given her kittens away to settlers in Manley.

I went out looking for her, calling her name. Andrew burst out of his cabin, acting defensive.

"I haven't seen your cat!" he barked. He went back inside and slammed the door.

"Maybe Andrew killed Callie and *ate* her," Sean speculated.

Andrew's metamorphosis, the souring of his personality and the darkening of his mood, reminded me of Stephen King's *The Shining* and a character in it who became possessed while isolated for a winter in a closed-down mountain resort with his wife and son. He took after them with an axe. Although Andrew hardly knew how to use an axe, I nonetheless made sure our door was securely locked when we slept.

His dark presence only a short distance down the creek made Les's absence even more intolerable. I developed insomnia and sometimes got up in the middle of the night to peer anxiously out the window. I imagined him down there, wild-eyed, wild-haired, and unshaved, brooding and stewing over perceived injustices done against him and blowing them all out of proportion. Every morning, the kids and I eagerly turned the radio to *Pipeline of the North,* hoping to hear some word from Les. Finally, the message we hoped for came through: *"To the Cobbs at Minook Creek and Lost Creek, from Les Cobb: 'My eye is okay now. Returning home on December 2.' "*

Once Les returned to the valley, his eyes almost fully restored, thanks to God and a fine Colorado surgeon, the kids and I ceased being afraid. Andrew even seemed to get better, temporarily. He ventured out of his cabin once or twice before more weather came and he retreated into further hibernation. We knew he was alive by the signature of smoke rising from his chimney. I couldn't help feeling uneasy about him nonetheless. It was a queasiness of the stomach, a sense of foreboding, a feeling that Minook Valley was being poisoned by ill will. Maybe we should, as Les jokingly suggested, lock Andrew up until breakup.

"He'll come out in the spring and apologize," Les predicted, typically optimistic.

56

To Alaskans, the Iditarod sled dog race was like the World Series in baseball. Iditarod was the name of an old mining camp through which the trail ran. Joe Reddington Sr. organized the first race in 1973, the same year we Cobbs arrived in Alaska. The event immediately captured the imagination of the world. It was the second-longest race of any kind, 1,049 miles long from Anchorage to Nome, exceeded in distance only by the Tour de France bicycle race, and certainly it was the most hazardous. It commemorated the daring feat during the 1925 diphtheria epidemic when three Indians made a nonstop run to deliver serum needed to rescue Nome.

Our neighbors in Eureka, Rick Swenson, Susan Butcher, and Bud Smith, intended to compete in the race come March. As it turned out, Swenson would win the Iditarod with a new record of sixteen days, sixteen hours, and twenty-seven minutes. He would win it again four more times after that—in 1979, 1982, and 1991.

The fame Rick earned as a result of his wins was nothing compared to when Susan Butcher became the second woman to win the Iditarod in 1986, and then claim victory three more times after that. At this time in her career, however, she was still years away from fame. She competed only in local races such as the one at the annual festivities at Rampart.

Susan was a solid woman with her dark hair in pigtails—not attractive in any real sense. Her face was too broad and roughened by weather. She seldom wore makeup and went around her kennels in Eureka wearing baggy jeans.

Her husband, Dave Monson, had been an attorney who gave up his practice to make a career of helping Susan achieve her goals. A hard-working man helping her train and care for several hundred dogs, he played a definite role in her later successes. Les was unaccustomed to seeing men taking the subordinate role. To him, Dave was "henpecked." Wasn't the fact that Susan kept her maiden name after her marriage proof of that? Les always greeted him as "Mr. Butcher."

"Jerk!" I scolded.

In spite of Les's attitude, the two men became friends. Dave merely ducked his head shyly and smiled, accepting the macho bushers for what they were.

Like fellow musher Susan Butcher, Rick Swenson wasn't much to look at, being shortish with a slim Norwegian face. When he was out training his teams, he made a point of dropping by our cabin on the long run down the Minook to the Yukon. It soon became obvious, even to Les, that Rick's frequent visits were not because he had formed an attachment to my coffeepot.

"Norma," he said, out of Les's earshot, "you sure do have long pretty black hair."

"Why, thank you, Rick. That's nice of you."

"Norma, you sure are the prettiest woman around these parts, if you don't mind my saying so."

"I don't mind at all, Rick. I'm flattered."

Les thought Rick's mooning around like that was funny. I felt almost insulted that he wasn't at least a little jealous.

"You know, Rick," Les said one day, his eyes twinkling. "I think I'll just let you have her."

A sheepish look spread across Rick's face. Les hit him with his big grin. "And when you come to take her out, Rick," he added, "why don't you gather up them five kids and take them along with her?"

That put an end to Rick's compliments. "You dirty booger you," I mock-chided my husband. "I was kind of enjoying that."

Les and Sid were fortunate to have world-class mushers like Rick and

Susan near enough to offer pointers on mushing and racing dogs. Although both racers were closemouthed about their training tactics, not wanting to teach someone else to come in and steal the Iditarod from them, my men nonetheless learned a lot about training, feeding, and racing dogs by simply hanging around, observing, and asking questions. It warmed my heart to see father and son working together with the dogs. They began talking of running the Iditarod themselves. Excitement filled their voices.

I had a feeling mushing for my son was a true passion, although it would be several years yet before he was old enough to race the Iditarod. For Les, I suspected, mushing was more or less a diversion because it was winter, there was snow, we were in the valley, and there weren't a lot of other things for him to do.

"We *will* win the Iditarod someday!" Sid proclaimed. "Sid Cobb, victor!"

57

The huskies of the North Country were noble animals used for a particular purpose, without whom life in the north would be far more difficult. They were muscular, heavy-furred dogs ranging in color from white to black, averaging sixty to eighty pounds in weight but with certain individuals exceeding one hundred pounds. Our dog Lady was typical in color and size, being a silver-gray with a white mask, while Black weighed over one hundred pounds and was somewhat darker.

In the bush country, dogs were not kept merely for pleasure and companionship; they were also used for work and travel. One of the oldest forms of all transportation, dogsleds had been tried and proven over and over again in the Arctic—four-footed animal power in the twentieth century when jet airplanes routinely traveled faster than sound. Unlike the previous winter when we were cabin-bound, this winter we were *mobile*. We had transportation.

Les had brought one husky home from the Fairbanks animal pound, a white long-legged dog we called Arrow. Two of our bitches from last year littered, providing an additional fourteen dogs. Sid "dog-sat" for other mushers around Eureka, acquiring six pups that way. Susan Butcher and Rick Swenson both contributed their "shy pups."

Dogs for the harness had to be aggressive, bold animals. If their mothers were shy, diving into their doghouses whenever something threatened, mushers generally assumed their offspring would also be shy. Such pups deemed unworthy for mushing were commonly killed and tossed into the woods for bears to eat. Sid begged Susan and Rick for their discards. It was impossible for a pup to be around five boisterous youngsters and remain bashful.

The clamor of dogs yelping and barking filled the woods at Minook Creek. As time went on, as many as two hundred dogs, counting those being dog-sat, would be chained to the little barrel houses made of oil drums, almost enough animals to supply all the mushers in the Iditarod.

"I betcha Bushman and bears won't dare come around now," Sean decided with relief.

Les bought a used training sled from Joe Pumper to replace the old one from Rick Swenson that Sid had repaired last year. A dogsled was a low sturdy vehicle with no frills; it had wide, heavy runners and after runners and no sides. Sid and Les worked with the dogs constantly. They had Iditarod on the brain. Whatever time Sid wasn't studying his lessons was spent with the dogs. Les, on the other hand, often became distracted by other projects.

Sometimes I watched Sid through the window, admiring his patience and perseverance. The previous winter he had trained Lady, Black, and eventually Lady's six pups to pull water and wood on the old sled. This year, he added a real lead dog to the team and placed more dogs into harness. At first, he tried Yukon on lead, then Bandit. Finally, there was Captain, a big young dark dog who, years later, actually made a trip with *National Geographic* explorers to the North Pole.

The three most important dogs on a team were the lead, swing, and wheel dogs. The lead dog was boss. He disciplined the others, designated the track, and kept the dog team moving forward. Number two in the hierarchy, and right behind the lead dog in harness, was the swing, whose responsibility it was to transfer the leader's decisions to the dogs behind. Last in harness, just ahead of the sled, came the wheel dog. His task was to make sure that the moves of the other dogs did not imperil either the safety or the progress of the sled.

The rest of the dogs were lumped together as "the team" and could include as many dogs as practical for any particular situation. They could be harnessed in either of two ways: as pairs, each pair yoked side by side, with a lead dog in front, his chain locked into the chain that ran down the center and attached to the sled; or hitched in tandem, one directly behind the other, with each dog's harness tying directly into that of the follower. In estimating the load that a team could pull, the number of dogs in harness was multiplied by a factor of fifty to sixty pounds. For example, a team of eighteen dogs could be expected to haul a sled load of 900 to 1280 pounds.

The lead dog had to be trained first, using a small sled to which he was hitched alone in harness. Sid walked patiently next to him, teaching by repetition that *Gee!* meant turn right, *Haw!* left, and *Whoa!* Stop. Once the leader was taught, the others followed him and learned in turn by repetition. Training the lead was the hard part.

Sid added more dogs and increased the distance of his runs. He ran ten dogs, then sixteen and eighteen. Dogs yodeling in excitement, snow spraying from runners—and there went young Sid all grins and skinny arms and legs wrapped in frosted furs, flying over the white crust of the earth and through the trees at amazing speeds. Taking different trails each day so the dogs would not be able to anticipate which one headed home. Making the nineteen-mile run to Rampart in forty minutes to pick up the mail and pal with Boots Newman, then trying to shave minutes and seconds off each new time record. A dog team at full speed could do twenty-five miles an hour and cover 125 miles in a day.

Knowing both Rick Swenson's and Susan Butcher's best times to Rampart, Sid worked hard to best them. He would burst into the cabin full of excitement whenever he got close.

"Mom! I'm only three minutes behind. We can beat her, Mom! I can beat her and Rick. I can win!"

Mushing the wilderness held certain hazards for a young boy, but I would have had as much success at harnessing the wind or containing the snowfall as slowing down Sid. I worried about him when he was out alone and not with Les, but a boy grew and became a man by trying his wings.

One morning while running his trapline with the dogs, he caromed around a blind corner at full speed to confront a larch tree toppled across the trail from the weight of snow. The sharp branches of the tree were spiked uptrail toward him. There was no way to stop the sled at the speed he was going, in so short a distance.

The racing dogs fit underneath the tree; Sid did not. Too late, he attempted to throw himself to one side off the after runners he was riding. A tree branch like a spear ripped open his parka and coveralls underneath, cutting open his chest. He could have been impaled. He returned home matted in frozen blood.

On another occasion, he was mushing across the creek on his way to Rampart to hang out with Boots when the ice gave way, dropping him and the sled into waist-deep water. A soaked human could freeze to death in a matter of minutes when the temperature was thirty below and a slight breeze of even two knots was blowing.

Levelheaded and calm under pressure, Sid waded out of the creek, busting ice. His legs below the knees and his toes already felt numb. One of his mittens was soaked; he was losing feeling in those fingers.

He removed the mitten and stuffed the hand inside his coat next to his skin. Using only the dry hand, he quickly gathered firewood from the dry underside of a fallen spruce. His teeth chattered uncontrollably by the time he coaxed a small fire into life. Battling the clock and the creeping numbness trying to consume his body, he stumbled around dragging up more logs and throwing them on the fire. Soon, it blazed as tall as the surrounding alders.

Only then did he strip off his wet clothing to dry. He stood as near the fire as he could without blistering himself. His close call was another reminder that this country had many ways in which it could kill you.

"You're becoming a real Alaska hand," Les praised the boy.

I learned to put all my faith and trust in God. Otherwise, what with five half-wild kids and a husband more than half-wild himself, I would have gone stark raving mad.

EVENTUALLY, EVEN I learned to mush and thrill to the speed and exhilaration of whipping through the trees at breathtaking velocity, riding the after runners and hanging on to the sled with all my strength. Imagine the newfound freedom! It was like when you received your first driver's license.

Along with the transportation came communications with the outside world. We added a battery-powered citizens band radio, a CB—*Come in there, good buddy!* and all that—to the old car radio and *Pipeline of the North*. We were now linked in our lost world to civilization.

"Come in there on Lost Creek, Hatchet Lady . . ."

Hatchet Lady became my "handle."

"Hatchet Lady, you and your ol' man and kids harness up them mutts and mush in to the Straks in Manley for the big Christmas party . . ."

It was our first big social event. We were so thrilled. It was all we talked about in the household for a week. Anticipating, planning. We mushed two dog teams to haul the seven of us up over Dead Horse Pass and across the Minook Flats to Manley. Our spirits remained undaunted even though we had some trouble with the still-undertrained dogs. Arriving at the party by dogsled was as fine as driving up in a Cadillac.

58

Les proved even more prone than Sid to getting into situations, some of which were dangerous, others ridiculous, and some a combination of both. He was a restless, energetic man driven by an overactive thyroid like a team of horses under whip. Whereas our hired hand Andrew Farnsworth was a ground hog afraid to venture out of his burrow for fear of seeing his shadow, Les hadn't the time or inclination for cabin fever. The dog teams and an occasional borrowed sno-go provided him the freedom to explore. Winter was actually the best time to travel the bush country, as long as you watched the weather and practiced caution. Les was never real long on caution.

Les and his buddy Pete Pasquali liked to fish for lake trout in the winter. They took off together on a pair of sno-goes pulling akios, a type of light runnerless sled that resembled a flat canoe, used for hauling cargo. Their destination was a lake two days away beyond the Top of the World.

They set up camp at the end of the first day. Pete gathered green spruce boughs as a mattress for his sleeping bag. Les decided to roll out his bag in the akio. That night, the temperature dropped to fifty-two degrees below zero.

Next morning, Les could neither get out of his sleeping bag nor rise from the akio. Body condensation in the subfreezing air froze him solidly, sleeping bag and all, to the fiberglass sled. Chuckling and teasing, Pete built a huge bonfire and leaned akio and Les in it at an angle facing the blaze in order to thaw him free.

UNLIKE BLACK BEARS, grizzlies were not true hibernators. They only slept, a quirk of nature that led to near catastrophe for Les, Pete, and a friend from Manley named Mike. The three of them were returning by dogsled from a cross-country excursion for lake trout when cloud cover turned the night too dark for travel. They decided to make camp against a high deadfall that offered both a windbreak and a reflecting backdrop for a fire.

They unhitched their teams of dogs, fed them, set up a small tent, and built a big flame in front of the deadfall over which to boil water for coffee and cook a meal. After eating, they sat around the fire sipping coffee and shooting the breeze. The warmth of the fire after the day's exercise lulled them into a near stupor.

Sighing contentedly, Les readjusted his log seat so he leaned against the deadfall. The deadfall consisted of the roots of a great spruce blown over by the wind. A cave of sorts had been left in the ground around the roots, covered over now with snow. The fire gradually softened and rotted out the snow that concealed the entrance to the burrow. It was precisely against that weakened snow over the entrance that Les leaned, coffee cup in hand.

To his surprise, he fell backward through the snow crust. He landed on something soft, furry, and big.

The sleeping grizzly was just as surprised as Les. Grizzlies were rarely in good temper, even under the best of circumstances. To be awakened abruptly like this was enough to make even a hare cross.

With a roar that shook snow off nearby tree boughs, the startled bear lurched erect, hurling Les out of the cave and rolling across the campfire, showering sparks. He sprang to his hind legs, bellowing with anger and prepared to take on all comers, towering over the three puny men who cowered wide-eyed at the fire, overcome with astonishment.

Bedlam erupted. Dogs barking, bear roaring, men yelling. Everyone went for the pistol he carried underneath his parka to keep the action from freezing. It was like turning a rattler loose in an Old West saloon where every drunk was armed. Guns went off everywhere. Bullets zinged in all directions. It was just as dangerous to be one of the shooters as it was to be the bear.

Fortunately, the griz was still a bit groggy. Before he fully realized what had happened, he was filled with so many holes that his hide looked as if a colony of moths had attacked it in storage. He fell across the campfire and extinguished all light. The men stood breathing heavily in the dark while the dogs continued their uproar.

"Pete?" Les finally ventured.

"Yeah."

"Mike?"

"Okay."

"Bear?"

No answer.

"Whew!" Les exhaled. "I guess all of us made it except Bear."

ON A COLD, CRISP MORNING during that silver-gray half-light existing a short time between dawn and dusk, Les was on his way home, mushing up and over the Top of the World, when he spotted something moving far off across the white flats. A mere black speck against the snow. It walked upright and was making fair progress.

"Whoa!" he called out to Captain, the lead dog.

He squinted against the snow glare. Surely no one was out here all by himself. No one *sane*.

Recalling his own ordeal in the blizzard in this same vicinity, he mushed the dogs forward at a gallop, veering to the left to intercept the lone figure. When he drew near, he saw it was a cross-country skier carrying a backpack. A kid actually, nineteen or twenty years old, wearing an old parka with an artificial fur hood.

The kid smiled. "I thought you were an Eskimo with your furs and dog team."

"Eskimos are little bitty short guys." Les introduced himself. "What are you doing out here by yourself?"

The kid explained that he was a college student from California. He had come to Alaska in order to get some firsthand experience to write a thesis about winter in the Arctic. He was on his way to Manley Hot Springs.

"You're sixty miles from Manley!" Les exclaimed. "You want me to give you a lift on the sled?"

"I'm okay. Really I am, Mr. Cobb."

Freedom on the frontier meant having the right to make your own decisions without being second-guessed or coerced by others for your own good. Les thought it a goofy reason for a kid to be out here alone, but even if he wanted to strip off all his clothes and walk from Nome to Fairbanks, he had the right to be a fool. Greenhorn *chechakos*, which we Cobbs had been not so long ago, often failed to recognize the awesome power of North Country nature. The north was totally dispassionate in its cruelty.

"If you're sure . . . ?" Les said, then continued his journey home.

When Les told me of the encounter, I chewed him out roundly. "You shouldn't have left him out there by himself. Don't you remember what it almost did to you?"

"What should I have done, Norma? Kidnap him?"

"It's suicide."

"It's *his* life." That macho bushman attitude!

I couldn't get the kid off my mind for two days. I prayed for the safety of this stranger I had never met. I kept thinking of how Les had been lost in the storm and almost perished. Finally, I could take it no longer. I asked Les to run an errand to Manley.

"On your way to the trading post," I casually suggested, "why don't you take the long route to the Top of the World and check on that skier?"

"That's a two-day trip! He should be in Manley by now anyhow."

"What if he *isn't*?"

Les relented. "If it'll make you feel better, Norma . . ."

I usually got him to do what I wanted, *usually*, if I kept at him long enough.

He hitched the dogs and took off. Up on the high snow- and wind-blown flats, he cut the trail the skier should have taken to Manley. He turned the team down it and followed it for a number of miles, expecting nothing more than a long roundabout trip to the trading post.

There was new snow of four or five inches. Captain swerved off the trail to avoid a snow-covered hummock blocking it.

"*Whoa!*"

The mound of snow looked like a grave. Wind had cleared the snow down to a small patch of green-brown fabric underneath. Les dropped to his knees and pawed away the snow until he came to a sleeping bag, an old one torn and patched as though it had been well used. He unzipped it. There was the kid. Les would never have seen him if he hadn't been lying across the trail. He seemed to be frozen solid. His face was so pale it blended with the snow and was cold to the touch.

"The poor dumb bastard is dead," Les said to his dogs. Men who spent long periods of time alone in the wilderness in the company of animals soon learned to talk to them. "We might as well gather up the carcass and haul it to town."

He dragged the body still inside its sleeping bag to his sled and started to hoist it aboard. He hesitated when he thought he saw it move. He looked closer. An eyelid fluttered, as gently as the pulse of a butterfly's wing. He quickly felt for a pulse. Found it. Weak and fluttery, but the kid was still alive. His lips moved stiffly; he tried to speak.

"He ain't dead!" Les informed the dogs, and immediately went to work reviving the kid. He rubbed the body vigorously inside the sleeping bag, attempting to restore circulation.

The kid murmured, slowing coming around. After a while, he opened his eyes. It took them another while to focus.

Les quickly built a fire next to the sleeping bag. Its warmth gradually revived the kid and returned him to full life. It still took another hour before he started eating a two-pound bag of Snickers candy bars Les had; he needed them for their life-restoring energy.

When he could talk again, the kid hesitantly explained, "After I saw you that day and you left, I got real sick and couldn't go on. All I had left was a one-pound can of Crisco lard. I ate that until it ran out. If you hadn't come along again . . . I could have died . . ."

"Yes," Les agreed. Another hour and he *would* have been dead.

The student ate every one of the Snickers bars as he rode the sled the rest of the way to Manley.

"You know that boy out there?" Les said to me later. "He's on his way back to California."

Months passed before I discovered how Les had actually saved the boy's life.

59

We all missed at least something from our old lives. For me it was indoor plumbing and other women with whom to talk. For Les, it was *football*. He was a big fan of the Denver Broncos. It pained him not to be able to tune in *Monday Night Football* or watch a college game on Sunday afternoons. Newspapers with the scores would have had to be delivered by airplane. It surprised me the lengths to which my husband the football fan went in order to watch a game.

He bought a tiny battery-powered TV set with some of the Prudhoe Bay money, but received no reception at the cabin because of the surrounding mountains. He wanted to watch a particular Denver play-off game. He got up early, helped me with cabin chores, then drew on his parka, hood, gloves, and boots and hitched dogs to the sled.

"I *am* watching that game today," he vowed.

I prepared him a thermos of coffee and a sackful of snacks. A regular guy getting ready for the afternoon game. He took off mushing the dogs to Elephant Mountain, from the top of which, on a clear day, you could almost see Fairbanks. Its peak offered direct line-of-sight TV reception.

He located a good spot at the top, unhitched and fed the dogs to keep them quiet and comfortable, then got cozy himself among furs and blankets on the sled. It was snowing lightly, big flakes dusting the furs across his lap. He poured himself a cup of coffee and plugged in the TV to his freshly charged battery. He lay back to enjoy himself.

Kickoff!

Three hours later he came dragging into the cabin gnashing his teeth like a bear.

"Your best dog die or something?" I asked him.

"It was two minutes to the end of the game," he groused. "Denver is three points behind, ten to goal and last down . . ."

It was almost too painful for him to go on.

"And . . . ?" I prompted.

He flung his arms in frustration. "The damn battery went out."

MOST PLACES NORTH of Anchorage were unable to watch the Super Bowl *live* during the 1970s. Instead, the Fairbanks TV station used what was called "tape delay." A videotape of the game was flown to Fairbanks where it was aired on the following Sunday. Super Bowl Sunday for most Alaskans came a week late.

Les proved no hardships were beyond endurance for a dedicated fan. Determined to watch the tape-delay Super Bowl, he packed camping gear and food onto the dogsled and, with a jaunty wave and that grin of his shining through his frosted beard, headed toward Fairbanks, a hundred and fifty miles away. Because of the rugged terrain, he only covered about sixty miles a day. He camped nights by turning the sled upside down and building a fire in front to reflect its warmth on him.

He arrived in Fairbanks early on Sunday morning of the game and made his way to the winter home of our Eureka artist friend Rose Stowell and her husband, Charlie. Like quite a number of bush people, Rose and Charlie wintered over in the city, returning to their homesteads after breakup in the spring.

The game was scheduled to start at nine A.M. At eight, it was announced that the Super Bowl would not be aired this Sunday after all. Severe ice fog prevented the landing of the plane delivering the videotape. The game would be aired the following Sunday instead.

More frustrated than ever, Les mushed his dog team back to Minook Valley. Six days in the bush traveling to watch a football game that never aired. He looked travel-worn and gaunt when he drove up to the cabin, dogs barking and happy to be home. I couldn't help laughing at the woebegone expression on his face. I had already heard the news via *Pipeline of the North*. I had also learned the score.

"Want to know how the game turned out?" I teased.

"Norma, I don't want to talk about it."

"I can give you the score."

"Norma!"

He stomped into the cabin and flung off his parka. He went to the window and watched it snow.

60

Breakup came early that year, in April, 1978 with its threat of flooding. One morning a tremendous boom shook the cabin to its foundations, rattling dishes in the cupboard and knocking a coffee cup off the table. The kids fled from breakfast as though shot from a row of catapults. I screamed as debris rained down on the cabin roof.

Racing outside, we were confronted by a great billowing cloud roiling up out of the creek behind the house. Ice and water pelted us from out of the cloud. We rushed back to the shelter of the porch, where Les had knowingly remained. He laughed uproariously. Dynamiting a channel through the glaciering in the creek without informing the rest of us was his idea of a great joke. Andrew Farnsworth almost killed himself when he tripped running out of his cabin and fell facedown in melt-off mud. He appreciated Les's warped humor even less than we did.

"He should be locked up for the safety of everyone in Alaska," he grumbled, stomping back to his cabin with his sissy dog Zack.

I never stayed angry at Les for long. After all, the dynamite served its purpose of opening up the creek and saving our home without all the labor last year's breakup required.

With breakup behind us, it was time to get back to work on the tourist cabins and airstrip. Andrew's attitude improved little with the coming of spring. In fact, he seemed more rude and uncooperative than ever. Cabin fever had turned him from a mild, meek professor-type into the Grinch who stole Christmas. Les had picked up some disturbing news while in Manley.

"When Andrew was over at Joe Pumper's dog-sitting last week, he was bad-mouthing the Cobbs up one side and down the other," Les confided to me. "He said we were cheating him on the deal he made with us, that we were isolating him in his cabin and having nothing to do with him."

"That's his own doing!" I cried in righteous self-defense. "It was his fault that he sat over there hibernating all winter like a bear with a toothache. He's flipped his lid."

"Apparently, he's bad-talking like that to anybody who'll listen."

I was more stunned than miffed. It turned out my uneasiness about him was proving justified. We had taken Andrew in, provided food and a place to live, tried to treat him like a member of the family, and in exchange—*this*. So far, Les had squeezed very little work out of him. What was it about so many people, I pondered, who came out to start new lives but never seemed to leave behind old habits of blaming others for their own problems and shortcomings? On the frontier, you accepted people at face value, whereupon it became up to them to prove themselves one way or another. So many simply failed to prove out.

Les's straightforward nature never left anything in limbo. He confronted Andrew. The good doctor dug in defensively and acted insulted. Les finally issued him an ultimatum.

"Either you work this summer to finish out our contract—or you move. We'll pay you for any personal expenses you've put into the cabin."

"I will do neither," Andrew retorted. "This is my cabin."

"Not until you finish paying for it."

I had to hand it to Lester for demonstrating remarkable restraint. He neither challenged Andrew to a duel nor blew up his cabin. Somewhere in Andrew's befuddled thinking, however, he must have realized it lay in his best interest not to push Les too far. He let Les cool off for a few hours, then ventured over.

"I'm sorry, Les. I'll go ahead and work this summer."

I accepted the settlement along with Les, although I was suspicious of Andrew's continuing irrational behavior.

In the bartering that went on in frontier communities where cash was not always plentiful, Les acquired two weeks' use of a D-4 Caterpillar tractor after repairing it for Rose and Charlie Stowell, who used it in their gold mining operation. With Andrew deciding to work and with the D-4, we accomplished more in April and May than we had the entire previous summer. I even learned to operate the Cat. Norma Cobb, Cat skinner. Two more tourist cabins went up. We named them Minook Cabin and Lazy Man. Andrew's was called Oh, Brother!

We cleared a site for the *real* house we intended to construct one day. It was located on the opposite side of Minook Creek, on a rise of high ground in the vee-junction of Minook and Lost Creek away from the breakup flood plain. We then cleared the flats east of the creek for building an airstrip.

"One of these days we'll have our own airplane," Les casually remarked.

Andrew's attitude improved little. It wasn't so much what he said outright that caused concern. Les said the professor reminded him of a dog who never bit you face on, but instead slunk off into the shadows and waited for you to turn your back. He deliberately did annoying little things like chopping down trees Les wanted saved or stealing beer left chilling in the creek. I became anxious at the thought of spending another winter with Andrew as our neighbor, especially if Les had to leave the valley for a few weeks to work. Cabin fever did awful things to people, caused them to behave in insane and violent ways. Maybe it was this coming winter that would turn Andrew into an axe murderer.

In June, Andrew's girlfriend Ellen came up for a week's visit. She was a plump dishwater blonde. Les, never being one for diplomacy, described her as "all ass and mouth." It was while she was visiting that things came to a head. It started with a note I found in laundry Andrew asked me to do.

The note appeared in the truncated format a professor might use while preparing for a lecture. Evidently, Andrew scribbled it during a conversation between him and Gary Westbrook when they drove to Fairbanks to pick up Ellen at the airport. It seemed Andrew had attempted to file for ownership of his cabin and the one acre of our land upon which it sat. Unable to do that, he and Gary located a clause in our BLM homesteading contract that specifically stated that a settler could neither hire anyone nor make deals with outsiders to prove up his homestead. He had to do all the work himself—or lose his land. Apparently, that clause prevented rich people from "homesteading" and hiring someone else to live on the land and prove it out for them.

Gary Westbrook and Andrew were actually plotting to take our homestead away from us. I was both outraged and heartbroken. We always tried to be good neighbors and good Christians, to do unto others. We wanted no trouble with anyone. Yet, in this country, if you turned the other cheek, someone read it as weakness and slugged you with a ball bat.

I showed the note to Les, then made him cool off before letting him confront Andrew and his girlfriend. He offered to buy Andrew out, pay him for what work he had done—but Andrew was going to have to leave our valley.

"I'll do as I damn well please," Andrew snapped back.

Les's shoulders rolled forward and he thrust out his beard. "If that's the way you want it . . . ?"

Andrew slammed the door in Les's face.

To outsiders, Les and I might have seemed like violent people because of the "Hatchet Lady" episode and Les's run-in with Heckle and Jeckle. It wasn't that at all. In a land where there was virtually no law, you had to be strong enough and willing enough to enforce justice yourself. Either that or turn tail, give up everything you'd worked for, and run.

It was precisely because we wanted to *prevent* violence that we returned to the Oh, Brother! cabin well prepared for the confrontation. We drove up on the Bombardier. I got off with a rifle and hid behind a tree. Still hoping to avoid trouble, Les and Sid left their pistols on the Bombardier while they knocked on the door.

Ellen was the one who got mouthy. Les finally told her to shut up and mind her own business.

"Look, Andrew," Les reasoned, "we've read the note and know what you're planning. It won't work. You have a choice. Either do what you have to do and get off, or we're kicking you off."

Andrew flared. "I'm doing neither one!" He made a move for the gun he kept on a peg next to the door.

I stepped out from behind the tree with my rifle pointed. "Don't do it, Andrew," I called out. I was trembling inside, but I couldn't let him see that.

"Bring our guns, Norma," Les ordered.

I kept Andrew and Ellen covered with the rifle while I handed holsters and belts to my men. Les and Sid buckled the revolvers around their waists.

"I'm not accusing you of anything," Les said with remarkable control, "but you're stirring up trouble and we don't need that. We're hauling all your things out to the road on the Bombardier. You decide what we owe you for your work and send us a bill. We're not trying to rip you off."

Andrew and Ellen and sissy Zack rode out on the first load. Even the dog looked sullen and defeated. Les removed all the shells from Andrew's gun. He deposited the hired hand, his girlfriend, and the dog where the road began at Joseph Creek, then came back and hauled out their remaining belongings. We never saw them again.

I felt distraught and shaky. What would I have done if Andrew had kept going for his gun? Would I really have shot him? I thanked God we didn't have to find out. On the frontier, you had to be willing to fight for what was yours.

Not surprisingly, that summer turned out to be the Westbrooks' last in the valley. They left without saying goodbye and never returned, undoubtedly doubly embarrassed due to the wife swapping thing and now this. We would never again have neighbors, the Homestead Act having expired. From now on, only the Cobbs and our Kernels—and perhaps the Bushman—permanently occupied Minook Valley.

PART IV

Not in the clamour of the crowded street,
Not in the shouts and plaudits of the throng,
But in ourselves, are triumph and defeat.

—Henry Wadsworth Longfellow

61

We were into our fourth year of homesteading, 1978, with less than one year remaining to prove out our claim. The airstrip was almost finished, six cabins in addition to the main house now sat on the property, waiting for the first influx of tourists. They were utilized in the meantime by hunters Les either recruited himself for his guiding business or who were referred to him by his licensed mentor. The kids were sprouting up like the willows along the creek. It was hard to believe Sid was fourteen and the twins almost seven. Cara and Cora remembered almost nothing of life outside Minook Valley. Tommy recalled only a bit more.

Now that our homesteading requirements were almost completed and ready for government inspection, Les took his great energy and spent much of it in seeking gold. I knew it was a fool's pursuit, and told him so, but he was a man who had to have challenges. Pete and he worked on and off for large mines in the Wiseman area or puttered around on claims they acquired from old Harry Leonard, trying to make a strike on their own. Pete supported his family from one of his mines, but not very well. He would have done much better taking a minimum-wage job somewhere.

Les had gold fever, had it both acute and chronic. More and more I saw him becoming old Harry in another fifty or sixty years. He dreamed of gold.

"I make more gold dreaming of it nights," he readily admitted, "than I'll probably ever make otherwise."

He tried gold panning and hand shoveling, but the yellow metal eluded him. In addition to his Slate Creek digs, John Shilling owned a claim at Granite Creek on the other side of Norky's Mountain from us. He offered to sell it to Les and Pete if they wanted to work it.

"If I found enough gold in the valley to make wages," Les attempted to convince me, "it would save me ever having to go outside to find work."

I could only say "Amen!" to that.

Les and Pete hiked over to Granite Creek and dug test holes and checked around before turning down John's offer. It was not good gold ground.

The major characteristic of gold, other than its alluring appearance, I learned through my husband, was its dense weight and its reluctance to react with other elements, staying stubbornly to itself instead. When the earth was created, gold began as gold and remained gold, unlike diamonds. It moved upward from its originating cauldron by squeezing through fissures in rock formations, depositing itself here and there in arbitrary and diverse patterns. It was never found in great concentrations like lead or iron ore or coal, but scattered itself so widely that no logical reasoning explained its placement.

Gold was found under two dramatically different circumstances. First, it might rest well below the surface of the earth in concentrations laid down millions of years ago, like copper and lead or other metallic elements. It was commonly found in quartz rock in flecks so minute the unpracticed eye scarcely recognized them. A tremendous value might be discovered in quartz whose cross sections revealed traces of gold no larger than widely scattered pinpoints. This could be mined, crushed, and sluiced with water. Mining gold like that required courage to burrow deep into the earth, dynamite to break the quartz loose, and a ready supply of flowing water to sluice the crushed rock for its treasure.

The second circumstance under which you found gold was called "placer mining." Over millions of years, the upper crust of the earth shifted and rose and fell, exposing to the elements rock containing minute veins of gold. Abrasion took place. Freezing winters fractured the quartz.

Incessantly dripping water further broke down the rock. Gravel at the bottoms of swift-moving streams acted like sandpaper on wood. Volcanic displacement coughed to the surface new deposits to be abraded. Gold, being heavier than rock, fell to the bottoms of streams and came to rest somewhere—in ancient gravel bars of now extinct rivers, in black sand, in low hills, along existing streambeds like Minook Creek.

"There's still gold in the valley," Les insisted. "I only need the right equipment."

EACH YEAR, Anchorage hosted a three-day-long Fur Rendezvous. Susan Butcher and several other dog mushers we knew in the area were going to run in the Fur Rondy races. Sid intended helping native friends from Rampart with their dogs; in another year or so he anticipated racing himself. The family trekked out of the valley and enjoyed a holiday in Anchorage, touring the arts and crafts shows, snacking on hot dogs and smoked salmon, and peddling the fur articles I had made over the winter. Les purchased a six-inch suction dredge and sluice box for the heart-stopping sum of $1,500.

"It's an investment," he rationalized.

"It's an investment in foolishness."

I wasn't won over. We knew too many sourdoughs who spent their lives in pursuit of gold, only to end up beaten and broken. Joe Pumper and Jeff Stoddard had been working their claims for more than ten years and barely made eats. I figured Les might pay off that $1,500 *investment* by about 1990 or so.

A dredge and sluice worked on a very simple placer-mining principle. A hose, in this case six inches in diameter, was attached to a gas engine to create suction. Gravel was thus sucked out of a stream and ran with a constant flow of water across the sluice box. The heavier gold particles and flakes settled against a series of ribs built into the bottom surface of the box where they could be harvested.

The entire thirty-three-mile length of Minook Valley had already been claim-staked for mining. A state mining claim encompassed twenty acres, a federal claim forty acres. The only places left available for mining were the streambeds themselves. Les and Sid joined up with a couple of Washington loggers, Warren Waldbillig and Jerry Banner, whom they met at the Fur Rondy, and formed a partnership. They stretched a tent at the junction of Minook and Slate Creeks, about seventeen miles downstream from home, and launched their gold-mining enterprise. I stayed home with the smaller kids. For days at a time, I only saw Les and Sid when they marched in to drop off their dirty laundry, eat a home-cooked meal, get a haircut, and pick up supplies.

Dredge mining was hard, cold, dangerous work. Sid's young shoulders and chest broadened and he developed a macho, can-do attitude. Just like Lester's. I scarcely faulted him. The fourteen-year-old kid did a man's work.

The temperature of the water in Minook Creek averaged thirty-four degrees, with an occasional spell when it warmed up to thirty-six. Dredging required the miners to be in the water with the dredging hose for hours at a time. Even though they wore wet suits, they came out so stiff from cold they could barely walk.

At times, rain in the mountains caused flash floods, raising the creek so rapidly that it surprised the miners and threatened to wash them and their equipment downstream. Even on the best days, they toiled eight to twelve hours at backbreaking labor. For most of that summer, providing the equipment functioned properly and required no emergency repairs, they averaged one-half ounce of gold a day. The gold market rate was $90 an ounce. It didn't take a mathematical genius to cipher out that $45 worth of gold divided four ways was $11.25 per man per day, about a dollar an hour.

"Getting rich yet?" I chided my husband whenever I saw him.

One afternoon Les was thigh-deep in the cold creek suctioning gravel for the sluice when he spotted something large and shimmering in the water. He picked up a gold nugget nearly as large as the end of his thumb. He stared at it.

"Look at *this*!" he shouted, displaying it for Sid and the two men. They abandoned their stations and came running. "I bet it's almost an ounce!"

In the excitement, he dropped the nugget back into the creek. Warren and Jerry jumped into the water, followed by Sid. The four of them dived and splashed frantically about until they recovered the nugget. This time

Les clasped it in his hand until he waded ashore and secured it against further mishap. He could hardly wait to get home to show it to me.

"Honey, this is our first. I want you to have it as a present for good luck—and because I love you."

What else could you do with a man like that except hug him?

62

Timber wolves were decimating caribou and moose populations. Contrary to claims by conservationists and animal rightists, wolves in Alaska were not endangered. They reproduced so rapidly that they often ate themselves out of a food source. Since grizzlies also lived off caribou and moose, feeding competition drove them off their range and reduced their numbers. Les was concerned about it since his hunting guide business depended upon plentiful supplies of grizzlies, black bears, caribou, and moose.

He and the other Alaskan guides petitioned the Game Department to permit wolf hunting to thin out the packs and help nature keep predators in balance with prey. The Game Department dispatched a woman wildlife biologist to Manley to meet with area guides. Les found her to be the typical liberal transplanted New Englander morally opposed to all hunting, but especially opposed to the concept that anyone should find pleasure in it. Self-righteous and opinionated, looking down her nose at this gathering of rough backwoodsmen, she stood up and declared that she would recommend wolves be live-trapped and surgically *sterilized* to control their numbers rather than allow them to be hunted.

Les and the other guides shook their heads in stunned disbelief. It seemed you couldn't escape, even up here, the Bambi attitudes sweeping the nation—that hunting was an evil to be gradually eliminated. Les shot to his feet and responded with a rowdy rebuke that brought down the gathering in spasms of mocking laughter.

"Lady, them wolves are *eating* them caribou, not *screwing* them."

Many people did not understand hunting. Hunting was not merely the bloody act of killing something. It involved a complex ritual of the hunt that was essentially male and that extended into the extreme depths of mankind's beginnings. Male comradery, being in the wilds—that was the essence and purpose of hunting, not the killing. The vast majority of outdoorsmen held a vested interest in preserving wildlife and wildland and fought with their time and money to ensure that preservation. Les always said that when hunting was outlawed, it wouldn't be long afterward before moose pastures were paved over and bears were locked up to "protect" them.

Although Les hunted bears, he both liked and respected them. He insisted he never wanted to live in a world without bears in it. They were dangerous beasts, to be sure. If you stayed in bear country long enough, if you didn't watch out and stay prepared, bears had a pretty even chance of getting you sooner or later. Even a single spine-chilling encounter with one of the big animals was enough to send most people packing back to a climate where the most dangerous transaction was trying to cross a busy street. Yet, Les always said he felt safer trapped on an island with a mad grizzly than he did in a New York subway station trapped with muggers and dope fiends. At least in facing a grizzly he was allowed to carry his forty-four and fight back.

"Honey," Les said one day during hunting season, "I don't care whether a bear gets me or I die of old age, what I want you to do is dump my ol' carcass out in the woods and let the bears eat me. That way I'll be a part of this country from now on."

LES'S GUIDE BUSINESS, not gold mining, supported us. Six bear hunters showed up that fall of 1978, among them a California attorney named Mel Najarian. Mel was a tall, slender man of about fifty with a thin face and a manicured iron-gray beard that made him look distinguished and urbane. Like many of our clients, he became a personal friend who returned year after year.

Mel thirsted for all pioneer knowledge. He wanted to know everything about the plants and trees and minerals and animals and seemed enthralled with the pioneering way of life. He was an Armenian, he said, who became wealthy and very successful in America. Our "old ways" reminded him of when he was a kid growing up.

Hunting season started with two near tragedies and ended with one. Eleven-year-old Sean was driving the Bombardier when one of its tracks flipped up a log and smacked him on the head, knocking him cold. I took four sutures in the wound to repair it.

The next morning as the hunters were unloading gear and fuel barrels from the Bombardier at the end of the road past Joseph Creek, Sam Hedstrom caught the ring finger of his left hand between the rims of two barrels and ripped flesh down to the bone. Since Sam chose not to make the long trip to Fairbanks for emergency surgery and therefore lose out on the hunting, Les volunteered to take care of it on our dining room table.

He first plied Sam with enough hot whiskey toddies to make him both deliriously happy and immune to pain. Then he cut off the mangled wedding band and carefully stitched the ragged wound so neatly and professionally that the doctor who later looked at it said he couldn't have done better himself.

Bear hunting was poor. Les blamed it on the wolf overpopulation. The six sportsmen finally bagged a single black bear. Two of them, Dick and Roger, along with our Sean, stalked the bear for most of a morning before they realized to their horror that the bear was also stalking *them.* When he charged, he roared out of the woods with mind-boggling speed—directly at Sean. Once again, poor Sean found himself in the pathway of an enraged bear.

Dick and Roger were at opposite angles from the beast, with Sean between them. Neither dared fire for fear of hitting Sean.

Sean fell belly-down to the earth. His quick thinking allowed the hunters to open up, dropping the attacking bear before it reached my boy. Although Sean was unharmed, the incident rekindled his old fears that the bears had it in for him.

Tanning bear hides for hunters was a good way for me to earn extra money. Mel helped me with butchering the carcass, then fleshing and cleaning the heavy pelt. Elbow-deep in bear blood and gore, I smiled at the picture I must have created. Little hometown girl Norma Cobb from Wichita. Well, pardon me, Toto. I certainly wasn't back in Kansas anymore.

63

A client friend sent his twenty-two-year-old son to Alaska to hunt moose with Les. Stewart was soft-looking around the middle, pale-skinned from lack of sunshine, and so uncoordinated he found it difficult getting into a canoe without overturning it. The father asked Les to "make a man out of Stewart" by taking him into the wilderness and forcing him to confront hardship and challenge. Les agreed, but shook his head with doubt. The kid, Les said, was a "sissy."

They set out by canoe down the Tanana River. It was a glacier river, dull milky white in color with a good current. It emptied into the Yukon. Two days out, they spotted a nice bull moose browsing on a low alder-and-willow island. The moose saw them at the same time and disappeared into the buckbrush.

"Let me out at this end of the island," Les instructed. "You take the canoe down to the other end. I'll go through the brush and run him out to you. You shoot him. Got it?"

Stewart trembled all over from excitement. He nodded. Les got out of the canoe and looked back.

"Calm down," he soothed.

Les heard a splash after making it halfway across the island. He took off running, assuming the moose had gone into the water to escape. Instead, he found Stewart standing dripping up to his waist in the river. In the excitement, he had actually fallen out of the canoe—and the canoe was heading downriver all by itself, pushed at a good clip by the current. The canoe contained everything they needed in order to survive—food, sleeping bags, rifles, tent. It would take days, maybe weeks, for them to get out of there on foot—if they made it at all.

"Grab the canoe, you idiot!" Les bellowed.

The kid frantically stripped to his underwear so he could swim. He was too late. The canoe was on its way to the Yukon.

Les also stripped and took off barefooted in the rind of mud that laced the stream. The canoe hung up on a gravel bar. Les dived into the river and swam for it. The canoe dislodged and continued its escape.

Yelling at each other, running and swimming from gravel bar to gravel bar, the two men pursued the fleeing boat. They were thus occupied when a sightseeing airplane containing a load of tourists from Fairbanks appeared flying low upriver out of the horizon.

The tourists received an astonishing eyeful of one half-naked man chasing another half-naked man down the river out in the middle of a desolate wilderness. What the tourists must have thought! The plane nosed abruptly upward and climbed rapidly. *Don't look now, Mildred!*

Later, after it was over and the canoe secured, Les sat down on a log and laughed until tears streamed down his bearded cheeks. Stewart grinned sheepishly.

64

Death and a near-deadly accident combined to drop a gold mine into our laps. It began when Ira Weisner died in his bathtub upstairs above his trading post in Rampart. Because he lived alone, a couple of days passed before natives broke into the post and found him. They ransacked the store. What was left of his estate went on the auction block. We bought the old-fashioned bathtub in which he died; no one else wanted it. A salmon fisherman from the Kenai Peninsula ended up with Ira's gold claim on Hoosier Creek, a couple of miles into Minook Valley from Rampart. Ira had worked the ground on his claim on and off over the years but had done poorly. Les found the big gold nugget in that area.

Don Lucas, the fisherman, was about sixty years old, a string bean of a Mormon with lots of energy and a dream to give up commercial fishing and try his hand at mining. He hired Les and Sid and our Bombardier to haul mining supplies for him down Minook Creek to his site. He intended launching his enterprise in a big way.

"Everybody says there's no gold there worth mining," Don confided in Les.

Les disagreed. Over the past several years, he and Pete Pasquali had spent a lot of time around Wiseman with old Harry Leonard. Les had listened and absorbed a geologist's amount of mining lore from the old man. As he always said, practical education was more valuable than "book learning" alone.

"I think the reason Ira and everybody else who tried never found gold," Les theorized, "is because nobody ever went below the false bottom. Look at the grain in the surrounding hills. It's a flood plain with Hoosier running downhill toward Minook, but the bedrock runs downhill *the opposite way.* If you divert Hoosier Creek into another channel and mine below the bottom down to real bedrock, I think you'll find gold. You just have to stay with it."

Les helped Don move in a D-8 Caterpillar tractor, suction dredges, sluices, and other equipment when he wasn't busy with improvements on our homestead to ready it for government inspection. In the middle of these preparations, Don's wife died of cancer. Tragedy followed tragedy that winter while Don was busy on contract work at Prudhoe Bay. He was driving his Suburban along Haul Road, rounding a curve blinded by piled-up snow when he collided head-on into a snow grader. One man died. Don was rushed to the hospital in Fairbanks unconscious with head and other injuries. From intensive care, he sent word through *Pipeline of the North* and CB radio that he wanted to talk to Les.

"I'm going to be laid up for a long time," he began from his hospital bed. "It'll take years and miracles to repair me. I'm concerned about the Hoosier Creek Mine. Do you still think there's pay dirt?"

"There's gold," Les affirmed.

"Do you believe in it enough to consider a proposition?"

We acquired 30 percent ownership in the Hoosier Creek Mine. Later, that became 60 percent, with 40 percent going to the Lucas family in royalties. Don needed the income if Les could pull it through—and Lord knew the Cobbs' trip sock always required cash.

Mining started in April and ended in September or October when the stream froze. The operation began small that spring of 1979. Les hired Ralph Pike and Tony Yenson, two roughnecks he had met during our pipelining days. With their help and that of Sid and Sean, he hauled in fuel, pipe, and other supplies. The Bombardier often broke down under heavy loads over the rough terrain. It was wearing labor and Les drove everyone, himself most of all, to his limits.

Old-time miners and prospectors laughed at his efforts. "Thar ain't no gol' out there, but you can't tell that greenhorn nothin'. That young buck movin' in like this, don't know nothin.' "

Talk never deterred Lester Cobb and his overactive thyroid. He confronted a new challenge. He didn't care how much work it took, how many hours a day he had to labor. The finding of gold possessed his waking hours and in countless dreams he struck it rich.

Clearing ground, freighting, diverting Hoosier Creek in order to begin digging down to bedrock consumed most of that first season. Using the D-8, the little group of miners dozed soil and gravel into stockpiles, then used hydraulic water to move it down through sluice boxes. Their first efforts produced twenty-two ounces of gold at $90 an ounce—less than $2,000. Les sunk $600 of that into a new dredge and generated sixty ounces of gold—$5,400. Not enough to cover expenses, but he proved his theory. Hoosier Creek at least had gold potential. I even began believing in it; Les's optimism was contagious.

His main problem was investment capital. Don Lucas supported most of the operation, but his funds were also limited due to hospital bills and his recuperation. Les believed in the mine so much he was willing to sink everything we owned—or would ever own—into it. Gold prices were going up and would eventually rise to more than $600 an ounce from a low of $90. At such prices, those first mere twenty-two ounces of gold would have been worth more than $13,000.

"We have to hurry," Les said. "Get it now and make the money while we can. It's our big chance, Norma. We don't want to ever look back one day and know we had the chance but turned it down. I need to get bigger, faster."

"Are you sure, Les?"

"Trust me, honey."

He met with Mel Najarian, the well-to-do lawyer-hunter with whom we had become friends.

"I need to buy another Caterpillar," he proposed. "Banks won't loan bushers money."

Mel thought about it a serious minute. "How much do you need?"

"Fifty thousand dollars."

"That's a lot of money. What do I get in exchange?"

"You name the interest rate and I'll give it back to you in gold."

Gold was a tax deduction until you turned it into actual money.

"You're that confident you'll find gold?" Mel probed.

"I *will* find it. I've already found some."

Mel took out a pen and checkbook. That fall when he came to Minook Valley to hunt, he mused, "You know, Les, you're the first man I've ever loaned money to without a twelve-page contract to protect every dime."

The confidence touched Les and left him almost speechless. "That's . . . that's very nice," he finally managed, embarrassed.

"It's not *nice*," Mel said. "What it does is say something about you as a man. That I would trust you with fifty thousand dollars and no signature."

I prayed Les was right and there was gold in Minook Valley. If the mine failed, the Cobbs lost everything, including our homestead.

65

To everything there is a season, as it says in the Bible. Life, it seemed to me during those philosophical times when I took my strolls alone by the creek and pondered and talked to God, was a series of seasons, each coming in its own good time and each following the other in its place. We were into what I believed to be our fourth season as homesteaders.

The first season, our springtime that now seemed so long ago, began with dreams and almost nothing else in a haunted, rented farmhouse in Colorado. They led us to Alaska and to Minook Valley. Spring turned into a summer of trials and tribulations and challenges during which God asked that we prove ourselves. Summer became autumn and a gathering time; we gathered our lives and our resources and we built a life in the valley. Now it was the fourth season, the winter of our homesteading, when life consolidated and took a look at our accomplishments, when it took into account all that we had done and prepared to bloom into an ever better spring.

Les's Hoosier Creek Mine started to pay off. At least gold was high enough that the mine made expenses and provided wintering-over grub so Les didn't have to go outside the valley for work and leave the Kernels and me alone. I began to think Les might find gold after all.

"I need to get bigger, faster," became his new mantra.

Sid worked at the mine with Les; the younger children and I went into the farming business again with three goats for milk, a flock of laying hens for eggs, and a new batch of rabbits. We picked up the menagerie from friends on 49 Mile Elliott Highway and transported it by truck to the end of the road. The last eleven miles of the journey was by tracked Bombardier with all the animals and kids piled onto the back while I drove the slow familiar trail back to the homestead.

I assigned each kid his own particular chores with the animals. When Cara and Cora gathered our first nest of fresh eggs, we all thought we must have died and gone to heaven. We had eaten powdered eggs for so long. To Sean fell much of the labor in preparing for the stock's own wintering over. We built a snug, low-profile shed to protect all from the wind and weather, then used kerosene lamps inside as a source of heat to take off the chill. Preventing the animals' water from freezing became the real challenge; it necessitated Sean and Tommy making trips to the water hole every day. They soon learned to keep a bucket of water inside the house and portion it out to the stock several times throughout the day.

I sometimes wondered what happened to the Bushman. We experienced his presence a number of times during our first three or four years in the valley. Only Tommy ever saw him again; he glanced up from getting water and saw him walking through the forest. Otherwise, we only heard or smelled him—the sound of something heavy striding through the woods past the cabin, preceded always by his strong, offensive odor.

Late one night Les was hiking home from a hunting trip. A terrible screech echoed across the darkened valley and brought him up short. It sounded human but, at the same time, *in*human. Les felt as though he had been dipped in ice water.

"I don't know what the scream was," he said, "but I do know that none of the animals I've ever seen make a sound like that, not even the lynx."

Bushman was a scary being at first, until I realized he could have hurt us anytime if he really *wanted* to. Contrary to the Indian legends about his stealing human children, he never offered a direct threat to the Cobb Kernels. I concluded that he was merely curious about us—a big male on his food-chain route who happened to encounter us. He observed for a few years, then moved on. We never saw him again.

Years later a scientific expedition came through looking for signs of Bigfoot and questioning locals about him. I doubt they uncovered anything. If you went searching for Bushman, you never found him. You had to let him find you.

Of more immediate and continuing threat were bears. You never got used to them, not really. You simply learned to live with their presence and to stay prepared.

One night at Hoosier Creek Mine, Les stepped outside the little clapboard bunkhouse to use the bathroom. He was going about his business in the open silvery light of a summer night when he spotted a male grizzly and a female strolling by about seventy yards away. A sighting like that was enough to cut off water.

The male glanced casually at his girlfriend, as though to say, "Get a load a this." Then he turned without warning and charged. Although Les wore only his longhandles, he habitually carried his handgun everywhere, even to the bathroom. No time to run for the safety of the bunkhouse. He drew his forty-four and opened up. He laid his first two shots in the monster's right and left shoulders. The beast flinched, but that was about it. The next two shots punched into his back. He came on. The fifth and final shot parted the griz's backbone and stopped him. He skidded to a stop at Les's toenails.

Although mortally wounded, he was still not dead. He couldn't get up because of his severed spinal column. Sid reloaded Les's gun and finished off the bear. Les sat down and nursed nerves and fatigue for two hours before he was able to rise again.

"I know they're going to get me sooner or later," he commented, "but if I had my rathers, I'd rather it be later."

Home schooling progressed. It was a struggle, but my kids were going to be educated. The airstrip grew to a length of nine hundred feet. It was only a bit wider than the wings of a bush plane and left no room for error, but we now had a means for tourists to reach us—if they were hardy souls willing to have an adventure. Once we had the money to buy our own airplane, the Cobbs would be linked to the outside world.

Our new cabin, our *real* house, took shape on the rise above the flood plain. It was going to be big and it was going to be beautiful. Les and Sid and their mining crew, which now numbered three hired hands, worked on the cabin during mining breaks and during the better days of winter. The walls rose and remained up for three years before the roof went on.

The deadline came for proving out our homestead. One morning in 1979 the BLM field examiner walked in to check our improvements. We showed him all the cabins, sheds, campsites, barnyard, dog runs, and airstrip. He seemed impressed and took many photographs for his files. After all we had been through, the procedure seemed somehow anticlimactic.

"When will we know?" Les asked him.

"Probably not until next year," the examiner replied. "The evaluation takes time. But if I were you, I wouldn't worry about it. It's only routine from now on."

"If we make it," Les said in one of the nicest compliments he ever paid me, "we'll owe most of it to Norma. She has done things out of the ordinary. She's the one who held it together."

66

Lester Cobb never did anything the usual way. I should have become accustomed to him by now. First, he built the airstrip. He bought the airplane. *Then* he learned to fly.

An airplane was a necessity for anyone needing to move about in the bush with any speed. The mine was doing well by its third year of production; it required a constant resupply of machinery, provisions, and other materials, the obtaining of which necessitated Les's driving the slow Bombardier seventeen miles up Minook Creek to the homestead and then out of the valley to where the road began and our vehicles were parked. From road's beginning to Fairbanks and back was another two days' journey. All in all, if something malfunctioned at the mine and a new part was required, the mine could be shut down for two or three days. Les needed an airplane.

"Bigger and faster," he said.

His first aircraft was an ancient Aeronica Chief two-seater. Someone had to "prop" the propeller from outside to get it started. It was little more than a kite on wheels. A pilot flew it in and landed on our airstrip. Les taxied it up and down the airstrip to teach himself the controls. The eccentric Manley pilot who flew Sean to the hospital after his gunshot wound, B. J. Baker, offered Les some sound advice on flying the bush. There were certain rules to follow, he said: stay away from whirling props; always check your gas before you take off, circle any unknown landing strip first before you land, to look over the surface; if caught in a fog, never hesitate to sleep beside your plane rather than push your luck; keep all cargo securely tied down inside the plane in case you hit turbulence, which you *would* encounter in Alaska.

Young bucks who tore the place apart, challenging the far north in their frail aircraft, B. J. warned, invariably wound up dead.

"There are bold pilots, Les, and there are old pilots like me. But there ain't never been any old, bold pilots in Alaska."

Realizing that the Aeronica was too light to handle the mine's business, Les sold it and bought a Cessna 206, a three-hundred-horsepower single-engine, fuel-injected four-seater with a tricycle landing gear. He built a landing strip at the Hoosier Creek Mine and hired a pilot, Bob Coskins.

Things went along for a while; it was a real convenience for the mine to have a plane readily available. It afforded quick access to the Fairbanks hospital in case of injuries. Replacement parts for broken-down machinery were only hours away instead of days. The airplane, Les said, was paying for itself in preventing loss of production.

A dispute soon arose between the young pilot and Les, however. Bob wanted to stay in Fairbanks with the Cessna and fly out to the mine each morning. Les insisted the plane and pilot remain at Hoosier Creek in case they were needed in an emergency. The mine was operating twenty-four hours a day. The disagreement came to a head one afternoon when Bob flew Les to Fairbanks to pick up some equipment.

"I'm quitting, Les," Bob said after he landed the Cessna.

"If you're bluffing, trying to get your way," Les replied, thrusting out his beard and rolling his shoulders forward, "it ain't gonna work, pal. As far as I'm concerned, you're no longer on the payroll."

"But . . . how are you going to get back to the mine?"

"Leave that to me."

Les gathered up the Caterpillar parts he needed and returned to the airport. He knew the fundamentals of flying from having practiced on the airstrip with the Aeronica. He had also carefully observed Bob during their flights. After stowing his purchases, he climbed into the pilot's left seat, took a deep breath, cracked the throttle, turned on the ignition, and pressed the start button. The propeller caught and whirred smoothly.

"Well," he murmured to himself, "this is the day I learn to fly."

An hour later, young Sid looked up from working the sluice at the mine to observe the Cessna approaching the landing strip from upvalley. He straightened up to watch more closely when he realized the plane failed to make its usual smooth approach. It behaved more like a Canadian goose with a crippled wing than an aircraft. It porpoised in the air, yawing and crabbing. Sid and most of the crew raced toward the airstrip as the plane's landing gear touched—more a controlled crash than a landing. Les stepped out of the Cessna alone, grinning.

"Dad, I *knew* it had to be you," Sid cried merrily. "You bounced from one end to the other."

Les spent the next two weeks practicing touch-and-go, learning to fly the Cessna. He was mechanical and he was bold. On the last Sunday of practice, he took off for home to surprise me, like a kid with a new toy. I heard the Cessna buzz the cabin and rushed outside with the younger kids in time to watch it land. I thought little of it until Les walked up the trail from the strip by himself.

"Where's Bob?" I asked.

"He quit me. I'm flying it myself."

"Lester! I'm in no mood for your pranks."

"Really, honey. I'm a pilot now."

It took him a while to convince me Bob wasn't hiding out in the bushes.

"Come on out," he coaxed. "I need you to snap a picture of me taking off from the home strip all by myself. I have to fly down to Fairbanks to get some parts for the mine."

"Les, do me a favor while you're there."

That grin of his. "Honey, all I want out of life is to make you happy."

"Lester, pick up some life insurance while you're in town."

LES MET MEL NAJARIAN at the airport when he arrived that fall for his annual hunt and to check on his $50,000 investment at the mine.

"Mel, I've just started flying. I fly pretty good. We can either drive in the pickup or jump in my airplane and go."

"You don't have a license?"

"I'm strictly illegal."

A slight smile and a shrug. "It's been a wonderful adventure every time I've come up here," he said. "So, let's take the airplane."

He climbed into the plane and turned his ball cap backward on his head and glanced over at Les.

"Look at the bright side," he commented cheerfully. "If you have any problems, you have your attorney with you."

67

The letter arrived at our P.O. box in Rampart while Les, Sid, and Ken were over on the Yukon cutting spruce logs with Boots in order to build Bony and Liz Newman a new cabin. Ken was a young man, a Seventh-Day Adventist from California who wandered into the valley one summer with two companions on a hiking expedition. The Three Musketeers, as I called them, were like Mel Najarian and others who somehow discovered Cobbsville and kept returning. Ken often volunteered to work with Les and Sid.

They cut Bony's logs for him, dumped them into the river current about ten miles upriver of Rampart, rafted them together and let them go. At Rampart, Bony sat in his boat and waited for the floating logs to appear, at which time he was to tow them ashore near his building site. Only, Bony fell asleep while waiting and the logs floated on down the Yukon. Some other Indian or Eskimo enjoyed a windfall. Bony's cabin had to wait.

The letter Les picked up at the Rampart trading post and post office, re-opened under new management after Ira Weisner died, came from Les's folks. His dad, Lyman, was ill and wanted us to come to Colorado to visit for the winter. The last time Les saw his father was when he injured his eye and flew south for treatment. Lyman had visited Minook Valley once a few years ago, but the kids and I hadn't been out of Alaska since our arrival in 1973. It was now 1981. We had been in Alaska over eight years.

"Let's do it," Les decided. "As soon as mining is over for the year, we'll lock up and head south. It'll be like a family vacation. We've never had one."

"I don't know, Les . . ." I hedged. "Remember what happened to the cabin the last time we left it over the winter?"

"Bony will drop by once in a while to keep an eye on it."

I was still uncertain.

"Honey, we have the money now. The mine is doing fairly well. I really need to see my dad."

"I can stay at home," Sid eagerly volunteered. "I have to stay to take care of the dogs."

Sid would soon turn sixteen. He had grown into a strapping young man with blond hair and blue eyes. He was not a big kid, but his body was as lean and sharp as his face. For the past two winters he had trained his sled dogs hard in anticipation of running the Iditarod in March. We owned about forty dogs now. Sid needed this last winter before the race to get his teams in shape and tune them up.

"I really can't go," he insisted. "Let me stay and work with my dogs. What about trapping? And school?"

Ken listened to the discussion with interest.

"I have a solution," he said.

Eyes turned toward him.

"Really. Let *me* winter over and take care of the place and the dogs."

Sean, Tommy, and the twins were all for it. They wanted to go on the trip. Sid frowned disapproval. I hedged.

"I could stay in Oh, Brother! cabin and it would solve everything," Ken argued.

"You've never wintered over in Alaska, Ken," I pointed out. "You don't know what it's like, what it can do to you."

I was thinking of Andrew Farnsworth.

"It can get real cold and lonely," I continued, still trying to discourage him.

In the end, however, both Sid and I relented. It was settled. He would stay. The entire family would go; we would return in December still in time for Sid to get his dogs ready.

Firewood was cut and stacked, food stored. I baked twenty-three loaves of bread for Ken. Les and Sid taught him how to care for the dogs and prepare for the birth of puppies in November and December. We stockpiled sacks of dry dog food, as that made it easier on Ken than his trying to mix, cook, and feed salmon and rice. The goats, chickens, and rabbits that had survived last winter were given to friends in Manley; farming wasn't proving lucrative anyhow.

We departed Minook Valley on October 23. Sid looked back as we pulled away from the homestead, all of us and our luggage loaded onto the Bombardier. He shook his head sadly.

"I don't know . . ." he murmured.

WE RETURNED TO ALASKA on December 16. Ken's fiancée, Donnell, a pretty dark-haired girl of about twenty, accompanied us. Weather this time of year made it difficult to get home from Fairbanks. There were two ways to make the journey: either bush plane to Rampart and mush or sno-go the nineteen miles upvalley; or drive to Minto and mush or sno-go sixty miles across the Top of the World.

It was finally decided that Les and Donnell would form an advance party and fly to Rampart. Les contacted Ken through CB relay radio and asked him to meet them with a dogsled. The rest of us stayed with Rose and Charlie Stowell in Fairbanks, it being impractical and expensive for all eight of us to fly. In a few days I would drive to Minto where Les and Ken would pick us up with dogsleds.

The first indication we received that something was wrong in Minook Valley came in a CB message from Les two days later. Ken had not met them in Rampart; Les and Donnell started out walking from Rampart, thinking Ken was surely on the way. He wasn't. They overnighted in the Shilling cabin on Slate Creek, then finished the exhausting walk through snow to Cobbsville the next day. Les omitted details over the radio; he simply advised us to scrub driving to Minto. Instead, we were to take a bush plane to Rampart and hire someone to sno-go us home.

Sid's face sharpened with alarm. "Dad talked to Ken on the radio, so he's okay. It's the dogs! Something has happened to my dogs!"

His worst fears were confirmed as soon as we came within view of the cabin. Instead of the usual clamorous welcome by forty exuberant dogs and half again that many puppies, there was only a tight silence. Most of the half-barrel doghouses were snowed over and empty, the snow around them untracked. Six dogs remained; they looked ravished and sickly and tried to hide from us.

Tears in his eyes, Sid dropped to his knees and frantically dug into one of the houses. Inside, frozen stiff, lay the body of a dog. Similar spectacles awaited him in most of the other houses. Other dogs had been dragged away into the woods where wolves and wolverines and other animals dug them out of the snow and left their bones and hair scattered about. Ken hadn't met his fiancée and Les in Rampart because he had no dogs left to form a sled team. Most of them were dead.

Sid's dreams of racing the Iditarod had been destroyed. He had worked hard the past several years building up his teams, training and testing them. Now, this . . .

"I shouldn't have left them . . ." he agonized. "I'll never leave them again."

Ken came out and stood at a distance. He looked thinner and paler with dark circles around his eyes. Obviously, the winter so far had been hard on him. Most people underestimated the cold, the dark, the isolation.

"What have you done?" Sid screamed at him.

He lunged at Ken, anger as fierce as that of any charging grizzly roaring out of his lungs. Only Les's quick intervention prevented a fight in the snow. Les hugged the boy tightly to his chest, his feet kicking off the ground, until Sid ceased struggling. He glared at Ken.

"You've killed my dogs!"

"Sid, I'm sorry." Ken tried to explain. "A dog team came through with kennel cough. The dogs caught it and they started dying . . . What could I do?"

Lady and Black were among the casualties. Lead dogs Captain and Bandit were weak and sick, but they survived. When breakup came and snow melted, it revealed the true tragedy. Fortunately, Ken, who later to his credit attempted to make amends, was long gone; even Les could not have held Sid off him.

It took days to clean up the mess of dogs left dead underneath the snow, of dog food strewn in the weather to ruin, of houses and runs left in filth. While some of the dogs might have contracted kennel cough, most of them died due to neglect. Ken had burrowed up in Oh, Brother! with cabin fever, becoming more and more depressed and unresponsive until he finally stayed inside and let the dogs starve and thirst to death. I wept softly over the remnants; how those poor animals must have suffered. Tears welled in Sid's eyes every time he looked at Captain and Bandit.

He never recovered from the crushing blow of losing most of his racing dogs. He continued to mush through his high school years, but his dreams of running the Iditarod gradually died. I guess he felt dogs were a poor investment if they could be done in so readily after all the effort put into them. He turned to sno-goes to replace his dogs. To my way of thinking, that compounded the tragedy. A machine never substituted for the closeness of communication and companionship with a live animal. The roar of those engines! You became so much closer to nature without all that noise.

Bandit and Captain became outside house dogs. We discovered Bandit curled up on the porch one morning, dead in his sleep. A couple of years later a musher named Bob Mantell rode through the valley, training dogs for an attempt to reach the North Pole by dogsled. He was having trouble finding the right canines. Sid gave him Captain with the stipulation that Captain be returned afterward if he wasn't wanted.

While Sid may never have raced the Iditarod, one of his dogs won a certain amount of fame.

On May 1, 1986, an expedition consisting of seven men, one woman, five sleds, and forty-nine dogs reached the North Pole, the first time since Robert E. Peary in 1909 that an expedition conquered that goal by dogsled without resupply. The lone woman, Ann Bancroft from Minnesota, was the first woman to reach the Pole.

Captain was among the dogs. His photograph appeared in *North to the Pole,* a book by expedition leaders Will Steiger and Paul Schurke, published by Time Books in 1987. *National Geographic* also used the photos in its September 1986 issue.

I always felt that a part of my son went with his dog to the North Pole.

68

One good thing about living in the Alaskan bush, one good thing among many, is that the rest of the world could end and bushers probably wouldn't find out about it until months later. No newspapers with headlines of murder and mayhem, no TV with politicians yapping like geese. It was living at its raw basics, from day to day and for the moment without the hustle and tension and urgency of the rest of the nation. A busher had time to reflect and live his life the way he chose without everybody else telling him how to do it.

Of course, isolation and news deficiency also had a downside. As Les discovered when President Ronald Reagan and the Pope came to Fairbanks. Naturally, we knew nothing of it in advance. While Fairbanks went into an uproar of preparations, Minook Valley continued life as usual. I always said that if there was trouble anywhere around, you always found Les right in the middle of it.

Machinery at the mine was always breaking down. Les jumped into the Cessna and took off for Fairbanks to find replacement parts. Flying at 2,500 feet, he approached the city outskirts on a bright summer morning. He intended landing at the Chena Marina strip that lay next to the international airport. However, as soon as he entered controlled airspace, the tower came up on his radio.

"Cessna four-three-seven entering Fairbanks airspace from the northeast . . . ?"

"Roger, tower. This is Four-Three-Seven. I'm approaching final for Chena . . ."

"*Stand by, four-three-seven . . .*"

Les noticed U.S. Army helicopter UH-1 gunships hovering like bees over the International. Crowds of people milled around the terminal. He dismissed it as being some kind of army war game until two of the army choppers broke away from their stations. They nosed down in the air and barreled straight at him with obvious purpose. The tower passed him over to one of the gunship pilots.

"*Cessna four-three-seven, abort Chena. You'll have to land at the international . . .*"

The two helicopters took up positions one off either wing, so uncomfortably close in the air that Les saw the reflection of his red and white airplane in the pilots' helmet sun visors. All this because someone found out he didn't have a pilot's license! The FAA must take these things seriously.

"I think I'll turn around and go back out to the mine," Les replied, nervously eyeing his escorts.

"*Four-three-seven, see this gunship?*"

What did they think—he was flying blind as well as without a license?

"*Four-three-seven, you're going to land at the international—or we'll put you down one way or the other. Is that clear?*"

Well, put that way . . . Les made the touchdown. A little man wearing a black sharkskin suit with wires running out of his ears pulled up after him in a black sedan. Why did government types always run around in funeral black? Les then learned he had blundered into the middle of a visit by President Reagan and the Pope, who were at that moment inside the terminal. Guys were running around everywhere with guns and radios.

"I want to see your license," the man in black demanded.

Les's shoulders rolled forward. He took out his driver's license and handed it over.

"Oh, boy, what's this? You trying to be funny?"

The FAA slapped a lock sock on Les's airplane propeller, issued him a ticket for flying without a license, and scheduled him for a federal hearing the following morning. The judge shook his head with suppressed amusement.

"Bushers!" he exclaimed. "Half you guys out there never have licenses. It's just bad luck that you stumbled into the middle of the Pope and Ronald Reagan."

Les received a lecture and a sentence to attend flight ground school and take a check ride. Passing the check ride permitted him to fly cargo, but no passengers. The FAA pilot directed him through a series of air maneuvers—eights around a pylon, tracking, turns, climbs, high-altitude stalls, and emergency procedures.

"You fly this aircraft very well, Mr. Cobb," the government pilot said when the test ended. "Now, I want you to line up on the international airport. Take the first right turnoff and taxi back to the terminal. You've passed your check ride."

Les touched the Cessna down at the beginning of the asphalt strip. From touchdown to where the big air carriers pulled out to warm up was a distance of only three-hundred feet. Les braked the Cessna hard and whipped onto the warm-up turn-in.

"No! No! No!" his surprised passenger squealed. "I meant the next turnoff."

Les grinned. "You said the *first*. That's what I did. This airport is so big, I can land on it sideways."

The FAA pilot wiped his brow. "I'll bet you could," he said.

Les flew his Cessna back to the mine that afternoon.

69

Gold mining was tough for the first two years. We barely had clothing for the children. But once Les got everything in gear—"Getting bigger, faster!"—he gradually upgraded to bigger and better equipment. That led to his making what had to be considered one of the finest strikes in recent history. He was right all along about there being gold in the hills. *Strike,* however, may not be the word for it. *Strike* carried the connotation of an accidental discovery. I preferred to believe my macho bushman husband *willed* gold out of that ground at Hoosier Creek. Only Les, I think, had the stubbornness to find it and make it pay.

By the third year, he and Don Lucas, partners in the Hoosier mine, owned three dozers, two hydraulic loaders, an excavator, an airplane, and a valley full of other modern equipment. Crews of men worked shifts around the clock. Gold was up to $600 an ounce and still rising. Les shrewdly took the entire pay channel of Hoosier Creek from rim to rim and washed it all for gold, the two-dollar-a-foot gravel along with the thirty-dollar-a-foot, the lean and the good ground together to average it out. The amount of gold recovered was calculated per cubic foot of earth washed.

Nine cubic feet of washed earth yielded approximately $72 worth of gold. The operation went through eighteen thousand cubic feet of dirt every twenty-four hours, thereby grossing over *one and a quarter million dollars* every year. The mine operated one hundred days from spring breakup until first freeze and snowfall in the autumn. Les's gold mine literally changed our lives. We went from being struggling hard-scrabble homesteaders to, more or less, moneyed landowners. For the first time since we left Colorado, we enjoyed certain comforts denied us until now.

Mining also produced an unexpected encroachment upon our way of life. Although old-timer miners at first chuckled at Les's endeavors to go after gold on a large scale, their laughter soon froze in their throats. Gold prices were up. As soon as word got around about Les's "strike"—and word about gold *always* swept the North Country faster than wildfire—it started a minor gold rush. John Shilling at Slate Creek, Jack Jones and Howard Lemm on Granite Creek, Lozonsky, and all the others who owned mining claims in the valley hurried to get in on the find.

We spent a few days visiting Pete and Gloria Pasquali at Wiseman. When we returned home, I was devastated to find the valley torn apart from road's end at Joseph Creek down into the valley and past our cabin. Dozens of miners were moving Caterpillars, Bombardiers, and other equipment downvalley, pushing over trees, digging ruts directly in front of our cabin, trenching our airfield, cutting trees, and in general laying destruction in their wake as they rushed to get in on the action.

When this valley was marred, so was I. Tears in my eyes, I jumped in front of a Cat and shouted at the driver.

"This is our homestead you're tearing up, not public land!"

"Lady, we're going to our gold claims. This is the only way there. Get out of the way!"

Les wanted to get his gun. I stopped him. That wasn't the way to handle this. Civilization was coming to the backcountry; I sensed it would come with or without our permission, around us, through us, or over us—but it was coming. Law came with it.

"We fight this battle the legal way," I told Les.

Les shook his head and stuck out his beard. "Then we lose," he predicted.

The war raged all summer. I scolded the miners responsible; none of them as much as said he was sorry or that he would mend his ways and repair damages. I wrote blistering letters to the Fairbanks newspapers. I complained to the Federal Bureau of Land Management. Meetings were held by the BLM to mediate between us Cobbs and the miners. No settlements were reached. Confrontations with the miners grew more heated.

In desperation, I contacted the state's only FBI agent whom we had met a year or so previously.

"You have to listen to me if you want to avoid bloodshed," I warned him. "You don't know my husband, and you don't know me. If this issue isn't settled by spring when the miners start to come back into the valley, there's going to be big trouble. That's our home down there. Les will block off the trail and keep them out at gunpoint. Somebody's going to get killed and somebody's going to prison. I can't live with that."

Apparently, the agent believed me. Another meeting was called. Present were BLM representatives, some state people from the Department of Transportation, the miners, Les and I, and the FBI agent. An agreement was hammered out. We granted right-of-way across our property. In exchange, DOT and the miners built an all-weather road from Joseph Creek down into the valley. With the completion of the road, the Cobbs now had vehicle access to the outside world—and the outside world had access to us.

"It all worked out," Les said, shrugging philosophically. "Look at it this way. You were telling me how you read about Minook Valley being full of miners back in the 1890s gold rush. They came, then every one of them left again. The bears and your Bushman returned. You couldn't hardly tell anybody had been here since the beginning of time. The same thing will happen again. The gold won't last. In another two or three years, everybody will leave again. There'll only be us in the valley once more. It will be the same way it was."

I looked at the new road winding down from Dead Horse Pass, paralleling Minook Creek and passing directly in front of our door. Perhaps subconsciously, I fought the miners more to preserve our way of life than for any other reason. Things were changing. Pioneers inevitably brought civilization with them wherever they went. It was human nature.

"No," I disagreed, a little sadly. "Things will never be the same again."

The American pioneer era was ending. Not only was I the last official woman homesteader to file for land under the U.S. Homestead Act of 1862, we Cobbs may in fact have been the last of the nation's *real* pioneers to stick it out. Of 110 claim filings made in our region of northern

Alaska during the last years before the Homestead Act expired, only two families proved out on them and obtained legal deed to homestead property. We were one of the two.

I felt a certain melancholy in its ending. By 1983, more than ten years had passed since we Cobbs first set out North with five small children in a blue Mustang Fastback and a two-ton Ford truck pulling a psychedelic-painted Willys Jeep. We arrived in Alaska with only the two-tonner intact, $35 in the trip sock, and a list of reasons why we should homestead. I was a long way from Kansas now; unlike Dorothy, I could never go back. I had no desire to go back. I had found my home in Minook Valley. God tested us, I think, and found us worthy.

Time passed so fast, as it did when you were busy living. You were often so busy that you didn't see it happening. Sid was now almost nineteen; Sean sixteen; Tommy fourteen; and the twins twelve and taller than I. I looked at them, sometimes through a mist, and remembered when we first fought our way to Alaska, across Dead Horse Pass and down into Minook Valley to build our home. Accidents, floods, bears, disasters, poverty, Bushman, isolation, lawlessness . . . We had dealt with all that. But there was more, so much more. Our list of reasons for homesteading, for coming here in the first place, explained it all.

I walked along Minook Creek and stopped to talk to God as I had almost every day for a decade.

"Thank you, God," I said, "for giving me so much."

That was the same year we also moved into the *real* house built on high ground away from the annual glacier flooding. We simply outgrew the cabin with its one big downstairs room and its loft. The new cabin was huge by comparison. It had a big porch; an entrance hall for holding parkas, boots, guns, snowshoes, and whatever; a kitchen; dining area; living room; two downstairs bedrooms, one for the boys and one for the girls; a huge twenty-by-thirty-foot bedroom-den in the loft for Les and me; and a root storage cellar. The bedrooms had closets and plenty of shelving.

And electricity! Provided by a gasoline-powered generator. Indoor plumbing with the water always cold and fresh—pumped out of Lost Creek—and an indoor bathroom. Soon we had a TV and a radio tuned in to stations other than *Pipeline of the North*. Perhaps it was primitive in comparison to what outsiders were accustomed to, but there were certain aspects of civilization that were pure luxury.

My birthday was special. Les arrived home with a diamond watch, a mother's ring he had had made from the gold nugget he found in Minook Creek, a mink coat, and two round-trip tickets to Tokyo, Japan. My dreams had never included a fur coat or a foreign trip.

"We need some time to ourselves before Sid takes off on his own," Les explained in that grinning way of his. "Besides, Japan was on special at the travel agency."

He hesitated, glanced away. That big man's eyes actually misted over. Les worked awfully hard at maintaining his macho image.

"I wanted to make up for all those years when I could give you nothing extra except hardships," he said. "I wanted to show how much I love you."

I truly was going to love being spoiled. What else could I ask for? God's beautiful nature all around me . . . My family . . . Plus my own bedroom!

AFTERWORD

On a Christmas Eve years later after the five Kernels have grown up and left home to become full Cobbs on their own, as it is meant for the young to do, I stand at the open door of the *real* house, the big cabin, and watch snow fall on the clearing and downhill toward Minook Creek and our original cabin on the other side. I am always filled with a certain nostalgia this time of year. Les claims it is because I watch all those tearjerking Christmas movies on TV—*Vermont Story, It's a Wonderful Life, White Christmas*—in which everyone is coming home and crying.

"Lester. Go plough the snow off the road. Maybe some of the kids will come home for Christmas."

"You gotta be kidding me, Norma."

"You never know. They might show up."

With a sigh, he finally gets up and goes out to plough the road in the snow.

The Hoosier Creek Mine exhausted itself, as we knew it must. The miners all departed and it was once again only the Cobbs in Minook Valley. We had about three good years of gold; the money we earned boosted Les's big-game guiding and provided us a start on the tourist business. We call the homestead Lost Creek Ranch these days. For a number of years we offered tourist horseback rides into the bush as well as hunting and fishing trips. It has been a good life, made more comfortable by Les's gold strike.

One by one the kids grew up and left. Sid is the only one who really likes the pioneering way of life, but he can never find a woman who will stay with him out here. Even now, in the twenty-first century, Minook Valley remains primitive and isolated by outside standards. Sid is currently employed with General Electric inspecting nuclear plants all over the world. He tries to make it back every autumn to help Les with the grizzlies during hunting season.

Sean has made a career of the U.S. Air Force. He is presently stationed in Florida with his wife and two children. He still enjoys returning to Alaska to hunt and help Les with his guide business.

Tommy is a dramatic mess full of inherent happiness. He and Cora, now divorced with five children of her own, have become housemates in Anchorage while Tommy attends college and Cora works on making a new start.

Cara, also divorced, has three children. For a while, she managed a Montana ranch, but eventually returned to Alaska. She lives near Wasilla, on the outskirts where she can be close to nature.

Our ten grandchildren are curious about the "old days" when the Cobbs came to Alaska to pioneer, but they are also addicted to video games, computers, paved streets, and "civilization." They are modern kids with no ties to the land.

I love my kids, all five of them. I was there with them when they were growing up, which is more than I can say for most American mothers today. So often in modern America, kids grow up with day care and TV baby-sitters. Perhaps my kids did experience certain hardships, but they also had responsibilities and challenges. They had freedom to grow into strong, capable, competent human beings. They know the value of common sense, of independence, of being *individuals* instead of mere numbers in groups. All these once-valued attributes, from what I can tell, are giving way to groupthink and the practice of victimology in which people feel helpless without handouts and support from government.

By homesteading, Les and I grew roots, deep. Homesteading was a commitment that left its mark on us, Cobbs and Kernels alike. It is such a part of me that my heart aches whenever I am away from the valley. Alaska haunts us wherever we roam and beckons us home. It is such a land of extremes, this last great wilderness in the world. You either love Alaska, or you leave it.

What has Alaska meant to us? That is a laundry list full of depth and meaning in its truest sense: freedom; independence; old-fashioned family values; faith in God; the seeking of understanding into mankind's place in the universe; roots deep in our own land; the privilege of having dreams and making them come true; the right to bear arms; clean air and water; a basic lifestyle close to the earth and each other; the splendor of nature and its wildlife always close at hand. We Cobbs were never isolated; we lived without the artificial barriers that truly isolate people from their own origins.

To be truthful, considering the time and effort we invested in our Minook Valley homestead, we could probably have bought a nice farm in the Lower Forty-eight. Everything you do in the wilderness is twice as labor intensive as anywhere else. There are no roads, no communications, no conveniences, no "necessities" other than those you build with your own hands.

Everything was achieved at much greater cost than required elsewhere in "civilization." Yet, Les and I have no regrets, except for having been separated from our extended families in the Lower Forty-eight.

There is an old saying. I don't remember where it came from, but it expresses what I feel about the adventure of homesteading in Alaska: *I've always been called a dreamer, but never listened. I did what others dare not do—lived my dream while they watched.*

I am now rapidly approaching sixty years of age. Les and I are considering selling Lost Creek Ranch to someone younger with the same love for it that we have. We talked it over. It is better to sell and retain the memories of it than, due to our inevitable aging and the onslaught of illness, watch what we have built slowly decay and come apart. Better to leave with the memories of good times and the way they were than to try to hang on and eventually lose them to a changing reality. If we leave now, we leave with all our memories intact.

I can only say, may God bless America and Alaska, where I found the keys to true happiness and success in faith, commitment, patience, freedom, and love.

I *was* America's last pioneer. A few years ago, Fairbanks constructed a huge monument downtown honoring the pioneer families of Alaska's interior. Our names were inscribed on it: The Cobbs—Lester, Norma, Sid, Sean, Tommy, Cara, and Cora. The Cobbs, Pioneers of the Far North.